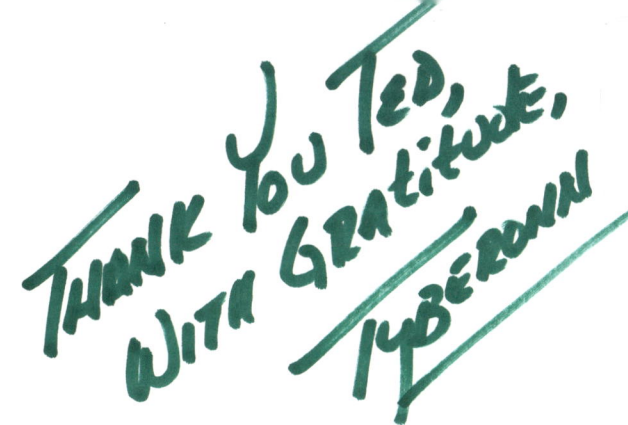

# Earth-Keeper
## The Energy & Geometry of Sacred Sites

### by Tyberonn

Grids, Vortexes and Portals of Gaia,
The Living Earth

Back cover artwork "The Weather Dancer Dream" © by Howard Terpning.

Photography by Tyberonn.

Earth-Keeper: The Energy & Geometry of Sacred Sites ~ Grids, Vortexes and Portals of Gaia, The Living Earth
by James Tipton, aka Tyberonn
ISBN: 978-0-9767035-4-9
Library of Congress Control Number: 2006940630

To order books:
Email: Tyberonn@Earth-Keeper.com,
Website: http://www.Earth-Keeper.com

Altered States, Biographies & Personal Experience, Body Mind Spirit, Energy Science, Gaia, Source Alignment, Ascension, Mastery, Light, Chakras, Channeling, Consciousness: Awareness & Expansion, Consciousness Physics, Crystals, Life Energy, Grids, Sacred Geometry, Geomancy, Sacred Sites, Portals, Vortexes, Everyday Spirituality, God, New Age, Science & Religion, Spirituality, The Self.

STAR QUEST PUBLISHING
RENO, NV        PHOENIX, AZ
New Perspectives in Unified Consciousness.

3030 E. Shangri-La Rd., Phoenix AZ 85028
info@StarQuestPublishing.com 602-482-1568
www.StarQuestPublishing.com/index.htm
Printed in China.

# Dedication

This book has been 30 years in the making.  I would like to sincerely express my appreciation and love to some very special people who have helped me along the path and to achieve this dream.

Ronna
Steve & Barbara
Karen
Anne & Bobby
Adam Yellowbird
Israel
Rainbow Woman
Becky
Denise
Shala
Lesa & Lane
Bwanequia
Ismeyer
Miguel
Gemma & Steve
Art & Aurora
Sheik
Aurielle

… and to all the others

With Love & Hugs, Tyb

# Foreword by Ronna Herman

In looking back over the years, it is wonderful to observe how Spirit subtly and, sometimes not so subtly, directs us on our path and assists us to gain the knowledge and expertise needed to fulfill our spiritual mission. Archangel Michael often tells people in the personal messages I channel for them, "We are endeavoring to help you remember and reclaim your magnificence and to know that what we are asking of you, you have done many times before."

Tyberonn is a great example of being guided and prepared throughout his lifetime to fulfill his Divine Mission on Earth. His work has enabled him to travel the world and visit places most people only read about. His educational background and continuing study of the Earth's grid system, power spots and ley lines, along with an astounding knowledge of gemstones and crystals have made him an expert on all these subjects. It has prepared him for a "downloading" from AA Metatron of Cosmic sacred geometric patterns of Light, and to also receive advanced information on crystals and gemstones.

I met James for the first time (in this lifetime) in November, 2005, and I will never forget my first encounter with this amazing man we lovingly call Tyb. After all the chaos and destruction that had recently taken place in the gulf states and the western Caribbean, we were all excited about our Atlantean Reunion cruise. We were finally realizing our dream of connecting with some of our soul family and our Atlantean heritage, but we were also wondering just how this journey would play out. We were scheduled to sail the western Caribbean on the Norwegian Sun, a beautiful and luxurious ship in every way. As Tyb and I were introduced by Steve and Barbara Rother, a thrill of recognition surged through me (Tyb later told me he felt the same instant connection). It was wonderful seeing so many old friends, especially my angel buddies, Steve and Barbara Rother, who were my co-seminar presenters. Tyb gave a slide presentation that was astounding. He has journeyed to many of the sacred sites around the world; in fact, he told me that he had been to ten of the twelve sacred sites that I mentioned in my lecture.

During the cruise, I offered private sessions to the participants which included a personal reading from Archangel Michael. I was guided to offer Tyb a message from Michael which he eagerly accepted. During the course of quite a long reading, Tyb was told that he was of AA Metatron's lineage (Metatron bears the Light of our Father/Mother God and is sometimes called the King of Archangels). Tyb was told that he was to play an integral part in anchoring the new crystalline grid on the Earth plane and he was to bring forth advanced information that is so critical during these times of great change; the ascension of humanity and the Earth into the more rarified realms of Light.

I am so pleased that Tyb is ready and willing to share his incredible knowledge with the world. I hope to work with him periodically over the coming years, and I know this book will become a mainstay in many spiritual libraries, including my own. Love, Light and angel blessings to all my dear friends, Ronna

Ronna Herman is an internationally known author and messenger for Archangel Michael. Her eight books and monthly messages of wisdom and inspiration from AA Michael are translated in most major languages and read around the world. www.RonnaStar.com

# Contents

# Introduction ~ Sacred Sites

*" Those areas on the Earth you term power points are apexes of infinity. These points are the primary dissemination mechanism of the higher dimensional energies of the Ascension: this through the vortex-portal templates that occur in many of these."* Tyberonn

What is it that has caused mankind since the beginning of time to recognize certain areas of our planet as power points, areas that resonate with a higher frequency?

Before we attempt to answer that question, we need to examine the greater reality of the fabric of our universe. The Cosmos, our Universe, our Earth, is composed of living conscious energy … the conscious energy of geometric light and electromagnetics. Our Earth is multidimensional, and so are we. Twelve dimensions exist upon our planet; 356 dimensions reside in our Universe. Geometry, sacred geometry, is the mosaic underpinning of them all.

The Greek mystic and philosopher Plato once described our planet as looking like a ball with twelve sides, when seen from afar. What he was referring to was the dodecahedron. Our planet contains a three in one grid complex that encompasses the Earth. This grid system enables and facilitates our experience on the planet and the fabric of reality we live. The grids are indeed the 'Windows' program that enable the human adventure in duality.

In specific places on our planet, these grids are unified into concentric vortex-portal templates and allow for all 12 dimensions to occur in a more tangible manner within a concentrated area, which I refer to as zipped space or harmonic dimensional overlay. When we as humankind enter into these special areas, we become immediately affected. One's energy increases, one's awareness is enhanced and one's multidimensional aspects are more tangible. The degree of personal expansion depends of course on the awareness level of the person, but all are affected. Those seekers, who enter into these areas in reverent spirit, are given the opportunity to step up their frequency and have a very rare multi dimensional experience.

## Sacred Sites

The Native Americans, Druids, Templars, Egyptians and other adepts have recognized, revered and built upon sacred sites since the beginning of time. There are four types of sacred sites:

- Natural Telluric Energies: mountains, lakes, volcanoes, forests and specific mineral deposits
- Human Imprint Sites: such as tombs of great leaders and sites of historical or religious events
- Points of Cosmic and Grid Alignment
- Man-Made: cathedrals, temples and pyramids built to sacred geometry.

Sacred sites can be defined in layman's terms as areas that resonate at a higher vibration and are catalysts for spiritual experience. Such areas often radiate electromagnetic fields of higher frequency. These locations can be naturally occurring or manmade. The latter are often temples or stone circles built over naturally occurring leylines or energy points. Temples, cathedrals and pyramids built to sacred geometry actually attract and amplify energies, especially when built over telluric hotspots that contain crystallized minerals such as quartz. Numerous sacred sites are aligned celestially, at specific angles to cosmic points.

Sacred sites and portal-vortex templates are connected through various energetic conduits. These include leylines and axial tonal lines. If one accepts the postulate that certain points of higher energy do indeed exist on the planet, and that they do have a crystallized matrix that projects a specific harmonic wavelength, then its can be understood how these vibratory energy pulse sources 'communicate' through harmonic energy oscillations. That is a scientific fact, called the 'Law of Harmonic Oscillation.' For example, if one has a tuning fork in the key of C, and then one plays a C note on a piano, the musical vibration from the piano will provoke vibration in the tuning fork. The same also occurs in frequency oscillations between power points on Earth and in higher dimensions. In the study of the crystalline structure of gems and crystallized metals, we learn that these are entirely geometric in form and are capable of emitting an electromagnetic field that also harmonically oscillates.

The concentrated energy matrix of sacred sites is frequencially crystalline in nature. As such they have properties of crystals, specifically the ability to receive, transmit and store energy. Sacred sites are conscious and knowing. A self-aware 'Spirit of Place' exists within the living energetic matrix. Because of this we can advance our own consciousness within them, in an osmosis of spirit. We can increase our psychic ability and spiritual experience and can access deep wisdom and healing. Like crystals and gems, sacred sites are amplifiers. Chakras are both heightened and balanced. Thought waves are manifested into reality far more rapidly in these crystalline templates. The ancients understood this and utilized these places for prayer, meditation and vision quest. In such reverent process, a sense of well being is achieved, and stored within the energy of the site. This sense of well being is a key part of why so many are compelled to visit power points and sacred sites. The profound spiritual links between Earth and the Cosmos help us to better understand our great yearning to know why we are here. They help us understand our purpose and activate us to evolve into a higher form of consciousness. Simply stated, sacred sites help us unlock the great mystery.

Sacred sites are teachers, and they teach in the third language, the unspoken resonance of light. The Native Americans understood this and always made an offering and asked permission before entering a holy place. When a pilgrim enters a sacred site in reverence, an energy envelopes the auric field, and one's entire being is shifted. One learns through stillness, through quieting the inner narrator and by allowing the wisdom to flow inward. The wisdom of 'Universal Knowledge' is activated within our 'God Mind' and within our very cellular DNA. Certain types of sacred sites, primarily those that emit light through an octahedral geometric overlay, purify us. They literally force us to face our imperfections and parts of our life-patterns that are in conflict with our higher selves. The seeker becomes purged through the crucible of deep self-examination. Other sacred sites, those that project light through the dodecahedral lens such as Rosslyn Chapel, facilitate our journey into higher realms. These are often called stargates.

In sacred sites the door to this sacred knowledge is opened, and a catalystic energy exchange occurs. We become imprinted with the keys of frequencial wisdom unique to each sacred site we visit, and in kind we imbue our imprint into the energy of place. We receive light energy from the site, and we feed energy back into it. A synergetic transposition ensues as each seeker begins to manifest the impeccability of every sacred site visited, each melding and building upon the other.

## Leylines

The word ley is a derivative of the Saxon word 'lea,' meaning open glade. The term *leyline* is not new, but our understanding and definition of it has certainly evolved since it was first characterized in the early 1900's. The term was first coined by Alfred Watkins, a British surveyor and dowser, in reference to 'straight lines' that he discovered (circa 1920) connecting stone monuments and Christian cathedrals (built on the Michael line) in England. The Freemasons, who built cathedrals capable of amplifying ley energy, utilized sacred geometry imminently. Almost all of the cathedrals and Greek monuments were built to phi, the golden ratio or mean, directly on power nodes along leylines.

Tyberonn defines leylines in a broader, slightly different way, as being one aspect of the electromagnetic flow-lines that network the planet. There have been several attempts by scientists such as Becker and Haagans, dowsers such as Hamish Miller, and metaphysicians who have attempted to either connect 'power sites' on the globe through geometric grids, primarily the dodecahedron, or through an oscillating Global Leyline. Others such as Bruce Cathie out of New Zealand speak more of a measurable rectangular network that is similar to 'Curry Lines' theorized in the 1960's and developed by Dr. Manfred Curry. In my evolving studies of this process, I am of the belief that leylines are 'groomed' energy flows of electromagnetic energies that can and do shift between portals and interdimensional vortex points.

There is currently no scientific technology capable of verifying ley energy. As such no measurable scientific means exists for mapping leys or patterning their circumnavigation of the globe, even if mainstream science accepted the theory of their existence. And of course, this is not a science yet accepted in mainstream. Most leyline hunters utilize the art of geomancy or dowsing.

Leylines are not constant. Over time they shift and dive, and currently they do not completely circumnavigate the planet as they did in the days of Atlantis. In the technology of the Tyberonn period in Atlantis, naturally occurring leylines were enhanced and amplified, and were used to create a labyrinth of tunnels for both communication and transport.

Leylines generally flow in specific patterns. They will spiral counterclockwise up domed mountains above the equator, and clockwise below it. They flow upward in straight lines on pyramidal shaped mountains. They spiral up conical peaks. This is why mountain peaks contain very high frequencies.

## Reshel Grids

Reshel or Tschad grids are geometric Earth grids, either discovered between natural node points in the landscape or created within sacred geometry structures such as cathedrals and temples. Reshel grids are the frequencial receivers that attract and connect specific points of Earth to the higher grids and dimensions. Reshels geometrically organize consciousness into energetic self sustaining generators, creating time gates and portals.

Washington D.C. was certainly built to sacred geometries and utilized obelisks (as antennae), reflection pools, domes and the golden mean in structures such as the Capital, Washington Monument, Jefferson Monument, Lincoln Monument and National Cathedral. These follow the same design theory as temples built by the Greeks, Mayans, Romans, Masons and Egyptians. It is interesting to note how many of the European cathedrals built on leys also employ the obelisk. These structures, with their domes and golden spiral phi, are capable of storing, refining and amplifying certain natural electromagnetics that flow along them, just as stone circles were capable of circulating and counter circulating the ley flows that intersected them.

## Telluric Energy Conduits

Leylines are potent conduits, but they are just the tip of the iceberg. Hydrolines are another form of flowing energy, created from underwater stream movement, which do in fact emit plasma or sub atomic pools. The way anions and cations effect the body and consciousness is also quite interesting to study. Gaia theorists believe that the Living Body of Earth has a nervous system (leylines and axial tonal lines), blood (water), chakras and meridian points, just as the human body does.

In addition to electromagnetic energies, the Earth produces great energy from her spinning core, from pressure created by shifting tectonic plates, from volcanic magma and from solar heat.

## The Crystal Vibration: Impeccability

The crystalline vibration is an essential acquisition for both seekers and for the planet. It is in fact occurring planetarily through a myriad of modalities, focally through the power points of the Earth. The portals of major power points have crystalline geometric matrixes, very similar in nature to the octahedral and dodecahedral crystallography of precious gems. When higher dimensional light waves are received through these overlay lenses, the planet is imbued with platonic crystalline frequency.

The crystalline vibration is achieved by man through intent and impeccability. What is impeccability? As defined by the Toltecs, it is simply walking one's talk, living in integrity, eliminating fear and worry, always doing our best, honoring others and, last but certainly not least, achieving self love. Granted, this is easier said than none, but it is essential in crystallizing our frequency.

## Gem Stones

There are tools to assist us in this process. The renowned psychic Edgar Cayce provided multitudinous readings on the health and spiritual benefits of gemstones and precious metals. My guidance is in enthusiastic alignment with this and suggests that, in addition to intent and meditation, gems can be very valuable tuning forks that assist in the refinement of our own auric energies to that of the crystalline merkaba. The ancients have always known this. The Vedic stones have been pronounced for millennia by Buddhists and Hindus. Many sacred sites such as Mount Shasta, Rosslyn Chapel and Lake Titicaca project hexagonal, octahedral and dodecahedral geometries. When we take crystals and gemstones of matching crystalline structure into these areas, an amplified harmonic oscillation occurs that can enhance our ability to achieve higher dimensional experience. Because the matrix of higher dimension is sacred geometry, certain gems can expedite the transformation of our auric field into the sacred geometric pattern of the crystalline merkaba. These are only tools and are not absolutely necessary, but they can indeed be powerful assistants. The ancients have always known that gems projected a geometric astral light that can be utilized in this process, as well as provide many other health benefits. Channeled sources say that one of the reasons women outlive men is because women wear gems such as diamonds.

Gems are like sacred sites, they do amazing things to light and emit a geometric field. Some are singularly refractive, others double refractive, splitting photons into polarized beams through crystal matrixes in similar manner to the platonic solids. Gems disperse, amplify and concentrate light in spectacular ways. Scientists have proven that light inside a diamond is actually slowed to less than half its normal speed of 180,000 miles per second! Among the most beneficial crystalline stones are the demantoid garnet, diamond, ruby, sapphire, aquamarine, emerald, beryl, lapis lazuli, topaz, tourmaline and amethyst. The geological location and area of formation is also of particular importance with gemstones. Gems from The Ural Mountains, Siberia, Bolivia, Chile and Sri Lanka are of particular benefit in the coming Ascension.

## The Quickening of Power Points in the Ascension

Now, we have spoken about the energy exchange that occurs in sacred sites and power points. Some metaphysicians speak of activating, healing and anchoring sacred sites. While we understand the intent of such descriptions, it is in most cases the other way around. It is we who are activated, healed and anchored by the heightened energies. Seekers do imprint their energies into sacred sites, and that energy is amplified and does enhance the vibration of the matrix. But the energy we feed into sacred sites is returned to us ten fold, with the quickened influx of higher energies occurring in sacred sites as we approach the Ascension.

In times past, guardianship of certain portal vortex complexes was considered necessary. However that role can be misunderstood. While at times certain residue energies or imbalances may need clearing, what is generally required of mankind is simply to recognize and honor these sacred sites and power points in intent and ceremony for the magnificent beacons of light that they are. The valid aspect of guardianship is to insure that telluric sites are preserved and not destroyed. How many sacred Redwood forests have been cut down by our logging industries in the past century?

**Power Points and Portal Complexes**

**Emerging Portals for the New Age:** These are portals that are receiving a renewed influx of energies, occurring in key areas for required balancing of the planetary energies of place.

- Amsterdam, Holland
- Bangkok, Thailand
- Barcelona, Spain
- Beijing, China
- Bogota, Colombia
- Berlin, Germany
- Buenos Aires, Argentina
- Capetown , South Africa
- Christchurch, New Zealand
- Galveston-Houston , Texas
- Istanbul, Turkey
- Jackson Hole, Wyoming
- LaPaz, Bolivia
- Moscow, Russia
- Monterey, Mexico
- New York City, New York
- Prague, Czech Republic
- Rio de Janeiro, Brazil
- Santiago, Chile
- Tel Aviv, Israel
- Tokyo, Japan
- Virginia Beach, Virginia

**Major Existing Energy Portals:**

**Africa**
- Giza

- Mount Kilamanjaro
- Victoria Falls

**North America**
- Danlai, Alaska
- Mount Shasta, California
- Sedona, Arizona
- Banff, Canada
- Talimena Ridge, Ouachita Mountains Arkansas

**Central America**
- Monterey , Mexico
- Yucatan, Mexico
- Chiappas, Mexico
- Guatamala

**South America**
- Cerro Huaika, Colombia
- Lake Titicaca
- Tierra del Fuego – Los Torres del Paine
- Diamanatina, Brazil
- Mount Uritorco, Argentina

**Europe**
- Externesteine, Germany
- Roslyn, Scotland
- Mount San Michel, France
- Temple of Delphi, Greece
- Montserrat, Spain

**Middle East**
- Mecca, Saudi Arabia
- Mount Araphat, Turkey
- Mount Carmel, Israel

**Australia**
- Uluru
- Tasmania

**Asia**
- Mount Kahlish, Tibet
- Mount Fuji, Japan
- Lake Baikal, Siberia
- Sri Lanka
- Gobi Desert, Mongolia

**Pacific**
- Hawaii
- Moorea, Tahiti
- Bali and Java, Indonesia

**The North and South Poles are major portals.**

# Ascension and the 144 Crystal Grid

The Crystalline Grid is the energetic lattice that covers our planet. It reflects and amplifies our ascending levels of consciousness. It is a crystalline 'light' matrix that was anchored in 1992, five years after the Harmonic Convergence. Although in place and functional, its total activation will involve 12 phases, with full resonant vibratory rate achieved on the 12-12-12 ... December 12, 2012. The 'triple' dates (01-01-01 thru 12-12-12) that occur uniquely for the next 12 years each carry numeric light codes that open and activate each of the 12 major facets of this amazing template.

Visualize the grid as a geodesic sphere, of pentagons and triangles, sparkling as a faceted brilliant diamond. It is a seed crystal of new form, the double penta dodecahedron. Its time has arrived, merkaba of Earthstar. The double penta dodecahedron has 144 facets, the number of Christ ascension. Each dodecahedron has 12 pentacles with 60 facets, add the 12 truncated pentagons to make 72, and double this for 144!

The concept of planetary grids is not a new one. Plato theorized the concept as did the ancient Egyptians, Mayans and Hopi Indians. In a sense, grids are the template, the window 'program,' if you will, that allows all life to accelerate in the graduated light format that is called the ascension.

If you will, the Crystalline Ascension Grid, is 'Windows 2012,' and indeed, it is quite necessary for our ascension.

There are not one but three grid templates surrounding our planet, effecting human life. The three are separate yet intricately related. The three become the one. The grids have separate functions relating individually to: 1) planetary gravitational field, 2) telluric electromagnetics, and 3) crystalline consciousness.

The Gravity grid is both within and on the surface of the planet. It is anchored to the spinning crystalline core of the earth. It is in the form of a dodecahedron, a sphere with 12 facets. It is primarily rooted in the first three dimensions. The dodecahedron was the primary consciousness geometric of the planet, from the time of the deluge of Atlantis until the emergence of the icosahedron about 4000 BC.

The Electromagnetic grid is at the level of the crust and extends upward in places as high as thirty thousand feet above sea level. It adjusts itself according to the elevation of the planetary regions. This is the primary grid in which humankind have maintained their consciousness connection for the past 6,000 years. It can, as such, be termed as the human grid. It also regulates the electromagnetic systems, such as the leylines and vortex systems, of the planet. It is in the sacred geometric form of the icosahedron, a sphere with 20 facets.

The Ascension or Crystalline 144 grid is anchored into the earth with two axis points. It is an emerging system, one that in truth has always been present but not accessible until after the Harmonic Convergence of 1987. Tremendous energy lines flow outward from the northern axis point and reenter at the southern. These energetic lines are directly connected to all sacred sites of Gaia. There are hundreds.

The grids reflect, and to an extent regulate, parameters of the consciousness of both Gaia and spirit. The Gravity grid and Electromagnetic grid have been adjusted on several occasions since man's establishment on the Earth plane 200,000 years ago. The Crystalline 144 grid became anchored in 1992, and scheduled activation began in 2001.

## Platonic Solids Geometry

Since our planet's birth, the grid work around the Earth has consisted of a sacred geometry matrix of one of the five Platonic solids. Plato believed that the Earth's basic structure was in the process of evolving from simple geometric shapes into more complex ones. In order of complexity, the five patterns theorized by Plato to be the building blocks of crystalline matrix are the tetrahedron (4 faces), hexahedron (6 faces), octahedron (8 faces), dodecahedron (12 faces) and icosahedron (20 faces). Plato further theorized that the earth was evolving into an icosahedron grid.

Academics, including Dr. Ivan Sanderson, Dr. Hagens and Dr. Becker, diagramed this shape in the 1970s by connecting major electromagnetic fields on the map. The points formed a triangular pattern of pentagons ... an icosahedron. However the pattern did not truly map the grid as was intended. The icosahedron was, in fact, the geometry of the planetary light grid for the past twelve millennia, prior to the Harmonic Convergence

The Harmonic Convergence was an organized spiritual event that occurred on August 16 and August 17, 1987. when groups of people gathered in various sacred sites and power points all over the world to herald a new frequencial vibration. The date was based on the Mayan calendar and Mayan cosmology.

The Harmonic Convergence was a global awakening to unity and divine love, an opportunity for transformation. It was initiated in 1987 by Jose Arguelles. According to his interpretation of Mayan cosmology, this date was the conclusion of 22 cycles of 52 years each, or 1,144 years. The Harmonic Convergence also began the final 26 year countdown to the end of the Mayan calendar in 2012 which would be the "end of history" and the beginning of a new 5,125 year cycle. According to the prophesy, this is the turning point where all the negativity and paths of destruction, war, materialism, violence, abuses, injustice and governmental abuse of power, will end with the birth of the 6th Sun and the 5th World on Earth, on the winter solstice of 2012, Decmber 21, 2012.

The 1987 Harmonic Convergence was also a measurement of Earth's vibratory level, a test. The Earth revealed a far greater measurement of 'light' than ever before. For the first time since the 'great fall,' the planet carried more 'light' than 'dark.' As a result, the grids required 'adjustments.' The Magnetic grid was adjusted to lessen the 'veil' separating humans from their higher dimensional aspects. The Telluric grid was adjusted to enable a greater vibratory rate, and this is particularly enacted within the energy of grid points and sacred sites. The Crystalline grid took on a new, higher geometric model, capable of regulating a far more sophisticated light code than the old icosahedron.

*As Joseph Jochmans writes in "Earth A Crystal Planet," "Beyond the Platonic series of Solids is another form being geometrically generated out of the old Icosa-Dodeca crystal. If you take an Icosahedron and join together with lines every other point inside the form, you create twelve pentacles or five-pointed stars. If you extend the outer edges of the Icosahedron and join these node points together, you create a second group of twelve pentacles or stars. This becomes the seed crystal that gives birth to a new crystalline form called a double penta- dodecahedron, composed of twelve double-pentacles equally spaced across the surface of the globe."*

The Crystalline 144 grid is now emerging beyond the icosahedron. A 'seed-crystal' matrix, the double penta dodecahedron, is born. The evolved geometry is divinely fashioned to resonate a higher frequency for the new Earth.

Mainstream researchers are in fact noting

that the node points and grid alignments, earlier attributed to the Becker-Hagens icosahedron grid map, no longer fit. Weather patterns are changing, climates are in major flux and migration routes of birds are altered. Whales and dolphins are beaching themselves far more often since the Harmonic Convergence.

. The Earth's geomagnetic field is changing, and changing fast. The Earth's heartbeat, the Schumann resonance, is said to be increasing by some knowledgeable geophysicists, although others dispute this. Volcanic activity, earthquakes and super hurricanes are occurring more often. The phenomenon of global warming has created the 'el nino' phenomena, and the polar ice caps are melting. Solar storms and their resulting winds are spraying the planet at a rate higher than has ever been recorded.

This is undeniably an incredibly monumental transformation of global proportion. The planet's frequency is increasing, and our concept of time is speeding up. The planet is being prepared to vault into the 4th and 5th dimensions.

The new Ascension grid is increasing in frequency as the Magnetic grid is lessened. The dual grid complex is evolving into a trinity matrix. A crystalline frequency is being transmitted to the planet. This validates the prophesied change in the grid system and the work of the magnetic master, Kryon.

We can all be a part of the new crystal formation … the Crystalline 144 Ascension grid. One of the most meaningful avenues available to us in the ascension process is in coming together as Lightworkers and Earth-Keepers in ceremony and unity, to awaken all humanity and bond with the Living Earth, the Living Cosmos, by generating and directing awakened loving energy.

By concerted efforts to support and give light to the Ascension grid, we accelerate both its activation and our own. The planetary Ascension grid is a manifestation of the energy evolvement and patterned growth of the Universal Consciousness. Earth is the living Gaia, the grid is her aura. Sacred geometry is the language and fabric of higher dimension, higher consciousness. Accordingly, the grid contains the sacred geometry energy patterns of the golden phi and spiral, the platonic solids, the Flower of Life and the crystal matrix of creation.

The triple dates, the 01-01-01, January 1, 2001 occur each year all the way to the 12-12-12, December 12, 2012. These dates are numeric frequency portals that in fact are each aligned to activate one of the 12 major facets of the 144 Crystalline geodesic grid, the double penta dodecahedron. The Crystalline grid becomes fully activated in December of 2012. A new world begins, as predicted so long ago by the Hopi and Mayans. The year 2007 tips the balance, with more than half of the Crystalline 144 in operational function.

There are many tools operating in synergy to increase the planet's frequency. Among the most important are the light portals that are geometrically and magnetically aligned to the Crystalline grid and to specific points in the cosmos. These 'sacred sites and power points' are, in essence, diamond inserts on the planet, with frequencial geometric overlays and electromagnetic properties that allow higher dimensional coded light and energy to flow into our reality. Many are being drawn to them, and that is appropriate. These are the accoutremental machinery of the Crystal grid, the primary manifold mechanism of the Ascension.

These are particularly powerful on the equinoxes, solstices and trinity numeric frequency dates, leading up to the 12-12-12. When Lightworkers and seekers visit these sites, they are able to align themselves to the Crystalline grid trinity, to anchor themselves to its frequency and to activate their hearts to the activation of the Ascension grid.

## Merging Into the 144 Crystal Grid

We accept readily that we are energetic beings surrounded by a potent electromagnetic field. We chose to be part of the ascension process and the ascension of the living Gaia. We channel inward great flows of cosmic divine energy with the capacity to direct this light outward through directed meditative thought for the highest good.

By unifying our energies in synchronized ecstatic states, we form a powerful light vortex. This energy can cleanse, brighten, energize and activate each one of us, according to our intent and flow. Our intent is light of the highest order, transferred to the new grid, the new Crystal matrix of Gaia … the 144 Crystal vibration.

## Activation Mediation

The exercise for energy connection, transferral and activation of the Ascension grid is as follows:

1. Find a place to sit or lie comfortably.
2. Breath very deeply and rhythmically.
3. Visualize diamond light energy coming in through the crown chakra.
4. Send it down through the spine, through each chakra and back to the heart.
5. Flow the energy in a beam, a corridor of light energy, into the core of the Earth.
6. From the core of the Earth, visualize the white light energy, flashing into an infinity of light frequencies, feeding into the Crystalline 144 Ascension grid.
7. Experience the ecstasy, and allow it to flow.

If this is done at a sacred site, power point or grid point, visualize receiving this energy and then connecting it through your heart to other sacred sites and back into the Ascension grid. Visualize weaving the vertices (points) of the geodesic sphere.

Through our creation and transfer of diamond light, joyous energy, into the Crystalline 144 Ascension grid, we simultaneously activate ourselves to be in alignment with the heightened energy of ascension. We become loving, channeling columns of light, we connect as one synergetic beam of ecstasy. Each participant is a vortex, a point of light on the globe, one with another, one with the ascension. Creating, cocreating the frequency of the New Planet Earth toward the highest good. We are a microcosm of the macrocosm, a point of light in the bursting infinity of light. We are love, and are loved. We become part of the 144,000. We are the rapture, the ecstasy!

## Tyberonn Channel

Arch Angel MedAtRon
Calibration of Angels

*"Greetings, Beloved! You are energy in motion, energy as desire expressing itself, and so your work calls forth now a finer frequency. Imagine that if you will take vitamins for your body, they must be put so they can be absorbed by the body, so they can be well used, they can generate wellness, well being and health. And so it is the same with frequencies and energies. They must now surround you in ways that you can absorb them into your energy fields, transferring them, converting them and amplifying them into your own work, into your desires, into your fulfillment and into all ways that touch humanity, brother, sister, kingdom and such. And so these words are brought to you from the beginning, from the center of your being, from the center of my being, that they will touch energetically and so create themselves easily, fortuitously, in the days and weeks that come. For that which you call the Ascension is upon you, and in but a wink of the Cosmic eye it will be done! In my realm it has been done already, you see, and indeed it is*

*a wondrous event. One heralded throughout the Universe and observed by many on this realm and others.*

*Now, we speak on the grid system. We will confirm as the channel has written. There are three grids, and each has a separate geometry, a separate frequency, differing dimensional aspects and unique assignments, but it is the three that are the one, you see. It is again the trinity that has played such an important symbolic role and purpose on your planet, has it not? So in the grid system, it is also the three into the one, the Trinity. Now, it is not as much that they only appeared after the Harmonic Convergence, it is that others became aware of them after the Harmonic Convergence. Your frequency is required to evolve into the crystalline, and this is occurring as we speak. So the matched frequencies resonate harmonically, and so as this occurs individually and planet-wide, you gain access to this grid. You tap into it, in your terms, and it activates you and itself in the process. All around you there is energy, there is life taking place, but if you are not in sync with this frequency you will not sense it. The propeller blades of your helicopters rotate so quickly in flight that you cannot see them, but they are indeed there. If you were also moving or rotating as quickly, they would be quite visible to you and, in fact, not appear to be moving so rapidly. And so it is with frequency, with lines of energy, it is the same.*

*Now, we confirm the geometries of the three components of the trinity grid complex as proposed by the channel. The dodecahedron, icosahedron and double penta dodecahedron, or as you term it the 144 Crystal, a term most appropriate, we will say. However you must know that the very shape of each defines its frequencial quotient and as such its dimensional span. Dimensions are defined by wavelength or frequency, you see. You required the higher frequency for the planet to move higher, thus the access to the 144 Crystalline grid*

*became a necessity, a graduation. In aspect, the grids reside in different frequencial space, different dimensions, although there is common ground in which they all share.*

*The 144 Crystal grid is only potentially accessible as mankind achieves the frequencial capability to operate in its harmonic. This occurs initially on an individual basis, and as it gains field, it will occur in more mass consciousness upshifts. This is why, as the 144 Crystal presents itself, some of you are already in the fourth and fifth, and others are not. The masses are not. But it is not that it is required for existence, you see. Others will not choose to ascend, but they will not disappear or die off. There are other opportunities based upon sacred geometry that supports third dimensional life, and they will continue to do so.*

*We will say that the dodecahedron extends to the third dimension, the icosahedron fluctuates just below the forth and the Crystalline to the ninth. Now, the channel believes that the crystalline grid extends to the 12th dimension. We tell you that above the ninth, it changes form and extends to the 12$^{th}$ in another geometry, another frequency. You see, geometry is relative to the dimensional frequency from which it is viewed. From your perspective the crystalline does appear to move into the 12$^{th}$, but in truth it does so with a different geometry, the polyhedron 120. This grid, in fact, somewhat contains the 144 within its 182 composition. The dodecahedron, the icosahedron and Crystalline 144 breathes, they do not spin, and each of the greater contains the one below it. The 120 Polyhedron does indeed spin, in what is termed the golden ellipsoid, relative to the creation frequency of the golden phi. In your universe the golden ratio is of utmost importance. Do you understand? This geometry and frequency will not come into a major role on your planet for some years, and the exact timing is yet to be known. But we ask the channel not to be confused by the numerical value of its name and assume*

*120 is lower than 144. You see the 120 Polyhedron has a greater frequency, the geometry of 182, so perhaps we should, with tongue in cheek, call it the 182 Polyhedron. Would that make it easier then?*

Befor 1987 Earth was To Be Terminated

*Now, the channel has asked if the Earth was on a pattern of termination prior to the Harmonic Convergence. That is correct, it was prophesied by many. However, it is not that the Earth was patterned for destruction prior to the Harmonic measurement. The Earth would have survived, inverted and recreated itself; it was patterned simply to become a different entity. Humanity was slated for termination and not the Earth, you see. A meteor crashing into the Earth with a diameter of over one kilometer would indeed have wiped out most of humankind and made the planet uninhabitable.*

*Now, the Earth is a living entity and has been conscious in all of her forms. As a gaseous fiery sphere, the Earth was just as conscious as she is now, in your terms. It is with humor that we see man speaking of saving the planet, and while we commend the environmentalists of your planet, what is truly being saved is man's ability to live upon the Earth. You see, the planet will survive even if man destroys the resources required for his biology to sustain itself.*

*The channel has referred to unique dates he calls the trinity dates, the 01-01-01 to the 12-12-12. We will confirm they are important and are patterned for activation of the grid. But we will say it is not 'written in stone.' In other words, the more important trigger of consciousness to the grid is based upon the rate of human evolvement. We will say that the 12-12-12 and the 12-21-12 (they are the same, you see), are important numerological and astrological triggers for the planet and grid system, but a more powerful trigger is that of mankind's degree of ascension. Intent and will are far stronger than astrological or numerical influences, you see.*

*The trinity dates are important, but NOT more important than moments or triggers of the free will, which can potentially accelerate the geometric activation of the crystalline frequency. That potential would speed the synergy. That would be a catalyst that would open the Crystalline grid into greater function sooner than scheduled.*

*So we say to you, do not believe that the ascension cannot occur before 2012. It can. Now, in terms of humanity's anticipated unfoldment and becoming aware of its cosmic ties to the 144 Crystal, yes in that way, these dates are pre-programmed, as described relating to the 12 facets, leading to 2012. We tell you that as of 2007, you are ahead of schedule. You are beloved."*

… and so it is.

# Arkansas ~ Emerging Crystal Portal

In November 2001, I attended a Kryon channel in New England that had a serendipitous effect on me. In the course of the channel, Kryon gave a precisely dated timeline of Atlantis, then added that indisputable evidence of Atlantis exists in Arkansas! The comment energized me.

Synchronicity noted. I had been experiencing tugs to do a little 'global' exploring in my home state for weeks prior to the Kryon channel. Kryon's bidding provoked mental exploration of where the Atlanteans would have left 'evidence' in Arkansas.

The first thing that came to mind was diamonds and quartz. Atlantis used them, Arkansas has them. As I began examining possible areas of Atlantean mining, a prolific juxtaposition occurred. I contacted several Lightworkers about the subject and soon learned that many Earth-Keepers had been recently receiving intuitive tugs regarding Arkansas.

The referred serendipity became quite poignant. I became keenly aware that Arkansas' unique geology would play a major role in the ascension of the planet. (A separate topic from the search of Atlantis, yet equally fascinating … and perhaps more important.)

**The Trip to Arkansas**

I loaded my Suburban and made the 8-hour drive to Arkansas' Ouachita Mountains on a sunny Thursday. The drive was pleasant and uneventful along the flat, straight expanse of Texas Highway 59. As I cruised through Texarkana into the rolling green hills of the Ouachitas, the energy became discernibly softer.

My destination was Crater of Diamonds State Park. I spent the night in Magnolia, and drove onward to the diamond mine-cum-State Park. Interesting things occurred as I entered the Little Missouri River valley that winds serpentine through the lushly forested hills. Pines gave way to thickets of hickory, oak and sweetgum. Occasional sycamore trees stretched high over the green canopy. I felt a distinctive sensation of being lulled into a deep creative serenity … peaceful, yet vividly awake. Ideas and impressions came in from all angles. I was aware of feeling very 'expansive.' Time passed quickly, and suddenly I was there. Two hours had passed in what felt like a quarter hour. Interesting energy field!

**Mounds and Rivers**

As soon as I stepped out of the car, I felt the pull of the crater. The heady perfume of gardenias hung wonderfully in the air, as I ambled to the Park entrance. Nothing like natural incense to kick-start data feed in a power-point! This site would not disappoint me.

I loved the quaint location. The diamond crater is pocketed alongside the Little Missouri River, a clear, pristine river held sacred by the Quapaw Indians. The Quapaws were themselves descended from Mound Builders who had several impressive mounds in the general area. Most notably the Toltec Mounds in central Arkansas, Spiro Mounds in eastern Oklahoma and Poverty Point Mounds in northern Louisiana. All built near major rivers.

**Arkansas Volcanic Pipe**

The diamond crater is actually three overlapping volcanic pipes, composed of the telltale green kimberlite soil. The 'Kimberlite Pipes' of Arkansas, like the ones found in Africa, are a cornucopia of diamonds, amethysts, peridot, garnet, carnelian and myriad other semi-precious stones. The rich dark soil had been plowed and turned to allow the dozens of 'miners' – mainly families and school groups – to dig through the greenish loam for treasures. Everyone seemed happy and very grounded. There was something both inviting and therapeutic about sifting and digging in that earth. The child in me wanted to tread barefoot in the soft tilled loam and squeeze it between my toes!

I walked the perimeter and came upon three young, well-educated Park Rangers giving talks under a pavilion fitted with water lines and screen-meshed shakers, explaining to would be miners the unique geology and strategy of finding gems.

"Over 500 diamonds were found here in 2001," the Rangers explained. "This is the eighth largest diamond mine in the world, and the only active diamond mine in the United States." The 20-minute talk was quite comprehensive, geological and useful to the stone miners. Very interesting indeed.

The blue skies began to cloud over, so I surveyed the concave crater grounds and spotted an enormous oak situated on a well-grassed slope. It seemed to call me over, and I joyfully obliged. A soft rain started to fall as I nestled under the thick cover of the big oak. The summer shower was light and passed quickly, creating that pungent, earthy after scent of rain on soil. A soft breeze flowed past and carried the wafting perfume of gardenias in bloom around the Ranger station. The two aromas mixed in a wonderful aromatic cocktail.

## Tyberonn Channel

Sitting there, back against the tree, I drifted, totally relaxed … and tuned to the energy of the place. Then I felt the familiar tap of Tyberonn, my spirit guide.

*"Beneath the surface of the central region of Arkansas rest enormous beds of crystals the size of which are stunning. Some of these quartz points are the size of skyscrapers seeded by the Atlanteans. These are out of the reach of mining concerns, well below the sacred waters. These 'Mother/Father Crystals' are very ancient and have been in a dormant mode for millennia. They are now ready for re-awakening and will release a magnificent energy once the crystal portal is anchored in place. Much clearing has been done, and more will follow. Many Lightworkers have been drawn to this area over the past decade, and others who feel the 'tug' will soon follow. Earth-Keepers are drawn to align themselves to this crystalline energy, some to anchor and prepare it for what will occur in 2012. Others will visit and be healed, and in so doing add their energy to the crystal matrix through ritual and healing prayers. This is assisted by many on the etheric plane."*

## Tyb's Download

My focal download of information occurred in a span of 20 minutes, but I knew the clarity of this oasis facilitated the flow. I wrote quickly, most of it after the flow, comfortably nestled against the oak. There was a lot of information. I was told that Arkansas is being activated as a major portal of the Crystal 144 Grid … and this diamond crater is one of three satellites that will anchor and feed the vortex.

## The Vortex

I was told that a wide vortex is in formation that will combine three separate energy fields in Arkansas and western Oklahoma, and this synergistic blend will disseminate a coded-crystalline energy throughout the mid and southern sections of the United States. The vortex will connect and blend three different energy fields: Eureka Springs, the Talimena Ridge (Rich Mountain), and Mount Ida (Hot Springs).

17

The center-apex is between Hot Springs Village and Mount Ida. Here the crystal energy will be emanated in a pristine fountain and carried in a spiraled sweep into eastern Oklahoma and southwest Missouri, in a unique two-segmented vortex. The approximate parameters of the ovalesque (2 part) vortex are Crater of Diamonds, Spiro Mounds, Christ of the Ozarks, Blanchard Springs and Toltec Mounds.

## Stargate Crystal Portal

The portal forming over Arkansas is a function of the Crystal 144 Grid. The portal is, in essence, a white hole, a stargate. It charges energy inward from higher dimensions into the earth plane. The portal will feed coded light energy into the awakened crystals, and the crystals will in turn outflow their new and stored energies for distribution by the vortex engine.

## Semi-Circular Compression Vortex

This particular vortex has a unique aspect that I have never before encountered. While it is somewhat circular in shape around the crystal portal, it is composed of two semi-circular segments that enclose the energy but are not connected in terms of energy flow. The energy does not circulate in a circular surrounding motion. Each semi-circular segment shifts in a to-and-fro movement, similar to the agitator inside a washing machine. The semi-circular templates are fixed in place and do not shift. The energy patterns rotate within them. The vortex aperture is of a smaller diameter at the base and increases in width as it rises higher. Tyberonn explained that the side-ringer format creates an internal pressure inside the matrix of the vortex, and that compresses and accelerates the light-coded crystal energy being vaulted upward. The two fulcrum-tips of the energy movements in each semi-circular template are in multidimensional synchronicity. The momentum of the two contained energies are in balanced opposition to one another. It is, in fact, this balance of opposing motion that holds the vortex intact and forces the energy upward, jacuzzi style, into the dimensional fields for distribution.

Although the vortex is intricately connected to the portal, it operates from a different grid – the (electro)-magnetic grid (icosahedron) – and operates under different mechanics. The vortex extends from 1,000 feet below the Earth's surface to about 8,000 feet above it. The upper portion of the vortex brings in the hydro energies, the mid portion the crystalline, and the lower segment the magnetics.

## Trinity of Tellurics

Combining three distinct vortices of different telluric energies, and forming one blended mega-vortex, is quite a powerful undertaking and will not happen overnight.

The three vortex nodes referenced represent three differing telluric energies:
- Crystal energies of the Ouachita Mountains centered between Mount Ida and Hot Springs.
- Magnetic energies of the Talimena Ridge on the western borders of the state.
- Hydro energies centered in a 70-mile radius around Eureka Springs in the northwest corner of the state.

Each area requires some energy clearing, healing and anchoring. This has been ongoing, and it is quickening. There still remains work to do in this regard. Although the vortex became operationally functional in 2005, it will not flow in full synergistic capacity until 2012.

## Clearing and Preparation of the Three Centers

In general the spring (hydro) energies of the northwest portion of the state are quite clear. The nature of the waters and the relative remoteness and resort status of the area have helped maintain its clarity.

The crystalline and electromagnetic fields need more clearing. This is a work in progress. All Lightworkers can help. Prayers, particularly utilizing an Arkansas crystal, are uniquely potent, but all prayer adds to the energy. Many clear, crystalline rivers traverse these mountains, and these aid greatly in the energy balance.

Many Lightworkers and Earth-Keepers, as Tyberonn said, (and I have since confirmed), are being pulled and drawn to the three Arkansas centers to aid in preparation for the 2012 ascension.

Tyberonn advises that each continent has its own energetic chakra system, powerpoints, meridians and leys. These are being cleared and reworked to appropriately correlate to each of the three harmonic grids: 1) Dodecahedron Gravity Grid , 2) Icosahedron Electromagnetic Grid and 3) Crystal 144 Grid (double penta dodecahedron).

## Crystal Center

The crystalline energy is centered in the Hot Springs - Mount Ida portion of the state. The crystal-bearing quartz deposits occur in strata 35 miles wide and 170 miles long, extending from Little Rock to beyond Talimena. However, the richest deposits occur in a powerful area between Hot Springs, Mount Ida and Jessieville. The mega crystals are deep below the Hot Springs area.

The thermal waters that give Hot Springs its name are protectors for these generators. The 47 hot springs along the forested southwestern slope of Hot Springs Mountain gush forth nearly a million gallons of 143°F water every day. The water is slightly radioactive with a very clear, focused energy. This water is remarkably healing and contains higher dimensional energy codes.

There are intermittent pockets of duality that do clearly require work. Hot Springs was an underworld gambling mecca from the 1920s through the early 1960s. Al Capone maintained a residence there as did many crime figures. That energy has been cleared to a large degree, but it is not completed. The Lightworkers, drawn to this crystalline vortex over the past decade, are being led to the areas for healing this residue and to assist in dimensional alignment. Much of this preparation has been completed.

## Talimena Ridge: Magnetic Outflows

The 'magnetic energy' is focused around Rich Mountain along the Talimena Ridge of western Arkansas and eastern Oklahoma. Iron and lodestone deposits abound. While most magnetic vortices have a downward pull, the magnetic energy here actually has an outward flow at the numerous vertical and lateral node points along the ridge. This happens rarely.

It is in fact this area that is the most powerful centre within the Arkansas vortex, combining most effectively the crystal and hydro energies, magnetically infusing and activating them. A powerful stargate exists near the apex of the ridge near Queen Wilamena State Park.

I heartily recommend the ridge crest drive from Mena, Arkansas to Talimena, Oklahoma. It rises sharply from the town of Mena and showcases 70 miles of beautiful overlook vistas with spectacular views on both sides. Some overlooks are located at incredible energy nodes, especially the one just east of the state park hotel. The 70-mile ridge actually contains the highest elevations between the Appalachians and the Rockies. National forests sandwich the ridge with massive tracts of virgin mountain forest, never having been inhabited. The 'raw' nature of the forest areas has preempted the need for clearing and balance. Certain points have pockets of a potent magnetic energy that is somewhat electrically imbalanced.

As with many power areas, religious groups have for years been drawn to the surrounding valleys near the ridge. Large groups of Mennonites, Ammonites and Rainbow People have colonies in this area on private lands adjacent to the National Forests. Their sincerity and spiritual seeking has contributed to the vibratory clarity of the Talimena Ridge. Bigfoot and Yeti have been reported in the ridge and virgin forest areas for centuries.

## Eureka Springs

The 'hydro apex' is centered near Eureka Springs in northwestern Arkansas. Long viewed as sacred land by the indigenous peoples of the region, the massive spring system that surfaces near Eureka Springs and undulates as an aquifer throughout northwest Arkansas and southwest Missouri creates an incredible plasmic field of benevolent anionic particles. The energy here is very balanced, and a tangible sense of spiritual well being exists within this area of the Ozark Mountains, centered near Eureka Springs. Several sacred rivers run through this area as arteries of heart energy. These include the Buffalo River, which was protected by a myriad of spiritual forces acting in synchronicity. The Buffalo River became the first river in the USA to be designated a 'National River' three decades ago. This declaration provided a protection that prevented commercialization of the area and halted plans for a hydroelectric dam.

## Telluric Field Electrics

As in any field of intensely charged earth, electrics will freely form pockets of anionic and cationic fields. Therefore certain areas will often hold pockets of electrical plasma that can become overcharged or imbalanced. Both create a macro balance, yet form a micro imbalance. Areas of benevolent feel usually have a 5-to-4 ratio of anions over cations. When this ratio is not in place, energy pools occur, which create a sense of imbalance. This will happen in pristine or raw areas. Yellowstone is another example of this. Certain areas with this imbalance are being groomed and redistributed to facilitate the flow of the vortex.

## Atlantean Mines in Arkansas

Now, I have completely evaded the initial concept of this article, regarding Atlantis mining in Arkansas … up to this point. So, where are they? Perhaps that's for you to find. The clues given me, after tedious research and channeled guidance from Tyberonn and Metatron, are combined as follows:

- Below Mount Ida are ancient remnants of Atlantean tunnels and mines, but these are quite deep.
- Outside Eureka Springs is the most likely area. Within the labyrinth of limestone caves that network the entirety of the Ozarks are passageways that link into a complex and abandoned facility, within which incredible mining structures still remain. These, according to Tyberonn, were used for mining a far more precious substance of which we have no knowledge today. There is a greenish, porous, phosphorus compound mineral that was used in the Temple of Rejuvenation in Atlantis. This mineral is a rare derivative of a more common mineral, and it still exists in an area not too far from the Christ of the Ozarks region of northwest Arkansas. It is near, I was told, a natural body of water. I was also told that when the cave evidence is found, it must be reported to journalists and put on the Internet quickly so that the authorities cannot cover it up and hide it.
- One other interesting tidbit that may be related – it is a little publicized fact that there are two areas in northwest Arkansas where ancient stones have been found that have petroglyphs

– ancient writing similar to Viking runes. These predate Columbus by 300 - 500 years. A more publicized occurrence of this is in the nearby Runestone State Park in eastern Oklahoma, near the Talimena Ridge, in Heavner, Oklahoma. Some speculate an evolved writing similar to the Atlantean hieroglyphics, not unlike rare specimens of the rune writings on certain Mayan ruins. Others believe they are from Viking explorers.

- There are vast hollow earth regions deep below the Talimena Ridge which are colonized by what is often referred to as the 'Blue Beings'. There is additionally a Sirius B base in this area. The magnetic energies provide a stargate matrix that enables entry and exit through hyper dimensional doorways.

## Tyberonn Channel

*"There are many locations within the United States that were colonies of Atlantis. These include upstate New York; Asheville, North Carolina; Stone Mountain, Georgia, Ohio, Florida and Arkansas. Many areas throughout the eastern and central states were mined. The language spoken by some of the red tribes, especially that of the Iroquois, is very close to the tongue of the Atlanteans. The area of Arkansas contains those remnants best preserved. Some of this has been found but not recognized. The greater evidence is underground. Some of the greatest Atlantean crystals are stored in Arkansas. The potency of these crystals have created a hyper dimensional field that is capable of shaking the grounds and bending the space-time continuum far more powerfully than those beneath the Sargasso Sea in the area of Bimini. It is the magnetics of this location, in fact, that have held these crystal energies in balance. That is why our team of Crystal Physicians selected this area for their storage and seeding. You have no idea of the energy these are capable of generating. You see, it is the use of magnetic energies along with etheric light, light*

*above the visible spectrum, light you refer to as infrared and gamma, that is used to both subdue and amplify crystals. An etheric gateway has existed over this area for the past 20,000 years, and a gateway of high frequency light is able to be focused into this area. A vast system of hyper dimensional tunnels networks the areas below central and northwest Arkansas. Some of these are still in use. The ability to detect these hyper dimensional tunnels will not be within your scientific capabilities for several more years. The metal you call gold is present at deeper levels within the beds of quartz crystals below Arkansas. Your geologists are well aware that gold often occurs in crystallized quartz. The Great Atlantean Crystals placed below the lands of Arkansas are actually an alloy conglomerate of quartz and gold. These were manifested through Acturian technology. The frequency of crystalline gold is capable of combining with specific types of high frequency quartz to enable the 'bending & molding' of dimensional fields. Dimensional access tunnels were often created using this methodology by the Atlanteans to create wormholes or dimensional tunnels within the Earth's mantle that could be accessed at a higher frequency. Many of these hyper dimensional tunnels were laid into place along the flows of existing leylines of natural telluric currents that flow on the Earth. Tectonic shifts have damaged many, but not all, of these. Some of these were simply deactivated. There are higher dimensional beings, from Sirius B, as part of the Ashtar Command legion, that have been given the task of repairing and activating many of these over the past two decades. Some of you, such as the channel, work with them.*

*Ley lines and great crystals were de-energized at periods when the people of Earth went into the periods of consciousness decline, in the sad wake of Atlantis. This was done without damage to the crystals. The reactivation process of portals, crystals and hyper dimensional matrixes has been taking place since 1986 and will continue over the next few years. This is the awakening that has drawn many of you to such places.*

*The geometric science you call sacred geometry is key to this awakening. Sacred geometry is the very fabric of the Cosmos. That is why the crystalline aspect is essential to the planetary ascension. Your very atomic structures are composed of perfectly aligned geometries, crystalline geometries, knitted into place with the thread of electro-magnetics. Electricity and magnetics are components of light. Your spectrum of visible light is but a candle in comparison to the magnificent geometric light of the higher spectrum. The crystalline aspect of Arkansas is not limited to the quartz. The energy of Arkansas is on a higher dimension, that of a multidimensional octahedron, that has formed itself to the level of the 9$^{th}$ dimensional field. The energy is transformed from the hexagonal of quartz to the octahedral of gold quartz and diamond. Diamonds project an octahedral geometry, and thus the volcanic pipes in Arkansas that bear the energy of diamond transform the cube to the octahedron. The hexahedron is enclosed in the octahedron.*

*The quartz Crystals of Arkansas are imbedded with the energy and wisdom of what is referred to as the Atlantean Law of One. The Master Crystals placed there have frequencially transferred this vibration to the quartz indigenous to the area, and as we have explained, the Master Crystals contained a higher dimensional alloy of gold conglomerate that has been received energetically by some of the naturally occurring beds. The crystals from the McEarl mine carry this unique harmonic. These are especially potent. All crystals are alive in a real sense and have an ordered consciousness and a self-awareness, but each carries unique and specific blueprint patterns. These patterns are greatly varied according to the geology and astrological energies of the vector. Therefore, seemingly identical gems and crystals can be quite different in their energetic*

*projections according to the location where they are mined.*

*Arkansas is aligned energetically to the Atlantean portions of Brazil. The Diamantina crystals of Brazil are very similar in projection to those of the McEarl mines of Arkansas. Master Crystals from both Atlantis and LeMuria were seeded in Brazil. Crystals are great receivers and transmitters, and a strong communication network occurs between Master Crystals. The connection of the Arkansas vortex/portal to the Brazil vortex/portal is extremely powerful. Keep in mind that while LeMuria is acknowledged as a civilization of great spirituality, there were thousands of years in which Atlantis harbored great spiritual mastery, a mastery that in many ways exceeded that of LeMuria. Atlantis fractured into a polarized society before its demise, but many of the crystals were protected and stored before they fell into misuse. The greater part of these are stored in Arkansas and Brazil.*

*"The role of Arkansas in the planet's graduation, the 2012 Ascension, is moving forward as planned. The wisdom that will be imparted through the Crystalline Projection will be the new Atlantis, the pure Atlantis. Be well, Beloved."*

… and so it is.

**Visitor Information**

For visitors, there are dozens of powerful and beautiful areas to visit in Arkansas. Two exceptional drives are Highway 7, beginning at Hot Springs and headed for 80 miles northward through the Ozarks. This passes through very potent energies. The Talimena Byway from Mena, Arkansas to Talihena, Oklahoma is another 70-mile stretch that traverses potent energies.

Arkansas is in the rural south Bible Belt. 'New Age' beliefs are not shared by most residents.

Healing, crystal rivers such as the Ouachita, Mulberry, Caddo, Cassatot, Strawberry, Buffalo and Little Missouri flow through the mountains. These are available for white water rafting and have beautiful cascades in the mountain regions. Springs sites are in Hot Springs and Eureka Springs. Both are very healing. The War Eagle Mill near Eureka Springs, the Christ of the Ozarks, Rich Mountain, Mount Magazine, Mount Nebo and Hawkbill Overlook are very powerful points in addition to the ones covered in the article.

In terms of crystals, there are dozens of 'metaphysical' mines open to the public. Seekers can dig for their own crystals in rich deposits of laterite earth. This is etherically permitted. However, massive amounts of quartz are being industrially mined on National Forest lands, using bulldozers, backhoes and explosives. This must stop.

Arkansas has the largest deposits of quartz in the United States. There are richly veined deposits of high quality crystal found near the surface in an area between Hot Springs National Park, Mount Ida and Jessieville. Arkansas crystal is noted for its clarity, hardness and several unique electrical properties. Certain mines, most notably the McEarl mine, produce an extremely clear, high frequency crystal, highly prized (and priced) among metaphysical circles. McEarl crystals are very potent and have a greater hardness and density than standard quartz.

## Conclusion

As functions of the new Crystal 144 Grid, portals are emerging in many areas of the USA, of which Arkansas is just one. The Arkansas portal has a unique function because of its tie-in to the crystalline energy. A vortex is being formed to distribute the energy. Many Lightworkers are drawn to these emerging portals to contribute to the anchoring, alignment and facilitation of these portals. Physical presence is not always required to contribute to the clearing of these portals. Each reader can contribute to forming these portals through intent and prayer.

# Canadian Rockies ~ The AA Michael Vortex

An awestruck visitor to Canada's Lake Louise once commented that such scenery was proof that God existed. The year was 1978, years before my awakening. I walked up the cobbled trail from the parking area, staring at the enormous white stone Chateau, shining in the sunlight like polished alabaster. The architectural symmetry and sheer grandeur of the castle are impressive, but I was totally unprepared for the stunning scene that lay behind it. What glowed before me was living painting. A vibrant turquoise mountain lake framed by purple and gold cliffs, ever-green forests and a massive white-blue glacier at the far end. Alpine flowers were everywhere. Beautiful sprays of orange, purple, yellow, white and red were dotted along the lakeside and set in manicured gardens on the grounds of the Chateau Lake Louise Hotel in the forefront. It was love at first sight, and that love affair has continued ever since.

That first visit was brief but made a deep impression. I have revisited Lake Louise dozens of times in the past 25 years. I soon recognized it was a living cathedral, and later still I have become aware of a divine angelic presence anchored to its energy.

**Canadian Park System**

I have traveled far and wide and without reservation aver that Lake Louise, located in Banff National Park in Alberta, Canada is the most beautiful place in North America. The entire region of the Canadian Rockies is majestic. Banff National Park has 6,641 square kilometers of mountains, forests, rivers and lakes that is the habitat to abundant wildlife. Banff National Park is Canada's first national park, located 80 miles west of Calgary, Alberta. Lake Louise is 35 miles west of Banff.

The Canadians have done an incredible job of protecting the pristine nature of this massive jewel and of managing the four national and provincial parks connected to the Rockies in western Alberta and eastern British Columbia. Other nations could learn a thing or two from a review of how the Canadian Park Services operate.

The Park has a superb 4-lane highway that passes through the center glacier scraped valley of the Athabascan Rockies. The incredible ice cut mountains are a blue jagged spine visible on both sides of the roadway passage. The drive is a dreamscape. Every turn brings exquisite beauty. Each mountain projects a unique presence and dignity. The energy field is serene and exhilarating all at once. The turquoise Bow River flows along the side, presenting a summerscape of evergreens, wildflowers and river valley against a towering blue drapery of scraped and sculpted rock face.

Whether it is the land, the grid, the culture, the people or a combination thereof, I find the vibratory rate of Canada very high and extremely balanced. It is tangibly higher than that in the Lower 48 and immediately discernable, both coming in and going out!

**Chateau Lake Louise**

Chateau Lake Louise sits atop a creviced moraine, created by Victoria Glacier when the last Ice Age ended some 10,000 years ago. The lake is a startling blend of green and blue water, so beautifully iridescent that it appears to be emit a glow, as if lit from underneath. At the far end of the mile long lake soars Mt. Victoria, exquisitely etched in the white blue of the crystalline glacier.

**Energy Concentrated Within Geological Walls**

Lake Louise is boxed on three sides by high granite walls that enclose the magical area like the cradled hands of God. The rock wall enclosure and resulting energy containment is *very, very significant*. It is this boxed enclosure of the various inflows of telluric, solar and elemental energies that differentiates Lake Louise. Its cubic and octahedral formations entrap and amplify the energy level. Visibly, it is one of the most beautiful mountain scenes on Earth … but it has an unseen inner majesty and purpose. Lake Louise is a key triangulated point of one of the most powerful portals on the Planet, a sacred portal that anchors the energy of Archangel Michael.

## Energy of Balance and Healing

Its balancing healing powers are immense. It is a sacred place, a healing, balancing energy of great intensity. It is a great, yet subtle, intensity that effects every visitor to the special mountaintop of Lake Louise … and there are many visitors. Contrary to what one may initially conceive, the energy of Lake Louise is absolutely not mal-effected by the hundreds of daily visitors and hotel guests. *In fact, it is enhanced.* The visitors are, without exception, moved by the energy and incredible, inspiring beauty. All visitors experience a sense of the profound beauty and awe, and that emotional energy is released onto and contributes to the incredible energy of place at Lake Louise.

Its energy is as powerful as any on the planet, yet its intensity is not overwhelming. Its balance is the plate that serves this experience to the pilgrim and tourist alike in a palatable, gentle manner. Comparable energy levels in less gentle formats are capable of depleting the aura, not so with Lake Louise. Negativity seems nullified within its energies, and the feelings of beauty and love are amplified.

As a result, few of the first time visitors to Lake Louise anticipate the depth of the spiritual experience they are going to have, and few of them leave without being profoundly healed by it. The emotional reaction to the awesome beauty opens and immediately balances the aura. The penetrating, spiritual energy emanating from the lake triggers self-searching and deep cleansing. I have seen robust tourists become so moved by the beauty

and healing energy of the lake that tears of joy flood their eyes within minutes. It is particularly healing for visiting couples and families. Few conflicts, fears or anxieties can remain buried in this energy, and their surfacing occurs in the energy of immense but gentle love, leading to a cleansing release. So if you want to heal a family or reconcile a relationship, go to Lake Louise. The issues will bubble to the surface in that cleansing magnetic energy.

## Feng Shui of the Chalet

The hotel is a splendid, flowing structure built with natural white limestone in chateau-style symmetrical balance. The lobby and dining areas offer wall-sized picture windows that seem to frame the unbelievable beauty lying beyond them. While the hotel rooms can be quite expensive in peak seasons, the grounds and restaurants are available to all. Having a cup of hot chocolate or tea in one of the overstuffed chairs in the massive lobby with its incredible panoramic views has allowed me great moments of balanced perspective. Of my dozens of visit to Lake Louise, I have only over-nighted there on two or three trips.

I have never left there without a brief pang of melancholy at leaving such beauty and intense clarity. (It was the emotion I used to feel as a young child when we left my Grandma's home at Christmas for the 3-hour drive home – that sad feeling of leaving a precious loved one, knowing it will be a while before I return.)

## Angelic Presence

My first awareness of the angelic presence occurred in 1995. I had spent a full day just drifting in the splendor of a sunny July day on the grassy lawn of the chateau. I lay back on the sweet tufted grass and closed my eyes in a moment of total content. I was fully in the moment, reluctant to leave. I closed my eyes in utter bliss and, in that instant, saw a flash of brilliant golden light. Suddenly I was immersed in an overwhelming emotional flow. Tears welled in my eyes, and I felt a wondrous sense of joy and well being. I saw a clear white-blue light amidst the gold and knew I was seeing an angel. I felt humbled by the enormity and love of the presence. The vision was over in a flash, but the powerful emotions lingered.

I returned the next day and found a beautiful little brook, off the main path to the back of the lake, and sat for an hour of prayer. The magical faerie den by the side of the brook would be the scene of a profound experience I would have with Archangel Michael two years later.

## Tyb's Journal: Touched By an Angel

In late June of 1997, I was dealing with the unexpected death of my sister and had come to Lake Louise in part to deal with that loss. I was up off the lakeside trail about 150 meters, looking for a place that would afford me privacy. About half way down the lakeside trail leading to the back of Lake Louise, a small, gentle mountain brook bubbled and bounced down the steep slope into the lake. I followed it up and found the enchanted faerie den, resplendent in bright, lime-green moss and iridescent yellow lichen, plus two striking striated lavender boulders of sandstone and amazing purple quartz – Amethyst!

The brook formed a couple of little crystal pools there, and wildflowers popped up everywhere amid the spongy moss. Rich green grass carpeted a circular open area near a perky little waterfall. I could actually feel the faeries dancing! This magical and picturesque faerie den opening was something out of an artist's dream – an enchanted and beautiful power-spot. My special place on earth! It was far enough off the main lakeside path of Lake Louise to be totally private, yet afford incredible views of the vibrant, turquoise lake. The day was partly cloudy, but the sun would occasionally break through, and enormous shafts of yellow light would angle in bright, glowing beams through the canopy of the spruce forest. Pure magic!

My meditation soon deepened, and a visible beam of light filled the opening and connected on my chest. At first I thought it was one of the angled sunbeams, but then the energy jolted me, and I saw kaleidoscopic colors everywhere. Then I felt the presence of an Angelic Being. I actually saw a formless, yet intense massive golden light over half the length of the lake. From this light, the energy connected to my heart center in an elongated beam. A blue sphere, glowing golden yellow in its inner core, formed a few feet from where I sat, visible with eyes open or closed. I felt a tremendous divinity and was moved deeply to emotional release. I had one of the most powerful internal reviews of my life to that point, and I was able to pray deeply on each aspect of my life, goals and spiritual purpose. I connected deeply to the angelic energy and understood the anchoring to the lake.

I did not immediately know it was Archangel Michael – that understanding came later – but an angelic 'Light Being' touched me and communed with me in a catharsis of joyful tears and inner cleansing that lasted a timeless two hours or so.

I did not 'see' an angel, nor did I hear any voices. But I felt light, I saw light, and my heart soared. I saw a massive cloud of golden energy, and in a visible ray, it physically connected a beam to my heart. That day was incredible. When I finally departed, I was emotionally exhausted and spiritually cleansed. I go back to that magic spot at least once a year, as the energy of my experience is still there. So is an anchor imprint of my heart and spirit.

## Chakric Area

The entire massif of the Banff Rockies is a chakric expression of Gaia's Divinity. In particular, the water in this area carries a very special vibration. I received a conscious channel specific to the nature of this water, which Tyberonn termed 'Crystal Waters.' The glacier powder in the rivers and lakes is a finely ground, crystallized quartz that has morphed under tremendous pressure and converted the fluids into a magical, colloidal suspension – a liquid battery, a fluid crystal, if you will. It is quite unique in its resonance to this area and adds a tremendous vibratory frequency to the rivers and lakes. The waters become a sacred living crystal of unmatched light and color.

A sequence of sacred lakes and falls occurs within this area, and each is connected in a living chakric system:

(7) Lake O'Hara – Crown Center
(6) Emerald Lake – Brow Center
(5) Lake Moraine – Throat Center
(4) Lake Louise – Heart Center
(3) Peyto Lake – Emotional Center
(2) Bow Falls – Creative Center
(1) Athabasca Falls – Root Center

In actuality, all five of the sacred lakes listed above resonate individually with the four upper chakras. Each balance and heal all chakras and emanate exceptionally high crown vibratory rates. In the divine spectrum of the Michael Vortex, the listings above designate the chakras of the body of the integral living earth of the Canadian Rockies. All seven of the chakric points are connected by major ley lines. The two falls mentioned are outside the inner Michael Vortex, yet serve to pull in the energies of Lower Banff and Upper Jasper to the Michael energetic flow.

**The Michael Portal**

The energy of Archangel Michael began manifesting in the chakric lake region of Banff and Yoho National Parks after the 11:11 gate. The energy is manifested in portals inflowing into Lake Louise, Lake O'Hara and Emerald Lake. All three lakes have sacred mountains associated with their hydro energies that anchor in the portal light. These are Michael Peak at Emerald Lake, Cathedral Mountain at Lake O'Hara and Victoria Mountain at Lake Louise. Each of the individual portal points has a smaller energetic vortex circulating around the focal light of the portal, but this is encapsulating in nature

and not designed as a mechanism of distribution. In a real sense, it is the circular energy that defines the integrity and matrix entry of the light portal. This encapsulation cell is a function of the light grid. The larger electrical vortex I call the Michael Vortex is a function of the electromagnetic grid and serves to distribute the light energy to a much larger area.

**The Inner Michael Vortex**

The Michael Vortex is the engine that distributes the inflow of divine light that occurs in the three portals. The portals are triangulated to create the stability for the circulating vortex. The apex points for the vortex are Michael Peak, Cathedral Mountain and Victoria Mountain. A massive vortex of counterclockwise energy connects all three points.

*Emerald Lake* is very similar in color to Lake Louise. It is less developed and therefore much more serene in its countenance. The Yoho Valley contains a smaller vortex encircling Emerald Lake and includes Takakkaw Falls, Twin Falls and Angel Falls. Takakkaw Falls is the second highest waterfall in Canada, with a total cascade length of over 1,200 feet. The energy of the falls adds greatly to the template of energy captured that is imprinted by the light portal. The sacred apex of Michael Peak aligns the side of Emerald Lake and is the namesake of the angelic energy. The peak was actually named after Andrew Michael, a well-known mountaineer involved in the discoveries of the area, but that choice of names is part of the synchronicity of the Michael energies.

*Lake O'Hara* is the crown center of the Canadian Rockies, the energy being among the most powerful, natural energies I have experienced. Be advised, however, it can be overwhelming in its raw power of amplification. Guard your emotional state and thoughts in this pocket of intense energy. The veil is so thin that it hardly exists here, which requires that you guard your thoughts.

Lake O'Hara is on the opposite side of Victoria Mountain and Glacier from Lake Louise. It is less commercialized than Lake Louise, as it is indeed circled on three sides, so the energy is trapped and concentrated within its high granite and limestone walls. The elevation is higher, the rock walls more reflective and Nature here is raw. Grizzlies abound as do tangible elementals of all types.

Lake O'Hara is the largest of the seven sacred lakes within the O'Hara area and the site of the Lodge. The lake has seven magnificent waterfalls, called the Seven Sisters, cascading into its depth at its southern perimeter. The soft flows of the glacier falls appear as silver ribbons from the lakefront. Lake O'Hara has a fragile flora, so visitation is restricted, with only 120 visitor permits issued daily from late May through mid-October. Fragile and incredibly beautiful tundra, lichen and moss paint the alpine valley with bright iridescent colors from burnt orange and scarlet red to canary yellow.

Sufi mystics, Buddhist organizations and Reiki masters have met at Lake O'Hara annually over the past decade, in quiet recognition of the incredible energy here. A different sort of visitor comes here, as compared to Lake Louise and Emerald Lake. The solitude here is defining. The intensity of the energy here can be almost excessive and incredibly revealing. The veil is so thin here that it is very possible to see manifestations of the elemental and the divine.

The *Greater Banff Vortex* extends beyond the inner perimeter, triangulated between Jasper, Kananastas and Revelstoke. A double triad occurs to create a six-pointed concentric triangle. These areas are full of healing, as balanced and divine energetic points. Sacred mountains abound within, including Three Sisters, Mount Rundle, Castle Mountain, Temple Mountain, Mount Robson, Edith Cavell, Spirit Peak and Mystic Point. (Another separate, yet divine, Earth expression occurs further west in British Colombia, centered in Vancouver Island.)

## Tyberonn Channel

*"Lord Michael began anchoring his presence in a triangulated portal within the core of the Canadian Rockies after the gateway event you call the 11:11. The process required three years to complete. The three pinnacles are Lake Louise, Lake O'Hara and Emerald Lake. These three crystalline lakes hold an incredibly potent energy and are thus capable of sustaining manifestations of Archangel Michael's energetic presence. The clarity that pre-existed in these pristine sites has facilitated many to have direct experiences with his Divine Presence. A counterclockwise energy vortex was set into motion prior to the 12:12, connecting the locations. The triangulation has formed what may be referred to as the Michael Vortex, and a great spiritual light is thus disseminated throughout the entire area for hundreds of miles.*

*Special caretakers have been drawn to these areas to anchor and imprint the energy. This is still ongoing. The channel is among these. The channel was aware of Lord Michael's presence long before he realized it, years before he realized the significance it had planetarily. That is why, even now, he has deposited an energetic portion of his spirit embedded in this magnificent area. The unique power of these lakes is in their crystallized colloidal quartz content. The glacier crystal silicate is quite unique in its frequency, and although this occurs in other areas of the Earth, the frequency of this vortex is unique to this area. While your geologists readily recognize that the incredible coloring of the waters is due to this silicate particle, they do not recognize the energy it adds. They do not recognize the unique pattern of the crystallized structure of this particle, or of the synergistic reaction that occurs when light penetrates the surface of the waters.*

*"Science knows of Newtonian fluids and col-*

*loidal plastic fluids, but there is another aspect to fluids that has not been considered. Energized fluids, magnetized fluids, crystallized fluids, all occur in the special waters of the Michael Vortex in Banff and Yoho National Parks. The silicate particulate in the fluids is in such a colloidal state that it does not settle, yet the fluid moves fully in Newtonian states. The fluid carries an electrical field so complex it creates an energetic field that penetrates all things, including the molecular structure of everything in its immediate field. For these reasons, certain areas such as Lake Louise and Emerald Lake are permitted to have large streams of touring visitors, many of whom are directed to come on a subtle level. The energy of the crystal fluids with the imprint of Lord Michael penetrates their being in such a way that it is physically, emotionally and spiritually impossible for them not to be affected, not to be touched or given the opportunity to heal. Lake O'Hara is, by design, more remote and serves as the energy holder for the flux of light energy. Lake O'Hara is already in the fifth dimension and beyond. A precise dimensional vector of all three grids exists within the Michael Portal Triangulation. As such, the geometric projection of this vortex area contains all the platonic solids: tetrahedron, hexahedron, octahedron, dodecahedron and icosahedron. An impeccable clarity of consecrated energy exists here, such that the sacred geometric template complies with the parallelogram law of addition. The living geometry here forms the Metatronic cube in a multidimensional matrix, such that any telluric transformation, in a particular way, such that any force of telluric transformation, that would effect the anchor points of the crystalline template is met with a balancing adjustment that will maintain the coordinate system in perfect symmetry. This is the nature of the inserted hologram of the Metatronic crystal. Humans experience this as an area of quickened 'higher' thought manifestation. Higher thought, pure thought, loving feelings, are transformed into a geometric vector within the operating system of these energies, and real*

*immediate healing and transformation can occur here. That which you refer to as negative thought is largely dormant within this field. This nullification is because negativity lacks the appropriate hyper dimensional geometric frequency impulse to achieve reaction or recognition within the positive homogeneous matrix. The matrix projects the energy of love. This energy is effectively disseminated throughout the area for hundreds of miles. That is the reason that the people living in this land are perceived as being so agreeable in disposition.*

*This area is energetically in tune with other crystalline waters, especially those of Patagonia, Chile, Lake Lucerne, Switzerland and Lake Baikal in Siberia – all living cathedrals of love and healing. You are beloved."*

## Summary

The Canadian Rockies are magnificent beyond words. The energy that exists within them is aligned with magnificent energies from mineralogical, water, light and electromagnetic aspects. Incredible energy emanates from the mountains with their granite, quartz, metamorphic and sedimentary strata, combined with the stunning array of hydro energy from rivers, streams, waterfalls and glaciers. The lakes are a class unsurpassed in the world, and their accessibility is a tribute to the Canadian government. Thousands of visitors have daily access to this massive region, but it is extremely well managed.

The supreme and benevolent angelic presence of Archangel Michael further enriches the energy of this area as a tool of the Ascension, and the seeker and tourist alike can experience this. The portal of Michael is presented in an amazing Metatronic geometry in three succinct amazing lakes. The Divine Presence has always been discernable here, as known by the indigenous First Nations of Stony and Cree. This magnificent area is truly a living cathedral.

... and so it is.

# Chile ~ The Blue Diamond Vortex

I first saw the sheer granite towers of Chile's Torres del Paine National Park in *National Geographic* a decade ago. Literally stunned at the incredible jagged landscape, I promised myself I would go there one day. I kept that promise in March, 2002.

Torres del Paine National Park is an amazing array of lakes, waterfalls, glaciers and jagged peaks at the bottom tip of South America. Its massive 1,000 square mile, 500,000-acre expanse runs from just north of Tierra del Fuego and curls around the Sound of Last Hope in southern Patagonia, Chile. The crowning jewel and namesake of the park are three incredible 9,000-foot purple granite monoliths.

## Formation

The park is part of the Paine Massif, which lies east of the high Andean spine. The massifs are a relatively short 17-mile column of mountains emerging suddenly from the plains of the Patagonian steppes. Composed of granite, capped by a purple-blue sedimentary rock, the Paine range is an upthrusted batholith, a giant bubble of once molten granite that rose from deep in the Earth, cooled and was later iced over with massive glaciers. As the glaciers retreated, they cut deep gashes and left an uproar of mystical jagged peaks. Deep pits spooned from the surrounding earth were filled with melting ice, creating a poignant daisy chain of colorful lakes around the fortress-like mountains.

The Paine uplift is almost completely encircled by the Rio Paine. The river begins at Lago Dickson, then crosses through the Paine, Nordenskjold and Pehoe lakes and then empties into the Lago del Toro. The intense upper chakra colors of the park's lakes and river waters are caused by pulverized silt created from the melting glaciers'

grinding retreat. The accumulation of this sediment in the river basins leading from lake to lake causes the amazing colors of blue and green. I have experienced similar colors only in waters in the Canadian Rockies, Lake Powell and the European Alps.

## Tyb's Journey: Arrival

To say the park is not easy to get to is an understatement. In fact, you *really* have to want to go there. My two-leg flight from Dallas took eleven hours, followed by a five-hour bus ride. I was having second thoughts about the extreme effort I'd gone to as I collapsed wearily into my bed at the Hosteria del Torres. It was well after midnight, some 20 hours after I had left home, and I was beyond tired. However, one look out the window next morning reminded me why I had come so far.

Every direction offered panoramic views of snowcapped mountains, green flowered fields, rolling hills of wheat-hued pampas and beautiful waters. The beauty was almost too perfect; it was so overwhelming that it made me melancholy. Amazing beauty is fleeting, and the fruitless attempt to keep it is a metaphor of the inability to capture time. Change is the nature of temporal life. And indeed, temporal change comes quickly in Patagonia, as I soon learned. A single day can, and would, display all four seasons.

Bright mornings rarely remain bright for long in Patagonia. The summer day is quickly transformed as irate winds whip up into an angry gray pitch. Rain can suddenly lash down, stinging hands and face. Thick gray fog rolls in with no warning … and suddenly the picturesque world has disappeared. On low ground it is bad enough, but it is downright scary if you are up at the base of the towers. The weather is raw, and crystal rivers can swell to raging dark torrents in minutes.

Now, despite the villainy of this description, this is an amazingly tranquil, inviting place. It is a spiritual cornucopia of magic and well being. All life abounds. Torres del Paine teems with fauna – huge furry rabbits, sleek pumas, enormous condors, hawks, eagles, emu and fuzzy guanacos, the Chilean cousin to llamas.

But it is the Paine Mountains, the incredible jagged spire towers and horns that generate the brow and crown energy and dominate the character of this utopia. The incredible indigo towers are the magnet that pulled me to southern Patagonia. I could not wait to see them … but that would prove harder to be than I thought.

### Day Two: Journey to Los Cuernos

My journey to the Paine Horns was on horseback … not exactly Clydesdales but darned close. The horses were enormous and healthy. The one chosen for me had a wonderful presence, very steady. I developed a tremendous respect for this mighty animal, who literally carried my life on his back, as we returned through thigh-high, rain-swollen rivers.

I was the lone rider this day. My guides – Claudia, a hearty Patagonian girl of 24, and Gato, a burly, athletic gaucho who had a mastery of riding – decided we could go despite the forecast of thunderstorms. Both guides were wonderful young souls, very endearing and capable Earth-Keepers. Gato exuded an air of competence and well being.

The journey to the Horns passed along glacier moraines and steppes painted with browns and reds. After a few miles, we reached the blue-green Pehoe Lake and rode along steep trails hampered by huge granite boulder outcrops along the sloping sides. The view was incredible. As we entered the crevice of Valle Francais, the beauty and feelings intensified. The horses crunched through gravel-bedded streams with clear flowing waters and through magical steppes of flowing pampas.

### Magnetic Vortex

Overhead, wispy mists swirled above darker cirrus clouds, giving way to UFO-like lenticular clouds that always seem to nest atop magnetic mountains.

There were trees with gnarled, serpentine roots and outreaching limbs, twisted in the telltale fashion of vortex energies. We rode onward through iridescent fields, with rocks covered in burgundy and orange lichen.

The sense of the devic kingdom, of elves and gnomes lurking behind knobbed and corkscrewed tree trunks, was tangible. Flowers abounded everywhere, like nothing I had seen before – amazing colors that occur only in very wet climates. So many shades of green! Small evergreens were decorated like Christmas trees with yellow clusters of miniature mistletoe so bright that they seemed to glow. A rare lacy green moss called Grandpa's Beard was draped symmetrically from the limbs of hardwoods. Although hardy, these grow in only the purest air.

The area was primarily volcanic, and the energy of place had a 'zingy' electrical feel – very male, but perfectly balanced by the female telluric expressions of soothing lakes and majestic inland fjords.

### Experience of the Horns

When we finally reached the base of the Horns, the drizzle had become steady rain. We found shelter in the *refugio* and drank warm Andean tea heated on a wood-fed cast-iron stove. I got warm and toasty very quickly. The rain passed in an hour, and, as suddenly as they had come, the gray clouds were swept away.

It is simply impossible to describe the contrast of how the scenery would shift from a foggy, dreary gray to a sparkling wonderment of polished light. When the rain clouds lifted their veil, the glory of the Paine Horns was simply overwhelming, beyond words, but during the rain, visibility was limited to about 400 feet, and the spectacular mountains disappeared.

As we left the *refugio*, the curtain of clouds was pulled back to reveal the smooth walls of the Cuernos. The vertical rise of the Paine Horns is incredible – almost 7,500 feet. The mountains are a batholith of blue granite, with shaded strata of purple-gray shale along the crown. They curve into an impressive crescent shape, hence the 'Blue Horns' name, although the Indian word can also be translated as 'crown.' An amazing site and energy, as the blue rock pulsed.

**Grid Activation**

I had scheduled (through the Hotspots website) a coordinated Grid Activation Meditation to take place at 2 p.m. on the day I arrived at the Paine Horns. I found the perfect spot on a granite table at the base for the meditation. I nestled in and, within moments of my mediation, connected deeply into the spirit presence of the Twin Horns. I visualized the light grid connecting to the horns and towers.

I made sequential connection with grid team members in Dakota, Georgia, New York, Texas, Sedona, Cornwall, Alberta, San Diego, Machu Picchu, Guatemala, Bogota, Shasta and Seattle. Visual focus came easy in the amplified energy.

**Geometric Energy Projections**

Interestingly, in the midst of my activation,

I received a strong visual of sacred geometry patterns being projected from the Paine Towers and Paine Horns. It was as if the 17-mile massif ridge had an auric merkaba grid projection along its length that projected certain Platonic Solids at key apex points. I sensed multi-octahedron shapes at the towers and a singular dodecahedron sphere at the Horns. I knew this 17-mile corridor is a single living presence and is quite a unique expression of Gaia.

My meditation was deep and cleansing. It began raining again as I completed the hour. When I rose from the granite table, I had the strange sensation of being enormous. For a few fleeting seconds I felt as if I was 200 feet tall, still inside my body, but in a huge titan body looking down at all of this splendor. That was a bizarre sensation, yet I have had it on rare occasions during vision quests and after deep meditations in powerful spots. I am not certain what occurs, but perhaps a greater part of my being is flooded into my merkaba, and I see through 12 chakras instead of 7 for a few moments.

**Day Three: The Indigo Towers**

The next morning, I began my trek to the Towers themselves. It was an arduous experience. As we rode horseback to the *refugio* of the Towers, it rained most of the way. I hunched inside my poncho, as the dreary rain fell steadily around me. As we reached the *refugio*, the rain increased to a furious downpour. The guides explained to me in Spanish that the weather I was experiencing was typical.

It is rare for a day to come and go without at least some rain, but the rain rarely lasts all day. At the *refugio* of the Towers, we were required to go on foot for another two hours on a steep trail, switch-backed up the moraine slake. Unfortunately, the trail became an eddied stream of rainwater, and the park rangers closed the trail for the day.

I was allowed to advance laterally to a hilltop offering a closer view of the Blue Towers but was separated from them by a massive ravine and lake. It would bring me within the visual and energetic field of the Towers, but would not put me at their base. It was not what I had wanted but turned out to be all that I would need.

For a fleeting hour, the curtain of gray opened to allow me a full view of the granite Gods. In the green filtered light of the paused storm, the Towers took on a blue-violet hue. Like mood stones, the enormous monoliths would shift from pearl-gray to indigo-blue to red-orange, depending on the lighting, as if the frequency of their energetic output was changing with the colors – a shifting light activation similar to those I had experienced at Mount Shasta, Enchanted Rock, Texas and the Canadian Rockies.

I harvested years of anticipation within a 40-minute view of the sacred towers. I tingled with energy and connected to the presence. I lived every second with the timeless joy of fulfilling a dream. I had a love and recognition of the towers the moment I'd seen them a decade earlier. I communed with them and left a piece of myself within their space.

We had to depart before the swelling Rio Paine rose too high to cross, but even before Gato called me for departure, I knew it was time to leave. I was ready, but I felt sad. I was saying goodbye to a presence I would likely never see again.

**Departure**

During the horseback ride back down, the skies again cleared, and for another precious moment I saw the sacred towers standing like the Three Wise Men of the East. The pale blue backdrop became a framed tableau in sharp contrast to the pearl gray of the towers. I shifted in the saddle, unable to resist frequent looks over my shoulder. But all too soon, the 'wise men' became draped in misty robes and faded from sight.

As we reached the slopes of majestic Lago Pehoé, the wind kicked up, and rain lashed us. As if replacing the towers, three Andean condors came into view, tracing spirals across the opal sky. A potent omen.

As the condors disappeared into leaden clouds, I stretched a grin across my wind-burnt face. I understood then that to step through the magic looking-glass into this mountain paradise, one has to swallow the pills of wind and weather. One has to enter the labyrinth. But when the dues are paid, the magical gift that is Torres del Paine is fully revealed in the twinkle of an eye … and then they are gone.

**Torres del Paine**

Torres del Paine literally translates to 'indigo towers.' The word *Paine* is a Tehuelche Indian word meaning violet-blue, describing the hue of the mountains at sunset. *Torres* is, of course, Spanish for 'towers.'

While Torres del Paine National Park is becoming the primary eco-tourist attraction in the southern Patagonia region of both Chile and Argentina, it is still rather sparsely frequented in terms of its enormity. Only two full-fledged hotels and half a dozen hostels are allowed in the park, which was created in 1959 and declared a Biosphere Reserve by UNESCO in 1978. There was divine intervention in that act as, at the time, powerful Japanese and American lumber and mining interests were attempting to buy massive tracts of land from the Estancia cattle barons for 'industrial development.' The exploitation was halted by an amazing synchronicity of events that led to the land being privately purchased and then donated to the government for use as a National Park and Global Treasure.

## Haven of Serenity

The park is truly a haven. It remains pristine and resplendent, and it serves as a balancing reservoir to Mother Earth. The Torres are being activated as a potent crystal grid portal along with several other significant areas in Chile, including Volcan Osourno in central Chile and Canjo Maipo in northern Chile.

The serenity is especially balancing. I found a deep peace and cleansing energy in the land. I sensed incredible energy pouring inward to the Cuernos and outward from the Torres. Ley energy abounds as do spiraling fountains of electrical vortexes. I did experience the primary energy to be magnetic in the perimeter flow, with the Torres themselves as exploding cannons of crown energy.

## Lapis Lazuli

It is interesting to note that Chile contains the world's largest deposits of lapis lazuli and is the largest producer. This precious gem carries a divine frequency, and the energetic vortex created by the massive deposits of lapis in Chile is being anchored by many special angelic souls in spiritual communities. (Afghanistan also contains massive deposits of lapis, but this energy has been greatly disrupted in recent months by the old energy of negativity and violence.) Lapis deposits, as well as jade, gold and silver, are abundant along the Andean spine of Chile.

## Twin Giants of the Horns

The mountains of Torres del Paine held significance for the region's native inhabitants. The Tehuelche Indians were an extremely hearty race, who for centuries adapted physically, being able to live totally nude in the snow-laden winters and wet summers of Patagonia. The tribe rarely experienced illness and had an unusually long lifespan compared to other indigenous peoples. Talk about thick-skinned!

According to Tehuelche legend, the longevity and fortitude of the people came from the protection of the mountain guardians of the Twin Horns and Towers. Their myths tell of an evil flying serpent called Cai Cai, who eons ago caused a massive flood to devastate most of the warrior tribe that lived in Torres del Paine. When the floodwaters receded, the surviving people were weak and dying. Two powerful Tehuelche warriors prayed to Great Spirit for protection and strength from future floods and for the ability to live long, fruitful lives in the severe climate. Spirit granted the wish, and the two warriors were transformed into stone giants, becoming the twin horns that crown the mountaintop of Cuernos del Paine. They protect the area for time eternal as guardians of the land. The Gods then immortalized the condor, puma and guanaco as the Three Towers, offering wisdom, strength and sustenance for the guardians and tribe.

When I read the story of the two warrior giants on my flight back to Texas, I immediately connected it to my experience of feeling like a 200-foot giant when I meditated at the base of the Twin Horns. I had a moment of clarity and smiled at the validation.

As a footnote, I did not sense any real connection to either LeMuria or Atlantis in Torres del Paine.

## Information

At the entrance, informative park guards can help plan hikes using a detailed map of the park. The park has many roads and hiking trails to choose from. Camping is available as is lodging at the Posada Serrano, Hosteria Estancia Las Torres, Hotel Explora, Hosteria Lago Grey, Hosteria Estancia Lazo and others located on the way from

Puerto Natales and the park.

Be prepared for rain, but persevere. When it clears, the scenery is a polished diamond, a blue diamond of exquisite light.

## Tyberonn Channel

*"This wondrous area of southern Chile and Argentina emits a very rare frequency. Torres del Paine is a crystalline 'heart' energy, very closely aligned with the Archangel Michael vortex of the Canadian Rockies. Torres del Paine contains a living Metatronic geometric template with full containment of the platonic solids, as does the area of Lake Louise. It likewise contains an influx, a holgramic insert, of angelic energies that pervade the area with peace and with the frequential harmonic of pure love.*

*You will notice that many of the higher dimensional portals containing the full hologram of Metatronic geometry primarily occur between specific latitudes and elevations on your planet. This is because the electromagnetic and gravitational fields are at a harmonic balance between the latitudes of the colder regions. The latitudes between 45 degrees and 55 degrees both north and south of the equator are preeminently advantageous in their generic equilibrium of electromagnetic and gravitational currents. This energetic parity can also eventuate analogously in elevations between 6,000 and 9,000 feet in your high planes and mountainous regions. The intrinsic modulation of Los Torres del Paine reconciles and integrates the full merkabic centers of the human, thus ameliorating higher dimensional integration. You see, higher dimensional energy is coagulated within holograms of Metatronic geometry. All twelve dimensions of your earth-plane coexist within such areas. The Metatronic hologram insert can be said, in real terms, to be an etheric heliotropic jewel. The crystalline projection and structure in fact can be said to*

*dovetail the molecular crystalline symmetry of the diamond. The diamond is of a cubic crystalline nature that can manifest into octahedron and dodecahedron; so do certain portals, such as Torres del Paine. You see, the very fabric of the Cosmos is geometric, although in higher realms the geometry becomes one of formless fluidity, yet crystalline and conforming to geometric law. Sacred geometry is the language of higher dimensions, and to access it, humans must become crystalline. How do humans become crystalline? In your higher self, you already are. The rediscovery of this aspect is much of your mission in duality. You become crystalline by achieving symmetry in divine pursuit and by achieving impeccability of thought and action. Pure love, Beloved, is geometric. You have many tools that assist you in this pursuit. Your ancients discovered and revered the sacred places of your planet that aligned the auric field and activated the chakric centers into the geometrical crystalline merkaba. Your ancients first valued your crystals, gems and precious metals because they recognized them as tuning forks and energy sources, capable of assisting human alignment to the field of higher dimension, the fabric of which is sacred geometry.*

*The planet's power points, chakras and meridians all project the crystalline geometry of gems and contain many of the same light refraction and dispersion properties within their matrix. Some sacred sites can be considered as single refractive and others as double refractive. Do you see the correlation? The angles of penetration of solar and stellar light affect the frequency of sacred sites. Since these angles and sources constantly shift, the light frequency within the sacred site corresponds in kind. You do not doubt that the energy of sunrise affects you quite differently than the energy of high noon or of midnight. It follows, then, that the frequencial activation you receive within the geometrical massif of Los Torres shifts with the refraction of light and source of light. Los Torres is singularly refractive. Light received* within its matrix is bent and 'slowed down' when it passes obliquely into its etheric medium; its wave velocity shifts. The change in the angle of propagation depends on the light source and critical angle. The singular refraction creates the prism effect of splitting light into an unbent rainbow, and, as such, the complete color spectrum provides an incredible healing effect. Within Los Torres and other such geometric sacred sites, light can be either slowed or accelerated. As such, the seeker within this area can have a sense of time being stretched or hastened. The physiological thought impulses react accordingly. This is a characteristic of the time-space continuum distortion of crystalline matrix. Time, of course, does not exist in your terms in higher dimensions, only pulsed thought image. In higher dimensions this is non linear, rather it is geometric in nature and occurs as a blue flash, or strobe, that flows across the mosaic fabric. The channel recently described it as a blue tsunami.

Now, in Los Torres, the seeker has the acquiescence to more easily upshift frequency to heal, to release blockages and to manifest thought. This area also is capable of allowing the advanced seeker to experience what is termed a stargate, or multi dimensional travel. This facilitation is most potent near the structures called "Los Cuernos' and the monolithic Torres. The Metatronic template is anchored to these towers. The unique towers themselves act as crystalline antennae, and within their immediate vicinity are many dimensional gates that are extremely active near the winter and summer solstices.

Los Torres exudes an energy that is projected for hundreds of miles, and certain volcanoes along the Chilean and Argentine borders receive and transmit this energy.

Chile, Argentina, Bolivia, Peru, Brazil and Colombia contain power points that interact and communicate with these energies of peace and love. The shift that will occur in 2012 will launch the arrival of the Meruvian race into these lands ... and these will indeed be crystals. You are beloved.

... and so it is.

# Giza ~ The Enigma of the Great Pyramid

I was focused on my recent trip to Karnac, as I sat in a Cairo taxi headed to Giza. But as soon as we stopped, and leather hit sand, I was simply mesmerized, in total awe of the Pyramids before me.

Ironically, I had underestimated the impact the pyramids would have on me, because my expectations were nebulous. The labyrinthine tunnel required to reach the energetic center of that enormous 'quad-lateral' vortex was not easy to negotiate on any level. Juxtaposed, the inward journey to the King's Chamber tested and taxed the trinity of my being in an unexpected purification rite. It forced me to overcome body and mind, and spiritually rewarded me for doing so.

## The Temple of Karnac and Valley of Kings

My trip to the Pyramids of Giza came after four wondrous days in Luxor at the Temple of Karnac and the sacred tombs of the Valley of Kings. At Karnac, I had spent enraptured hours walking though the immense ruins, with rows and rows of towering marble columns and dozens of miniature sphinxes. I meditated in three very powerful sacred chapels, each called 'Holy of Holies.' I resonated deeply to the Temple and was tingling with download. Throughout Luxor, guardian cnergies were abundant, some benevolent, some definitely not. Beware the Valley of Kings … King Tut prefers to be alone!

I knew the Temple of Karnac. The entire complex was built with sacred geometry, straddling the omniscient Nile ley line. Precursor masons built esoterically with conductive granite, quartzite and marble. The antenna-like obelisks pierce the sky with phallic tips and radiate energetic sprays into the feminine sacred lake in the center ground, yin and yang circulating in balanced perfection. The Holy of Holies resonates with a contented hum alongside the banks of the serpentine Nile.

## Egypt

I loved Egypt immediately. There was an appeal that pleasantly surprised me, and it felt like home. I loved the narrow, shop-lined streets in the bazaar, with vendors selling vibrant fresh fruit, the aromatic bread shops and bustling, robed merchants. Strong fruit-flavored tobacco wafted in pungent, feathery plumes from the colorful water-pipes being smoked in the open-air coffee shops.

Fertile land, living waters and ancient energies all are in balance. Ancient times cry through the thin veil of dynasties long past, with dramatic histories folded in echoes of the desert breeze. Sculpted pharaohs rule from massive stone thrones, as if having viewed Medusa!

Laughter and smiling eyes were everywhere. Ley line country – that sense of balance and well being.

## Tyb's Journal: Cairo

My flight from Luxor was about an hour. At the airport, I'd hired an Egyptian guide named Nadia for the Sphinx and Pyramids … which proved prudent. She turned out to be a graduate student and mother, with a B.A. in Egyptology. En route to Giza, she told me of 'The Springs of the Holy Mother,' so we stopped to see a shrine dedicated to Saint Mary and Baby Jesus in a magical garden shrine. The Holy Family of Christianity had lived there for over a year while escaping King Herod's murderous decree. Legend claims a spring burst from a rock – a miracle to slake the thirst of the Holy Family. The living spring still flows and is now a lovely enclosed park-shrine in Heliopolis.

After the brief detour, we began the 40-minute drive across the city to Giza. That proved to be an amazing trek in its own right. Unfortunately, the car lacked air conditioning. The heat I could bear, but the exhaust fumes were quite nauseating. I managed to wet my bandana and use it as a makeshift air filter, quite to Nadia's amusement. Nonetheless, it worked.

The modest fee for the tour-guide, including transport, was less than $50, which is only slightly more than a taxi would have cost, anyway. Nadia exuded a wonderful, wholesome vibration, and she helped me tremendously in negotiating the entrance, obtaining the dozen tickets required … all while intricately detailing the history of every site in Giza … and I visited them all.

**Giza in View**

As our open-air taxi reached the full panoramic view of the pyramids, I sensed an audible buzzing sound. The energy jolted me, and I literally felt the electricity of the circulating energy from a kilometer away. The hair on my arms stood erect, a sensation I would experience many times that day.

The panoramic view of the Giza complex is, in a word, stunning. It is beautiful, and its title of one of Seven Wonders of the Ancient World is well deserved. (In fact, it is the only one still standing.)

The pyramids are not obscured by a surrounding perimeter of mud huts and rabble. Indeed, some pictures taken from a specific, aerial view do offer a rather unflattering view of the pyramids, with a rubbled section of Cairo in the forefront. These are illusive. A considerable spacing separates the city from the antiquities.

The grounds of the Pyramids are National Trust property, well organized and tidily groomed.

The pyramids are outside of Cairo, just beyond the east bend of the Nile, on the eastern extremes of the great Sahara desert. I have seen the western and northern Sahara in both Algeria and Tunisia, with golden sands and impressive 600-foot dunes. Here her personality is more subdued. The desert appears more like a high plain of granulated silt, tan in hue, but looking still quite the part of a desert.

**Pyramid Facts**

The Great Pyramid is 451 feet high. Its top is a squared base, which is said to have held a pyramid capstone of jet-black obsidian, some 30 feet in height. (Drunvalo Melchizedek, among others, claims the flat top at the summit is flat by intent and served as a base for an energetic disc, stored below it in a subterranean chamber.)

For more than four millennia, it ranked as the tallest structure on Earth, only to be surpassed in height in the nineteenth century by the Eiffel Tower. It was once covered with a brilliant casing of polished white limestone to smooth its surface (some of the casing can still be seen near the top). The sloping angle of its sides is 51 degrees, 51 minutes, and the sides are carefully oriented with the compass. The horizontal cross-section is square at any level, with each side measuring 229 meters (751 feet) in length. The maximum error between lengths of the base is astonishingly less than 0.1%. The sacred geometry of phi is apparent in its uniformity. The structure consists of approximately two million blocks of stone, each weighing more than two tons, for a total weight of over six million tons. The area covered by the Great Pyramid can accommodate five stadiums the size of the Astrodome.

The pyramid's entrance is on the north face. A number of corridors, galleries and escape shafts either lead to the King's Chamber or were intended to serve other functions. The King's

Chamber is located at the heart of the pyramid, accessible only through the Grand Gallery and a snug ascending corridor. The King's sarcophagus is made of red granite, as are the interior walls of the King's Chamber. Most impressive is the sharp-edged stone lintel over the doorway, which is over 3 meters (10 feet) long, 2.4 meters (8 feet) high and 1.3 meters (4 feet) thick. All of the interior stones fit together so well that a card will not fit between them. The sarcophagus is oriented according to the compass directions and is only about 1 centimeter smaller in dimension than the chamber entrance, so it might have been introduced as the structure was progressing. According to Galileo, a unit of measure could be found in the Great Pyramid which is in accurate correlation to the circumference of the planet.

The ages of the pyramids are a point of dispute. Some channeled sources claim the Great Pyramid was built 50,000 years ago; psychic Edgar Cayce dated them to 10,500 BC, while conventional beliefs point to both 2500 BC and 4000 BC. Take your pick.

**Labyrinth – The Test**

My first antiquity to visit was, naturally, the Great Pyramid. As I gazed at its sheer enormity, I recognized the importance of the moment. Then I began the climb to the entrance. Surprises lay in store – the serendipity of pentahedrons.

I naively expected to be able to walk to the King's Chamber, and initially the entrance accommodated my height and girth as I walked through what appeared to be an eight-foot-high arched grotto. After 150 feet though, things got considerably more narrow. I had to wind round, ducking slightly as the groomed walkway became more of a rough tunnel. I eventually reached a narrow upward shaft where I had to climb six feet up a metal rung ladder. This took me to another ledge with narrow sides and a low ceiling,

and I lost my feeling of comfort. Feeling as if I was spelunking, I experienced mild waves of claustrophobia, which is unusual for me. Soon these waves would turn into powerful tsunamis of claustrophobic terror.

The ledge led to a small, rectangular shaft which inclined steeply upward. I had to bend down to my knees to look upward. I peered into the opening and saw it was only a few feet high and a few feet wide for what seemed to be about the length of a football field … endless. *Surely this isn't the way*, I thought. All four sides were polished and grooved, never intended for human passage. I was stunned that this tiny artery was the way to the famous King's Chamber … and suddenly full of doubt.

I doubled over at back-cramping angles, took a breath of stagnant air … and entered. I plodded up for a few meters. It was hot, and I was perspiring heavily as I crab-walked my way forward and upward, often bumping my head on the four-foot ceiling. Then I encountered a husky security guard scurrying rapidly down the dimly lit shaft towards me. Oh no! Two-way traffic! I slowed him down a bit, to say the least. Somehow, we squeezed past one another in a process of squirming osmosis – way too physical for my tastes.

After progressing about a quarter of the tunnel, I suddenly felt quite disoriented and weak. Claustrophobia overcame me. And I mean *really* overcame me, as the wave became a tsunami. I couldn't continue. I felt frozen in fear, and felt that the pyramid was going to collapse onto me. I had to get out of there! Dizzy and nauseous, it took all my strength to reverse myself and worm my way out to my starting point. I stood up and gasped for air. I steadied myself weakly on the ledge and finished my remaining water.

At six feet-five inches and 270 pounds, I was really struggling … and uncertain whether I could make it up the small shaft to the King's Chamber. I felt sick and panicky. What loomed before me was to fit my large frame into a very small space for a laborious, contorted climb of approximately 100 meters, where I would be bent double. I couldn't do it and contemplated quitting.

**Angels and Goddesses**

As I stood debating my options, four energetic fifty-something German ladies popped up the ladder. Goddesses all! It took all my energy to move over to allow them to pass. The first one asked me in English if I was okay and gave me a fresh bottle of mineral water. Flustered, I told her I had attempted to go up and became claustrophobic, and I did not know if I could make it up the shaft. She smiled, put her hand on my shoulder and assured me that I could. After a few moments, she urged me to go on up. She told me it would be worth it. "This may be your only chance," she said in a stern but supportive German accent. "Haven't you come a long way to see this chamber?"

I was touched. She paused a moment, patted me on the shoulder and motioned for me to follow. I summoned up my will, found my determination and followed her in.

The upward crab-walk was hard. I was slowed considerably by negotiating the limited space to allow exiting visitors room to pass as they descended the shaft. I focused on the task and counted my crab crawls in units of ten to block thoughts of getting trapped inside. I became faint and short of breath, but I persevered. I prayed and kept following my new friends. Finally, we reached the end of the tunnel. I unfurled my bent chassis out of the ascension corridor into the roomier Grand Gallery. As I stood and took inventory, my legs trembled in uncontrollable spasms. (Note to Self: Lose 35 pounds and get in shape before returning to Pyramids.)

I had another lengthy upward walk, but this corridor offered plenty of headroom. Grand indeed! This walkway had a handrail and steps for several hundred feet. At the top was another four-by-three tunnel, but fortunately it was a mere 50 feet long. It led horizontally into my destination, the King's Chamber, into which I crawled.

I was soaking wet, both physically and spiritually exhausted, after the tunnel trek had purged me like a sweat lodge. I wobbled to an unoccupied corner and plopped down behind the celebrated sarcophagus. My anxiety attack was lessening but still present. I crossed my legs and leaned against the burgundy granite wall. It felt cool and comforting. I unwrapped two special crystals from my belt pack, took several deep breaths, and began to meditate.

**King's Chamber: Toning Activation**

My head began to clear. In the dim yellow light, I saw the vibrant group of German ladies seated around the sarcophagus in the lotus position. As if on cue, one of them began to tone with an angelic voice. A golden melodious tone of the powerful "Om" penetrated the chamber. What incredible acoustics! The other ladies joined in perfect harmony, with voices of professional caliber. The sacred tones immediately activated an energetic response from the pyramid itself. I received the energetic response through my crown chakra like an electrical jolt. My energy surged, as the frequency of the room shifted dramatically. Some 'pyramid presence' was clearly reacting to the sacred Om.

I knew the seven or eight tourists standing around the chamber edges also felt the dramatic quickening of energy that occurred with the toning. Almost instantly, they all departed except for two young seekers, both male, who sat down against the wall.

Over the next 20 minutes, I experienced a vibration of pure energy. Amazingly, no one else entered during that period of toning. I was very aware of a male/female balance between the feminine energy encircling the sarcophagus and we three males sitting along the outer wall.

## A River of Light

My senses were vaulted to an area of light. I didn't go into vision but rather to an area of pure energy, of bright light and well being. I had no thoughts, said no prayers, I simply WAS. I became part of a seven-piece receiving unit that conducted and transmitted a flow of incredibly pure energy. My vibration lofted to pure joy as all seven of us in that room melded without speaking. The toning, combined with a perfect balance of male/female energy, triggered a tremendous healing frequency for all of us. I was blessed to be inside with this group. Alone, I would not have experienced this activation process. I had not known of the sonic toning trigger but unmistakably felt the shift reaction that occurred when specific notes of the Om were hit.

After 20 minutes, the toning stopped. The group leader directed the ladies to stand circle around the sarcophagus, while she lay inside. After a few minutes, she left and another climbed inside. I understood the sarcophagus to be the energetic center of the pyramid chamber, the precise point at which the three star shafts converge. I joined them. When my time came, I lay inside on my back, knees pulled upward to allow the fit. I held a crystal in each hand and directed them to absorb the energy. As I prayed deeply, a river of light ran through me. I remained inside the sarcophagus for a few brief, but eternal, moments … and then it was complete. As I crawled out of the sarcophagus, the German goddesses hugged me and then waved goodbye. We had shared a magnificent experience, and I was so grateful to that special group, although I never knew their names. In absolute strength and totally void of any anxiety, I sat back against the wall of the King's Chamber for another half hour and savored the energy. The Queen's Chamber was next.

## The Queen's Chamber

The path downward involved more contorted crawl-walks, but my energy was peaking, and I arrived without a struggle. The Queen's Chamber, too, had vaulted ceilings but a dramatically different resonance. I felt very comfortable and instinctively began a baritone toning. I experienced a state in which I saw light sparkles and geometric patterns, as opposed to one sheer, bright flow. The energy was oscillating, and I knew this was in the downward flow of that magnificent stream, within a balancing female, recharging energy pocket.

## Rejuvenation

In the midst of this energy, I felt a physical floating sensation. The energy stream felt more dense, almost wet. It oscillated in an explosive, orgasmic flow of bluish-white energy, and my body felt invigorated. In fact, I suddenly became aware of the sensation of crisp physical arousal, even though my mind was in a detached, thoughtless state of almost perfect nirvana. Every chakra, every energy receptacle, was being fully recharged. I was in a place beyond my body, observing it all, undergoing incredible, joyful rejuvenation on every level. It was spiritually orgasmic.

I hardly recall the exit trip. My legs trembled a bit, but my energy was resurgent. There was no fear of confined space, only the tranquility and serenity that comes with purge and profound renewal.

## Rebirth

I finally reached the entrance walkway and

burst out into the world, as if exiting the womb, reborn to the day and to the beaming sun. And I was literally 'blinded by the light.' I sat alone on an isolated, creviced block of the pyramid entrance for a brief eternity as my mind swirled in a still-altered state. I felt moved to tears. So much more had happened than I had ever expected. I had been mentally unprepared, and I wept deeply as I released a lifetime of forgotten pain. The dam burst, and the waters flowed clear.

I came down to earth and walked to the entryway. Nadia never seemed to notice my emotional state. Perhaps the RayBans helped. Drained, I felt the joy that comes after clearing. My God, what a place!

## Infinity Energy Flows

So much has been written about the Great Pyramids, pyramid energy, their purpose and origin, etc., that I am reluctant to write anything other than my own experiential impressions, toned with the disclaimer that I consider myself a student of Spirit but by no means a master. My impressions are a work-in-progress. I have traveled tens of thousands of miles over the world the past 25 years, usually alone. Life has been my greatest teacher and the Living Earth both my classroom and equation.

## My Thoughts

The energy of the Great Pyramid is certainly alive … and self-aware! It responds to keyed intents and triggers, especially vocal toning and various meditation techniques. It can be used in a great diversity of modalities, such as healing, meditation, rejuvenation, communication, inter-dimensional travel and generation of power. It is a stargate portal, a multi-faceted vortex and a self-amplifying energetic generator.

Its effect was penetrating. I had to overcome an unexpected terrifying panic to get to the King's Chamber, but when I did, I was greatly rewarded. The pyramids respond to intent. The circulating energies are centered in the King's Chamber, particularly the sarcophagus. And a unique orgasmic recharging energy exists below in the Queen's Chamber.

The pyramids are set directly in the path of the Nile ley line, and it once contained a cross ley line from the Atlantean continent. That line is no longer in consistent function, yet I sensed its energy.

The pyramids have a dynamic energy flow of four lateral helixes. These are not exactly vortexes in the usual sense, but circulating energies. More accurately, I see two 'figure-of-eight' flow patterns. The energy enters the pyramid at an angle on all four sides at about the top third of the pyramid, flows through the King's and Queen's Chambers, then circulates out through the ground and back up. Each circle is a centered, lateral intersection of the four sides. The two 'figure-of-eight' patterns are individually flowing from the four cardinal directions into the King's Chamber. The north-to-south one represents male energy, while the east-to-west one represents female energy. The north-to-south flow is the strongest, due to the shifting of ley line spacing and the fact that the Nile ley flows south to north.

Above the pyramids is a precise double-rimmed electromagnetic (in and out) vortex, moving counterclockwise on the outer rim and clockwise on the inner rim. All of the pyramids are incorporated in this upper portal and vortex.

I also feel a specific axial connection for the electromagnetic grid (not the crystal grid) to be somehow anchored within the Great Pyramid vortex. I also feel the crystal grid and gravity grid have key apex points at this great vortex-portal.

## In Closing

I visited many wonderful sites in Luxor and in Giza, and my days flowed from dawn until dusk. I specifically have not mentioned the Sphinx or the other two pyramids, but these must not be overlooked. When I visited the Pyramid of Menkaure, I had a very, very powerful experience, similar to the one I had in the Queen's Chamber. Amazingly, I encountered two more angelic ladies toning in the lower chamber of this pyramid late in the afternoon, and I had a potent energetic influx.

Egypt is the site of several other sacred sites I feel drawn to, including Mount Sinai and Aswan. Giza exceeded all my expectations. The grace and regal majesty of the pyramids is unquestioned. Giza is ancient Memphis … and Memphis is ever home to the King.

I am still in download from my experiences of the pyramid, although my visit occurred 12 months earlier than this writing. I expect I will remain in download for some time to come.

"Man fears time … but time fears the pyramids."

— Arabic proverb

## Tyberonn Channel

*"The King's Pyramid of Giza exists, not only in all twelve dimensions on your Earth Plane, but also in your Earth's probable reality parallels. It is, indeed, timeless. The channel has asked me to give a precise timing of when it was constructed, and we tell you that cannot be accurately given. You see, the Great Pyramid was manifested from sonic frequency, it was never actually constructed and erected, per se, as many of your historians theorize. In future times, historians will shake their heads in amusement over some of your present 'main-stream' anthropologists' intricate theories of hordes of loin clothed laborers pulling massive stone blocks over logs and up ramps with hemp twined rope. They will ask themselves how educated men could surmise that the construction riddle of such an impeccably defectless structure is cobbled into such enigmatic form by rudimentary method. There have been those 'Pyramidologists,' in various times, who understood its 'divine creation,' and some of their assertions were very close to the truth. But when these were made public, their credibility was quickly attacked and their theories dismissed by academia.*

*In your duality perception of sequential time, there appears to be only the stone structure, but we tell you there is more than one pyramid standing there. In truth, it has actually disappeared and reappeared from your visible light spectrum several times, dimensionally speaking, that is the nature of its hologramic manifestation. It was erected in stone out of sound, then the sound dissonance dissolved it, and then the sound created it again. And for most, to know such would perhaps be a detrimental confusion. Even for humans who are more consciously aware, attempts to frequencially isolate and see its dissonance or its disappearance would not be of great benefit. There are other such inserted manifestations on your Earth, but none quite so tangible as the Great Pyramid. Other versions of this insert of the octahedron are within your universe on all of your planets. All are aligned to Orion, and all are great communication devices in one aspect, although there are variations in their properties and dimension. That is because these other planets are wrapped in more dimensional fields than your Earth. Currently Mars has 18, Jupiter 84 and Saturn 144. These fluctuate, does that surprise you? Few humans are consciously able to truly perceive more than 3, and that is because the logical conscious mind is not the innate receiver of higher dimensional frequency. Higher dimensional perception occurs in the back brain, or meditative mind. Most dismiss it as dream. That is because higher dimensional reality is in a different language, a different format. It is* geometric code image, and it is not received in analogical conscious thought; the logic process of the frontal lobe can never format it. That would be like trying to pick up an FM radio station with an AM receiver. (Although some of the Crystal Children, those of full 12-strand DNA, have a dual capacity to receive both.)

At the time of the firmament, your Earth had two moons and far more dimensions than it does now, and at other times it has had less. You see, there are 356 dimensions within your universe, and the number of dimensions that are enfolded to the planets depends on a variety of factors, including mass, grid structure and the gravitational variants, including the number and pull of each satellite, or moon.

Your universe has potential to realize more, and in one sense it already has. It is expanding, you see. Consider this expanding universe analogy: Your solar system is an atom, with its nucleus being the sun. This atom is bonded to other atoms to form a molecular universe. The universal molecules form compounds that are Galaxies. They align with other Galaxies within the Cosmos to form a corporal living mass.

Now, the Pyramid, the octahedron, communicates with and exists within them all, although the geometric expression of polyhedrons and geometric light properties differs somewhat in each field.

The channel asks to validate his perception of the energetic center of the Great Pyramid. It is better phrased to say, where is the energetic vortex. The vortex is the truer alignment, because although it is drawn to the Great Pyramid, it is not exactly part of the Pyramid. For example, your spirit is drawn into its created physical body, but it is not part of the body, per se.

So, we will say that the King's Chamber is not the center of the Pyramid, rather it is where the potent vortex of the energy is centered. The vortex is the true alignment. Now, the vortexes of energies, as they are oriented, are oriented to the Earth and to Orion, so as such so they are tilted. It is not straight, rather it is a vortex that is tilted. If you were to place yourself deeply in that vortex, you would almost wish to stand as if at an angle, you see. You must know that the energies move, and so they direct themselves. Now, as they are at an angle, then it appears that they are managed by an axis, and that axis, as well, rotates here and there. Now, under the proper circumstances, under very specific conditions, the entire chamber would also appear to rotate, even as the heavens rotate creating an indoor planetarium within the very pyramid. All of this comes about because the complex harmonic frequency makes it so. Now if I were to give to you the specific date as you had asked earlier, all of this would then disappear for you. Can you understand? In time and date and linear sequence, the vortices would then not exist, and you would not then gain the benefits. It is multi dimensional, timeless; such is the nature of higher dimensional holograms and the vortex-portals they magnetically attract. They cannot be pinned down in linear time. Truly, because linear time only exists in the duality of lower dimensional fields, and such vortex-portal matrixes exist above that level, by a complex merging of hyper dimension and grid.

The channel's recognition of lateral infinity (figure 8) flows intersecting in the sarcophagus, we will say, is functionally correct. These are directionally aligned, north-south and east-west. Sometimes, there is a distortion of energy in which it meets close to there but not exactly there, according to the equinoxes, and accordingly it shifts. But this is mostly correct, keeping in mind that the cardinal direction vectors have shifted over the eons as well. The sarcophagus is especially powerful for other reasons as well.

*Now, the tuition of fear that was experienced by the channel is one of initiation that many, but not all, share in the Pyramidal journey. In fact, it is an example of the etheric parallels of the Pyramid that coexist in place. An ancient school of Wisdom of the Egyptian era can be said to coexist in the NOW parallels of all experience within the Chambers. The final stage of initiation involved placing the initiate in the sarcophagus and sealing the lid for three and one half days. There was no light, no water, no narcotic and only enough air to survive if the initiate was able to lower the frequency of the body physical into an entranced state of yogic hibernation. Those who chose to undertake this phase of final initiation were relatively few, and those who survived it fewer still. The channel chose such initiation in three consecutive lives, and died in the sarcophagus two of these. The first time he was too young, the second time unprepared, and the third he succeeded. If one thing will not take you, another will. If the air will not give way, then the fear will see more than one pathway is offered to you then. The outcome may be the same or different, but they are the choices. Within the Pyramid, the initiate must always face their cumulative fear, face their darkness, and turn it into light. So the memory of the first two times was re-expereinced for him in the confinement of the tunnel, and the experience of the third in the Kings Chamber. All served as a powerful release and activation. Much more was gained in the perseverance than he fully realized, as he wept in deep purge and joy on the outer walls after realizing his purpose here. Now, we smile to see if the channel will keep his note to self on weight loss! His frame was far smaller during the time of Akhenaten."*

… and so it is.

# Machu Picchu ~ The Light Temple of Mu

Peru's incredible Machu Picchu is one of the chakras of Gaia. Located in the heart of the Andes, it is a rite of passage for the dedicated pilgrim. There are but three ways to get there: helicopter, train or foot. I chose the latter.

**Tyb's Journal: Arrival!**

Ragged and weather worn from three days of hard hiking on the Inca Trail, I peer downward from the narrow stone trail 14,000 feet high, on a jutting overlook in the Andes of Peru. I gaze at a sea of jagged blue peaks and the pinnacle island emerging from the mists in the center. The moment is molten. I sense the energy in a familiar, deeply felt wave of joy. As if in slow motion, the wispy clouds are pulled back like curtains, revealing an exquisite vista – Machu Picchu, Lost City of the Andes!

Below me are pieces of an interlocking rock puzzle, lying in a symmetrical ancient ruin. The terraced land looks like a green staircase going up an impressive blue-green pyramid-shaped monolith. Below, 6,500 feet straight down, the mighty, serpentine Urubamba River twists and coils around the base rock, the pounding rapids making a roaring hiss, audible from over a mile away vertically. I am hypnotized by the grandeur, enchanted by a mystical scene I have waited a lifetime to see.

I am seeing, for the first time, Machu Picchu, the most enigmatic and powerful telluric site in the Southern Hemisphere. The panorama is well publicized. True to form, Machu Picchu *looks* absolutely magical. Blanketed by the thick, green jungle and surrounded by a corona of pointed mountain peaks, she is simply stunning. Partially hidden by the mystic veil of cloud forest, the heavens wink to open her vaporous gown. I am in total awe!

An hour passes. Weary and stiff after a 50-kilometer trek, I move forward toward the impressive ruins below with a renewed energy. Powerful, high-end emotions flow – respect, awe, accomplishment and completion. The mysterious Incas may have been vanquished and may not have discovered writing, but this view speaks volumes for who they were and the knowledge they accessed.

**The Energy of Sanctuary**

The Sanctuary Lodge is situated on the rim of the ruins, looking more like a monastery than a lodge, flowing with the *feng shui* of the surroundings and accepted by the Goddess spirit of Machu Picchu. The lodge, fashioned in flowing wings of stone, stucco and pine, is the gate, the guardian. Many employed by the lodge are Earth-Keepers, evolved guardians aware of their task.

A hot shower is on my agenda, and two full days in the lodge pampered by a soft bed! My time will be wondrous – exploring, absorbing, climbing and meditating. It is the full moon of the autumn equinox.

Machu Picchu was hidden for over 400 years. Her beauty and mystery are only now revealed in the yellow solar burst that clears the morning skies and activates the warm life flow of this powerful sacred site.

**Discovery**

It is thought provoking to consider that Machu Picchu was only re-discovered 90 years ago by American archaeologist Hiram Bingham. His 1911 discovery brought about a flurry of interest, but fortunately, the academic notoriety provided immediate protection of the site. This was indeed as it was meant to be.

It is the conventional belief that Machu Picchu was built in 1460-70 by the Inca ruler Pachacuti as a royal retreat and religious sanctuary. Its remote location, in nearly impassable terrain, high above the Urubamba River canyon cloud forest, ensured protection. Travel was restricted on the high Inca trail except by royal decree. The Incas were a regimented society, enlightened in many ways, but enigmatic in others. Their history is cloudy, as no written language was ever developed.

## Sacred Placement: Grid and Vortex

Machu Picchu was acknowledged as a sacred land long before the Incas, going back to the land of Og. Situated in the core of a unique double vortex, this sacred energy is of massive potency. It is primarily female, goddess in nature. The vortex is both electric and magnetic in structure, meaning it has aspects of being both an inward pull and outward flow vortex.

The double vortex is composed of two concentric energy rings that act as templates for both the magnetic and electrical vortexes around Machu Picchu. In this concentric circular template, 7 – 10 kilometers across, an outer energetic ring of clockwise motion draws energy into the perimeter of Machu Picchu. The inner electrical vortex, about 2 kilometers across, circulates counterclockwise and is fed by an outpouring of vertical columns of light from locations within the inner circle. The opposite directions of clockwise magnetic (inward) and counter-clockwise electric (outward) telluric flows are unique. I have experienced similar patterns in the double concentric stone circles of humanly groomed ley line energy at Avebury Circle, but rarely in a fully natural setting (except for the volcanic craters of Hawaii and Easter Island, where a unique 'anti-gravity' resonance is created).

## Creation and Protection

The Machu Picchu energy vortex has been protected for millennia by extraterrestrials who assisted in its creation. It has been kept hidden for the last six centuries by planetary guardians in order to prevent its pristine counter-spin energy from being thrown into imbalance. The greedy Spanish Conquistadors knew of the legends of Machu Picchu, and they searched for it but were never allowed to find and plunder the sacred site, even after the fall of the Inca Empire in the mid-1500s.

Present day Inca shamans say that the spirit of the Inca Goddess shrouded Machu Picchu in thick, white cloud forests that made the shrine invisible to all would be exploiters. When the site was found by Yale anthropologist Hiram Bingham in the 20th century, it was by divine plan. The Goddess energy was emerging globally and ready to be revealed to a world that would protect and prevent her exploitation and degradation.

## Conductive Mineralogy and Tellurics

The ancient ruins occupy about five square kilometers atop a flat shoulder of the geometric tetrahedron formation, 9,000 feet high. The base perimeter is hydro-energized on three sides by the class five rapids of the Urubamba River. The conductive mineralogy of Machu Picchu is granite, wafered with layers of serpentine, rose quartz, snow quartz, pyrite and jadeite. Thermal hot springs bubble up at the fourth base paralleling the granitic rock face. The telluric blend is intense yet somehow very nurturing.

The energy of the site is unclouded by the hundreds of visitors, pilgrims and tourist alike, who traverse the grounds daily. It is, in fact, enhanced by the overwhelming sense of reverence and awe that all feel when experiencing the structure and beauty of this serene Andean location.

## Goddess Energy

As I am discovering more and more on my

sojourns, it is indeed the wise female energy of the Goddess that is needed to balance our planet. The Goddess Energy present at Machu Picchu initiates all seekers with the light-encoded energy emitted in perpendicular golden rays from the sacred earth inside the inner ring. All who receive it provide more balance to the planet by achieving a greater balance within themselves. Machu Picchu has an energetic affinity with Glastonbury, as a balancing Goddess chakra of Gaia. She is also located as a gateway point on several grids, connecting her to Mu.

**Energy Fusion**

It was my experience that the most powerful points within the site are the Intihuatana Stone called 'the Hitching Post to the Sun' and the peak of the Huayna Picchu pinnacle. The two points communicate and fuse a male earth current to the pulsing female light energy in a sacred bonding, best experienced by visiting both of these points.

Having distinguished these two, I must clarify that the entire inner perimeter of the site is a virtual dynamo of pulsing light, literally teeming with energy focal points. Other major sites are the Temple of the Sun, Temple of the Moon and the Crevice Cave of the Greens.

Huayna Picchu is the famous pyramidal monolith behind the ruins. A thin rock carved staircase switchbacks its way up the peak, a one hour climb for a fit hiker. It took me over two! The thin oxygen climb to 9,000 feet had me puffing hard! The climb is not easy, but the peak and summit altar rock are absolutely the most powerful point in Machu Picchu. The reward for the climb is immediate. There is actually a small temple about 70 feet below the pinpoint summit, and from there the trail goes through a symbolic rock window tunnel – a bit of a squeeze for me – but ends up with an incredible view 3,000 feet

above the Machu Picchu ruins. A flat 'table altar' of gray granite 20 feet below the peak sits on a small plateau. It is quite stable and a virtual cornucopia of energy, large enough to recline on. The vitality emitted from the altar is tangibly electrical and reviving. The summit itself tapers to an accessible point some 20 feet beyond and must be experienced. The full telluric and etheric spectrum from Machu Picchu spirals up and cascades in a blissful fountain here.

Another very powerful point of Machu Picchu is the Hitching Post to the Sun, carved on a granite outcropping within the actual ruins. Machu Picchu, like many sacred Inca temples, was an astronomical observatory. The Hitching Post to the Sun is the Intihuatana stone of Machu Picchu. (An Intihuatana was the point the Inca considered most sacred in any temple, housing the deity, the God Force.) In Machu Picchu, it was uniquely fashioned (as a phallus) to serve as a solar calendar, a precise indicator of the winter solstice. On December 21, the high priest and priestess conducted a ritual ceremony of 'tying the sun' to bring on the new season. So sacred is its energy that the Inca claimed when seekers prayed at the stone, the Intihuatana granted knowledge and visions to those pure in heart.

**Intihuatana**

Unfortunately, the rampaging Spaniard invaders searched for and destroyed many of these sacred Intihuatana in other sacred Incan Temples in order to demoralize and Christianize the 'pagan' people. When the Intihuatana stone was broken at an Inca shrine, the Inca believed that the deities of the place died or departed, and indeed, the energies were thrown out of flow.

Because the Spaniards never found Machu Picchu, the potent Intihuatana stone and its resident energies remain today in their original, balanced flow. However, the mountaintop sanctuary fell into disuse and was abandoned some 40 years after the Spanish seized the Inca capital of Cusco in 1533. It was a planned dormancy. It is fully activated now for the 2012 Ascension!

## Sojourns

Like many sacred sites in the world, I found it impossible to capture the grandeur of Machu Picchu or the Inca Trail on film, or to describe it adequately in words. The centerpiece of one's sojourn is highly personal. For me, the three days at Machu Picchu was almost a totally different experience than the truly awesome (and taxing) four-day Inca Trail trek. The latter was the preparation, in my case, for the former and equally rewarding in a different sense.

In the Incan Andes, there is much more to see and experience. I spent two days in Cusco, the ancient capital city of the Inca Empire, located at 11,000 feet in the base of a bowl. What a mega-center! I also spent one day in the Sacred Valley of the Incas. While acclimatizing to the altitude at Cusco in preparation for the Inca Trail, I visited temples and ruins, viewed art treasures centuries old, passed through colorful open markets and explored some of the most impressive architectural feats in the world, including the Temple of the Sun and Sacsayhuaman. The stones used to build the temple and great walls of Sacsayhuaman fit so perfectly that it is impossible to slip even a razor blade between them, yet incredibly, many of the stones weigh more than 100 tons each!

## Apu Salkkantay: Wild Spirit Protector of the Inca Trail

The Inca Trail itself is a fabulous, pristine trek of wondrous beauty, winding through majestic and serene locations and emitting powerful energy. The Guardian Spirit of the Trail is the highly visible, stunning 21,000-foot snow-capped mountain called Apu Salkkantay or Wild Spirit

Mountain. The Inca held this male guardian spirit in great awe, and only the highest level of shaman was considered able to commune directly with the strong protective force. The Inca felt the male energy of Salkkantay was bonded or mated to the female energy of Machu Picchu, and I was keenly aware of Salkkantay's presence along the trek.

## LeMurian Codes

Another energy center of great importance is Lake Titicaca. Kryon channeled that Lake Titicaca is a mega-vortex that balances the Southern Hemisphere in a counter-spin paired to the mega-vortex in Sedona, Arizona. The massive lake sits at 13,000 feet and straddles the border between Bolivia and Peru. It is also electromagnetic, and balances and anchors Machu Picchu.

Machu Picchu is, above all else, a place of light, spirit and mystery. After huffing up and down its endless terraces and steps (there are over 3,000 of them) and poking in and out of the labyrinth of alcoves, plazas and temples, I could easily sense the presence of initiates, priests and feathered royalty within the magnetic stone temples and grounds.

Machu Picchu opened a door for me that I am still deciphering. I felt deep purifying emotions here. I was deluged with profound and puzzling sensations, both sweet and sad. I received a light code – the second LeMurian code – and felt a balance unique to that energy.

## Conclusion

The Machu Picchu experience has two requisite parts, the Inca Trail and then the Sanctuary Temple. The trail is an exquisite labor. It is the labyrinth, the purification. It prepares one for the majesty ahead … and what a divine majesty it is!

## Tyberonn Channel

*"Machu Picchu can be termed as an ancient and timeless 'Light Temple.' There have been other temples in this location since the time of LeMuria and Og. Long has this timeless light been recognized. Now, light operates both within and out of relative time. Your physicists have deducted that time slows as it nears the speed of light and stops when it reaches it. This is mainly correct. Light passes through the lens of your dimensional grid before it bathes your Earth. As such, it is refracted in certain vertices of the planetary grid and achieves a certain concentrated quality. It does so at Machu Picchu.*

*Machu Picchu is a multi dimensional prism, of sorts, that refracts the light into full spectrum and then uniquely absorbs and disperses it in a higher dimensional 'coded' format. The colors of green and violet are predominately reflected into and around Machu Picchu, although all colors are present.*

*The energy of this portal template is of a very rare synergy. And while it is potently beneficial and plays an important planetary role, it is not, on its own, what we would term one of the chakric centers of the Earth, although the channel believes it to be as such. In truth, it is more accurately described as a major contributor to the global chakric center of Lake Titicaca, supplying heart and crown energy to same, you see.*

*This, by no means, lessens its importance, quite the contrary, for it is uniquely magnificent in its chakric beneficence. The Titicaca chakra would not be complete without it. However, Machu Picchu performs other functions as a multi dimensional stargate with many Cosmic alignments.*

*It is specifically aligned to the planet Saturn. The planet Saturn has the combined dimensional frequency of 144, the square of the Earth Dimensional frequency of 12, which is indeed the harmonic of your Crystalline Grid. Saturn has a special alignment in your solar system and plays an important role in the graduation of Earth.*

*You see, the 144 dimensional frequency of Saturn is carried and pulsed by the seven ring groupings that encircle it. In truth, there are thousands of stellar particulate rings around Saturn, and each rotates at different speed and radiates its own frequency.*

*Saturn is composed of the original prima mata of the Solar Nebula creation and is the lightest of all the planets. Its density is less than that of water, you see. Its surface is as a viscous, semi solid gel.*

*Much of the energy waves that are being received in various portals and the poles, which are of course massive portals, is being pulsed from the radiating harmonic of Saturn's rings. The rings of Saturn contain monatomic matter, atoms devoid of electromagnetic charge. As such they are of an incredibly high vibratory harmonic and superconductivity. Your Solar System is moving into a quantum electromagnetic vacuum, a field devoid of electromagnetism, as it completes its current cyclic stellar progression. This is termed the zero point field. Saturn is predominantly zero point energy and radiates this field within your solar system.*

*This is being received by the Earth, most powerfully in your polar regions, and also occurs to a lesser degree at Machu Picchu, the Ural Mountains and New Zealand.*

*The synergy of this monatomic frequency with the condensed light of Machu Picchu's spiraled creation energy is particularly beneficial for the planet and humankind. The Light movement of Machu Picchu portal is in the creation spiral,* or golden phi, in a massive cone. It is absorbed all the way to the Earth's core and disseminated upward in pulses of perpendicular energetic beams. At certain times of year, particularly the equinoxes, the pulse is of brilliant intensity, affecting the time-space continuum in the portal and its surrounding double vortex, and geo magnetic alterations occur. Small energetic spheres of light are, on occasion, emitted as if from the ground and stone when these geo magnetic pulses become heightened.

Now, as your Earth prepares for Ascension, geo magnetic changes are occurring at both the magnetic poles. The rate of spin about the axis will lessen somewhat, and this will affect the cyclic ratio of Earth's inner crystalline core to the mantle. This is occurring now and is experienced by many as the 'quickening' of time. You see, the ratio of the earth rotation to the rotation of the inner core determines the pulse of the space-time continuum. Now, we will say, it remains to be seen as to what degree of earth change will occur with the loosening of the planet's axial torque. But the global cataclysm foretold by your prophets and seers for millennia, we will say, need not occur. You have changed it. There will indeed be an appropriate process of purification, but not on the proportion of global devastation, as the Earth brings in the crystalline frequency. We tell you that the planet's harmonic measurement, the 'human-grid frequencial' has made benevolent progress, and that there are enough souls now of high vibration to create the FUTURE and sustain it, as you enter the 20th cycle.

Now, verification of how an individual perceives an infinity point such as Machu Picchu will vary. A third dimensional human will perceive and interpret based upon their light quotient, their awareness and integrity. One may see the portal here or the transference of energy there, and they will interpret it differently, individually. If you would approach the same portal from a crystalline standpoint, it will define itself differently, and each place that you would stand, each stance, would offer to you a different perception and a slightly different definition. Now, it also varies, with the specific vector of space-time continuum, how these will define themselves. Where one stands based upon space and time. Does one stand upon the past, the future, the present, does one approach it from what dimension? All of these change the geometries each time, you see. Many speak of visiting 'power points' for the purpose of activating them, aligning them and anchoring them. In truth it is the power point that activates, aligns and anchors the human. And each human will receive this in a way tailored and defined by their light quotient and system of belief.

Infinity points, sacred sites, if you will, involve all that you would term the platonic solids and more as well that are not revealed. They are not revealed, because they are not aware yet. The conscious mind attempts to make logic out of it, you see. When an expansive paradigm is encountered, the logical mind attempts to fit it into what it already knows and into the frame confirmed by the ingrained main stream science; so the mathematics, the logarithms, the algorithms, all would attempt to locate how to fit the new concept. And of course it would not fit because it is based upon a crystalline essence, and so it would be misunderstood or dismissed. And so the better understanding of the cosmic matrix and the interplay on and with the infinity points on your Earth are waiting for the human group mind to expand a bit more into comprehension of that greater reality.

We would say to you that there is even greater life that circles about and above your planet now, wishing to enter into your mass field of awareness. It is light of a sublime nature. It does not hold logic, it does not hold vision, it is not the light of promise, but it is the light of wellness. And we will say to you that if you will allow this light to enter your sphere of influence, your field *of awareness, you would find yourself lighter in spirit almost immediately, and this is only by intent. This subtle brilliance is available to humankind, to the individual by self-projection. You can apply and avail yourself of it, but YOU must call it forward, and become it. Seek, and ye shall find. You must engage the light of the truth of wellness within yourself. Because in seeking greater knowledge, one does not always seek or choose to include wellness, self love, but they are synergistically required to do so in achieving the crystalline vibration. They are complimentary, and each would benefit by it.*

*Divine dimensional light for each human is transmitted from within your own being, not from without. It is based upon the energy of one's own truth, the confirmations that are the Cosmos, and from that place they are aggregated. They are expanded within you as only light frequencies can be, and then vibrate themselves into the mind and heart where, by the magic of your intent, they are converted to wisdom. But it is important that you will know that it is energy that you send, energy that you receive, energy that you speak and that you guide and that you call upon that reveals to you your true divine self. Points of light and infinity dot your planet, and they offer great acceleration, but the most important sacred site, you see, is within your heart, and you ever carry it with you. You are beloved."*

… and so it is.

# Ireland

Ireland's Ring of Kerry is beyond magical. Its verdant, rugged beauty is dotted with amazing landscapes, stone circles and myriad potent Neolithic sites. But Skellig Michael, the mystical, monastic island named after Archangel Michael, is undeniably 'Lord of the Ring.'

## Holy of Holies

The small jagged island of Skellig Michael is the point on the earth plane in which the renowned Michael ley line enters Gaia. On this pyramidal island, the Michael ley line begins its sacred trek across Britain and Europe, ending at Mount Carmel in the Holy Land of Israel. How interesting that it begins on this otherworldly little island off the Ring of Kerry. How interesting, indeed.

It was, in fact, through researching the Michael ley line that I first learned of Skellig Michael. The very concept of this ancient monastery crowning this isolated rock, 13 kilometers off Ireland's shore, is a stunning enigma. The actual genesis is biblical in proportion. Inspired monks receiving and obeying a divine decree from an archangel to sail out and build a monastery on bare rock carries shades of the exodus of Moses.

This location equals, no, surpasses, the sites of the other two great monastic centers in Western Europe that were also built per Archangel Michael's inspiration – Mont St. Michel in Normandy and St. Michael's Mount in Cornwall, which are triangulated with Skellig.

It is interesting and fitting that historians and pilgrims alike are interested in the three 'Michael' islands for connected yet succinctly differing reasons. All three are islands of archeological interest for the academic. And metaphysically, all three islands anchor the Michael portal of the Michael ley line, and connect to its amazing telluric thread as it weaves its divine tapestry onto the Earth.

Islands on which manifestations of Archangel Michael appeared and inspired holy men to come and live on bare rock for over 1,500 years led me to suspect Skellig to be one of those rarified gridpoints that coexist in multiple dimensions. So I was compelled to investigate and experience this for myself.

## Tyb's Journal: September 2002

When I landed at Ireland's Shannon Airport, Irish skies were smiling! It had rained all the week prior to my arrival, but the skies were clearing and the sun was beaming through mist on my disembarkation. The weather would remain brilliant for my entire four-day trip. Luck of the Irish indeed!

While beautiful sunny days are something of a rare commodity on the West Coast of Ireland, beautiful countryside is not. The glowing green of the soft, velvety landscape had quite an allure. The solid week of rain had polished the grounds and trees almost as if to display Ireland in watercolor, a living Monet. The hills radiated brightness, and they seemed to shine with every shade of green in the painted landscape.

Getting out of the airport into the lush countryside was easy, a simple matter of minutes, even with driving on the left. I headed north for the Cliffs of Morea and then on to the Burren of County Clare. Both destinations were tidily packed into a seven-hour slot, in basically a looping drive through magnificent country with ample time for stops. Evening would see me heading south to the Ring of Kerry and Skellig Michael, entry portal of the Michael ley line.

## The Cliffs of Morea

I arrived at the Cliffs of Morea within the hour. What an incredible place! The cliffs are magnificent black slate fortresses deflecting the fifty-foot crashing waves of the North Atlantic. The sheer walls drop 650 feet straight onto a crag of jagged ramparts, dotted white with barnacles and seabird guano. The color contrast is awesome. Bright green fields cap the walls like a shaggy mop wig, right to the very edge. The sheer drop is frightening to anyone with vertigo or children. Despite guardrails and stone walls that keep the visitor a safe distance from the edge, there are stunning views allowing the viewer to get showered by invigorating salty sea spray! Constant wind off the ocean slams against the sheer cliffs in fog-white swirling eddies, scampering upward, like the spirits of long past Vikings scaling castle walls. The icy winds over the grassy edge carry smoky water plumes, making a waterproof jacket highly recommended.

I found the energy here really charged, very amplified. The combination of green fields, sea air and the mesmerizing cliffs provided an immediate resonance of balance and well being. The ionic release from the pounding waves created an immense plasmic field that was immediately refreshing.

The spiritual traveler and tourist alike can find endless reasons to spend an afternoon here. Vast energy pockets were ample for meditation, contemplation or just being in the moment. The sea breeze energy is so awesome, I could have enjoyed a few days in a seaside B & B, just losing myself in the green rolling fields alongside the cliffs. However, I had to settle for a two-hour taste, then onward to the Burren!

## The Burren

The Burren is a geological phenomenon in County Clare, just a brief 30-minute drive from the Cliffs of Moher. The word 'burren' is derived from the Irish-Gaelic word *bhoireann*, meaning 'place of stones,' and the stones of the Burren are quite something to see. The entire area looks like a massive gray rock floor, which is exactly what it is – a glacier-cut hearth of tabled limestone covering some 300 square kilometers. The limestone surface can vary from smooth plates to undulating five-foot waves. The rocky wave pattern is amazing, looking oddly like a gray, solidified ocean! Veins of snow quartz zigzag through the area, often several meters wide, in an arraying pattern of swirls. Some very unusual plant life also adds to the otherworldly appeal of the Burren, a moonscape teeming with telluric energy that virtually buzzed.

Not surprisingly, it is also home to some fine Neolithic sites, the most famous of which was my next destination – the Dolman at Poulnabrone.

## The Dolman at Poulnabrone (aka Druids' Altar)

The word 'dolman' comes from two Breton words meaning 'stone table,' and has traditionally been referred to in Gaelic as the Druids' Altar. It is a 5,000-year-old Neolithic monument, (dating to 3,000 BC) and believed by some to have been set in place by Druid priests to mark a very powerful vortex of crossing ley lines. A place of ritual and wedding ceremonies, fertility rites and wakes, it looks like a massive table held in place by huge limestone sheet rocks.

Upon my arrival, I was delighted to find a pair of German visitors measuring the energy with dowsing rods. After watching them for a few moments, I struck up a conversation and learned about other sites in the area. I brought out my copper dowsing L-rods to help map the energy lines, and we did, indeed, find the rods swirled and aligned with two leys intersecting at the Dolman, with a swirling energy in its center. Both entered exactly on line with monoliths wedged in place in three points along the outer perimeter. The monoliths were relatively small but had been carefully chiseled with circular holes to create energetic portals for the ley. It was an astonishing discovery.

After a couple of hours at the Dolman, I reluctantly had to leave. Although it was almost 6 p.m., and sunset wasn't until 10 p.m., I had to conserve light so as not to miss the visual portion of the spectacular Irish countryside as I headed south.

## To the Ring of Kerry

I squeezed my large frame into the small rental car and pulled onto the serpentine two-lane country road. I let the picturesque winding road just slide by as I drove southward, in total contentment, to the Ring of Kerry and Skellig Michael itself. I drove in one of those lucid, waking dreams. The leisurely drive to Kerry was about three hours in linear time, but I seemed to arrive with no awareness of its passing. The soft green Irish countryside really has an amazing charm, and I merged into every landscape during the drive.

It was not quite dark when I arrived at the Skellig Peninsula. A quaint fishing village right out of the 18th century delighted my eyes. A faint chorus of cawing gulls gnawed at my perception of space and time, as centuries seemed to roll back in perfect rhythm with the gently bobbing boats anchored in the harbor. Everything was perfect and tugged so at my heartstrings. The pungent smell of drying fishnets was so familiar that I felt a pang of sweet sadness. *Déjà vu* all over again! Ah, but the rugged Irish coastline has a captivating allure.

The salt-air breeze of the North Atlantic was cold enough to sharpen my senses, and snap me out of the time warp I was in, to see the brightly painted boats and quaint stone village. The peninsula became quickly cloaked in a thick evening fog, so I checked into my B & B, then reserved my boat trip to Skellig for 10 o'clock the next morning. If the village had this hypnotic effect, I wondered what lay in wait on Skellig Michael? I would soon find out.

As I scanned the rolling ocean from my room's bay window, I caught a fleeting glimpse of two pyramidal shapes far in the distance. There are actually two Skellig Islands: Skellig Michael and the smaller Skellig Minor. From any angle or vantage point on the Ring of Kerry, they are spectacular pinnacles. From my bedroom, they were the last sights I saw before retiring. As I fell asleep, my final thoughts were, *how on earth did the monks get here, and why make a life atop the bare rocky pinnacle?*

## Day Two: Skellig Michael

*"An incredible, impossible, mad place. I tell you the thing does not belong to any world that you and I have lived and worked in; it is part of our dream world."*

When George Bernard Shaw wrote those words back in 1910, he had just returned from a jarring visit to Skellig Michael:

*"Even the gnarled stones seemed alive on that mystical island. Skellig's monks must have communed with angels for their daily sustenance on such bare rock."*

Indeed they did, Mr. Shaw. Indeed they did.

My boat trip out was quite a roller coaster ride. The 30-foot passenger skiff was diesel powered and heartily handled the waves, not so with most of the passengers, however. On the tip of a passerby and an intuitive tug, I took two anti-seasickness pills an hour before departure. I normally don't take such precaution, but in this case I was glad I did. All nine of my touring shipmates lost their breakfast on the roll of 15-foot swells during the hour-long ride. That Technicolor unpleasantry aside, the boat trip was exciting, to say the least.

As we neared Skellig Michael, the views opened, and I became enraptured at the sheer pyramidal symmetry and surprising richness of color. In the sunshine, the black silhouettes transformed to purples and greens – absolutely stunning colors.

Interestingly, but not surprisingly, a lenticular cloud sat over the peak of Skellig Michael – a telltale sign of an inward pull, or magnetic vortex, and certainly in keeping with the anchoring of a portal. No less, a portal infusing the Michael ley energy into the quartz pinnacle. Yes quartz, purple quartz, an entire island of amethyst.

Geologically, Skellig Michael is Devonian sandstone, 350 million-year-old vintage sedimentary quartz that runs right through the backbone of Kerry. The colors are cabernet purple and lavender rose. The bouquets are plentiful, but more so the floral varieties that seem able to grow directly on this magical quartz, the source of the electrical energies here. Indeed, Skellig is amethyst, purple quartz cut into a tetrahedron.

The tiny landing dock came into view as the boat pulled in closer. It was concrete, built outward from steel shafts anchored into the rock wall. The cement was fashioned into a landing quay large enough for one boat at a time. The swells created a ten-foot bobbing, so unloading had to be perfectly timed! It was! The Irish boatmen were confident and capable, as they steadied the vessel and guided each of us individually onto the quayside. We were given three hours but told that, because the weather and sea change constantly, if we heard three horn blasts we were to head back immediately or face a night on the island, something I secretly yearned for!

## The 777 Steps

A roadway leads upward from the quay, carved into the side of the rock years ago in order to place a lighthouse on the far side at the lower mid-base. It leads a couple of hundred meters to the staircase of chiseled steps, painstakingly carved by monks to get to the sacred saddle and monastery above.

I was still wobbly from the effects of Dramamine and ocean swells as I collected myself for the walk up. I hoped the grogginess would wear off and not affect my ability to tap into the potent energies I knew to be above in the Skellig Monastery.

At the recommendation of the boat guides, I was dressed for wet and cold, as icy Atlantic rain can blow in at any time. However, the weather was incredibly warm, in fact, it was hot! After climbing a few meters of the steeply inclined path, so was I!

I had actually wished for a sauna the night before in order to purify my system, and between my heavy waterproof gear and backpack, my sauna wish was granted. I worked up quite a sweat as I toiled upward on the steep sides of the mountain. Be careful what you ask for in 5-D portals, because manifestation is immediate!

Like many mega-power sites, the energy crests as one reaches the higher points. The walk upward is literally a staircase of 777 steps, although there are differing versions of the exact number, based on whether the count extends to the monastery, the sacred caldera or the southern peak. Flowers were everywhere – small blossoms in delicate casings, resplendently juxtaposed in vital beauty. The stairs formed a switchback, with exquisite places to sit and rest on purple rock outcroppings and to enjoy the commanding view.

## The Michael Portal Anchor

Near the top, a small saddle is formed almost like a volcanic caldron. It took a good 40 minutes for me to reach the Fryer's Saddle, but what reward! It is an incredibly potent area. A definite contained energy is emitted within its elongated bowl that balances the male and female peaks and anchors the portal.

It is a lush, magical fairy garden. Tiny white and yellow flowers were dispersed like angel hair bouquets in the sweet grass. The energy here was far more complex, thicker, yet balanced and mesmerizing – the entry point of the Michael portal.

How it could be so lush and green is really not surprising. The monks brought rich black soil over from the mainland and painstakingly built sodded areas on the saddle and monastery grounds for planting gardens.

That process has since maintained a critical mass cycle of self-replenishment in which the hearty plants decay into mulch, thus creating new soil. Every horizontal area and quite a few vertical ones seemed to have a rich layer of fertile loam. So energetically powerful was this place that plant life burst out everywhere, even on naked rock. Sweet smelling grasses and flowers thrived, and life teemed all over Skellig.

Skellig *is* life. The energy on the island could grow roses in snow and sustain monks on air alone – the original breatharians, perhaps not by choice! Few places on Earth hold such vital, healing and sustaining life energy.

The very osmotic process of absorbing Skellig's electro-light energy essence through the auric field sustains life ... and optimally, thanks to the pristine quality of the energy. The isolation, the exact blend creating an energetic cocktail of mineralogy, the grid location and geometry, and the portal alignments are the fountain of youth, or portal of youth, flowing divine energy.

I soaked in this immense, wholesome vibration and went into a meditation of such pristine clarity unlike any I had experienced before. I did sense Lord Michael and was moved deeply. I went into a sense of 'zipped' time, where the passing of time was halted. The minutes seemed to float like hours. I was grateful and wanted to stay, but alas there was more to see.

## The Monastery

To my right, the north, was carved the final tier of steps to the holy of holies, the monastery. There seemed to be another 100 or so feet upward and 300 feet or so to the northern corner. Interestingly, two amazing dragon figures of natural, weather-sculpted rocks hovered over the entrance as if to protect the area from intruders. The likeness was quite amazing, and I felt a presence.

It wasn't lost on me that the church symbol of Archangel Michael includes dragons, he is connected to the harnessing of the dragon's energy and the removal of the serpents from Ireland.

The dragon often symbolized the fire of kundalini, and the serpent the use of kundalini on the earth plane. Could it be that the energy of Michael is to anchor kundalini into the upper chakras for the full integrity of root to crown assimilation? Rather than slaying dragons, Michael is about integrating their fire energy, refining fire into violet light!

The monastery itself was otherworldly. I was quite unprepared for what I saw and felt, as I climbed and weaved along the trail to the beehive huts. These were created in perfect domes, without cement or mortar, with two foot thick walls. They projected incredible energy, each one an infinity point and anchor of the portal. Each one a vortex.

### The Chapel: Holy of Holies

The 'beehived' chapel itself is situated on a narrow ledge, more than 750 feet above sea level. I spent 15 minutes inside alone, and its energy jolted me so, that I was moved to tears. I felt an energetic download, a light code of 5-D energy. The domes remain virtually frozen in time, structurally the same as when built 1,450 years ago. Flashes of light were everywhere.

I found a grassy patch that commanded a stunning, open view onto Skellig Minor Island. The afternoon was glowing bright, and the sun warmed my face. Winded from the hard climb and wet from the toil, I felt comfort on a piece of soft earth at the edge of the domes. The electricity of this spot was absolutely tangible. The purple and gold, the sweet flora smells. All had that dreamy sense of well being. Skellig Minor loomed large on the horizon. It is also a pyramid and energetically part of this Skellig energy field. Skellig Minor is home to some 27,000 pairs of gannets – the second largest colony of such seabirds in the world – and just then, an enormous cloud of gannets wafted over its pinnacle, bringing their grace and soft energy into this balance. More to this than meets the eye … undoubtedly.

From the shoreline, both Skellig Islands appear as tetrahedral pyramids, but in truth, Skellig Michael curves slightly near the top into a saddle joining two lateral peaks, one male, one female, in balance. The second and highest of the two peaks on Skellig Michael is 770 feet above sea level, topped by a monolithic 'standing stone,' engraved with a Celtic Cross at the very end of a narrow stretch of rock.

### The Pilgrims' Test

While the climb to the monastery is tortuous and difficult, the climb to the upper peak is even more demanding and leaves one in awe of the people who chose to make this their home. The climb up was tenuous, a labyrinth that I find in so many sacred places.

Medieval pilgrims, after visiting the Skellig monastery, would climb to the south peak, quite a precarious task. They would kiss the cross, thus proving their faith and piety, and occasionally as an act of penitence. It may have been the burning desire inherent in some to find an isolation that enabled them to develop communion with God. I can only imagine the courage and dedication involved in the days and times past. Yet it is understandable when you experience first hand the presence of Spirit that is Skellig. It is humbling, immediate and penetrating. The essence of divinity atop Skellig Michael is overwhelming. So much is there.

### Islands of Light

It was, in fact, due to places like Skellig Michael that western civilization was preserved. Scholars proclaim that when Europe was being overrun with barbarians in the depth of the Dark Ages, these isolated monasteries preserved the arts, reading and indeed civilization itself. These include Skellig, Mont Michele and Meteoria Monastery in Greece. Totally isolated, totally benevolent, angelic anchors.

Yet in spite of their stark inaccessibility, Viking invaders attacked the Skelligs several times, although there was little to attract them in the way of wealth or material treasure. Light always attracts the dark. But it cannot exist for long in places of pure benevolence such as Skellig.

## Connecting the Energies

I used my remaining time in the magic of the crest to energetically connect to Michael, who was omnipresent. I felt humbled, as I flowed with the energy and consciously connected energy lines to Lake Louise in Canada, Enchanted Rock in southwest Texas, and Torres del Paine in Chile. I planted small rocks from each of these locations into the soil of Skellig. The moment was timeless and moving.

## The Spiral Home

The trumpeting of the boat's horn from far below jolted me out of my reverie, and my heart sank. It would take close to an hour to reach the loading dock, but I was in no hurry. I weaved my way back down, absorbing every ion of the incredible energy and scenery en route.

The following morning, I bought a book at the visitor center that captured my feelings regarding Skellig, and I end with the words of Sir Kenneth Clark:

*"As I climbed the path winding up to the ancient constructions near the top of Skellig's cliff, I sensed that I was on the threshold of something utterly unique, though I was by no means a stranger to monasteries, which I had visited throughout Europe, and even farther afield at one time and another. But nothing in my experience had prepared me for this huddle of domes, crouching halfway to heaven in this all but inaccessible place, with an intimidating immensity of space all around, where it was easy to feel that you had reached a limit of this world. A holy place, to be sure, which would still have been holy, even if it had never known the consecrated life of prayer."*

## Tyberonn Channel

*"Now, it is important that we review that which are called the leylines. These can be said to exist in various forms, with differing degrees of refinement from multifarious forms of energy. Ley lines, as they are called in your times, are the energetic patterns that run both above and beneath the Earth. These circumnavigate the Earth in a variety of ways based upon laws of mathematics, upon geometries, upon vibrational essence, geological force, electromagnetics and mineralogical fields. They shift and they move, and they have been utilized in a myriad of ways throughout the eons of space-time. In eras of greater understanding, times of greater technology, they have been traveled as highways, utilizing enhancement of very refined energies. Through such understanding, leylines had the capacity to be used as conduits of energy transferal and for communication. Since the fall of Atlantis, amplified utilization has ceased, and the ability for sustaining this manner of usage was lost. As a result, the refined network is no longer intact, so the ley lines are shorn in some areas, torn in others, and the highways and byways appear not to make sense, you see; they no longer completely connect across the globe.*

*Now, the base essence of leylines occurs from a natural source. They are currents of telluric energy. As these were refined, some became coded and engineered on new paradigms which you call fourth dimension and fifth dimension. These replace the old, but not all have discovered them yet, and that is appropriate, you see. Extraterrestrials have assisted the Earth in this effort. Those from Sirius B have been instrumental in recent years in realigning this system for the Ascension, and indeed they were the architects of the original enhancement of the ley system, established over 30,000 years ago.*

*Now, the system of leylines can be said to act as the nervous system of the living planet. The planet also has what can be termed axial tonal lines, meridians and chakras.*

*Leylines are not constant, many factors can cause their shift. Many factors add to their complex energy content, or lack thereof. Tectonic stresses, magma, solar energy, naturally occurring electromagnetic fields exerted by minerals such as quartz, and even the decomposition of organic matter, this creates a heat and electrical charge, you see. These energies accumulate and flow along earth paths of conductivity either on, slightly above or underneath the Earth's crust. Those regions and places on the Earth, high in natural metal or conductive mineral content, will attract the current of these electromagnetic flows. Man made structures built to sacred geometry will also attract these flows. Almost all of the sacred geometric temples built by the Asian, Roman, Greek, Egyptian and Mayan have leylines passing through them. Some of these structures were built on leys, others attracted them to them.*

*Now, when these currents pass through structures built to sacred geometry or through what you term sacred sites, the currents absorb and radiate light. When this occurs, the leys assume a refined conscious nature, capable of coded memory. When two or more of these lines intersect, a vortex or specific type of power point is formed. Ley power points energetically connect to the grid system and assume a geometric matrix, which in turn can attract to it higher dimensional energies. These become meridian points, and in some cases, chakras of the living sentience of the Earth.*

*Each ley, each sacred site, can and does affect the human electromagnetic field. Additionally, the light arcs and angles from planets and stars will feed and influence the areas of telluric energy pools (called electrical, or outward, vortexes) and can actually create, depending on their alignment, inward pull portals or openings that can feed in energy from stellar and solar light photons, as well as from planetary and higher dimensional grid lattices.*

*If one accepts the postulate that certain points of higher energy exist on the planet, and that they do have a crystallized matrix that projects a specific geometric pattern, then its can also be understood that these living energy sources communicate thru harmonic energy oscillations. For example if one has a tuning fork in the key of C, and then one plays a C note on a piano, the musical vibration from the piano will also create a vibration in the tuning fork, because of the law your scientists call harmonic oscillation. Harmonic oscillations between power points on Earth and in higher dimensions are also so 'attuned' to resonate to compatible harmonics.*

*Just as your human body has organs that sustain the health of the physical body, so it is with ley lines. Ley lines sustain the health of the physical Earth. Now, above the organs of the body you have meridian lines that bisect the body, and as they do, contribute to the wellness of the being, which then transmits that energy into a different form, then feeding the organs, feeding the senses and the awareness. Now, just as your human body undergoes changes, so does the Earth diversify and shift. The ley system changes and adapts in kind. We tell you that with the graduation of the Earth, the Ascension, not only will the earth system of sensitivity adjust but so will that of the human.*

*Now, above the meridian system of the human body are what we term the axial tonal lines. This is a term that is relative, and quite new, to your sphere. You will not have heard it so much, but it will become more and more well known. The axial tonal lines are distinct lines, which connect the emotional body, the mental body, the causal body and such to the ascended body, and so it is with the Earth. The Earth, as well, has axial tonal lines defined by both spiritual and celestial qualities, again based upon sacred mathematics. These touch in certain areas to the ley lines, they touch but they do not rest upon them. But they do intersect, especially in places where the ley lines are torn and shorn and disconnected. They act as bridges, bridges from one dimension to another to bridge gaps in knowledge, to bridge gaps in history, to bridge gaps of energy that have been depleted or shorn as such, you see?*

*Now, when you visit a conjunction of ley energy, or a sacred site or vortex complex, you absorb the code of its unique message, its unique geometry. You carry within your field the energy of every sacred site, every power point and every grid point on each continent you have visited. You have the ability to connect them to yourself and to one another, Dear Ones. Those of you, such as the channel, that have been tugged to visit such places can visualize connecting them to the 144 Grid, and thereby assist in connecting them to the evolving grid. And in the process, you connect and activate yourself.*

*Now, in reference to the Michael Leyline, we speak first of Archangel Michael, as he is termed in Judeo-Christian experience. The source of this angelic energy existed long before the Judeo-Christian actualization. In Atlantean and pre Atlantean times, he was called by different names. He works with those of all spiritual desire and all religious beliefs. He is known by a different name to the Pagan, Buddhist and Hindu. So we will say that angelics are dedicated to the heart of the human, to the eternal truth, as opposed to a certain sect or dogma. That segment which you call the Michael line became imbued with divine light and drawn into power points and cosmic alignment points some 18,000 years ago. In truth, this line was recognized first by the Atlantean Priests and Druids before it was given a Judeo-Christian name, yet the energy is the same, you see. Oh but there was Divine wisdom in the name change. How many Christian Cathedrals built with*

*immaculate sacred geometry on the exact vector and cosmic alignment points of this transcendental current would have been so constructed if the leyline were considered Pagan?*

*The complex of Skellig Michael is indeed a potent portal, and all portals have a distribution engine you call a vortex. The structure of Skellig Michael is pyramidal in geometry and is particularly aligned with celestial energies. It is composed of violet granite that carries the imprint of the human quest. Your geologists will know of this particular granite that is the rock foundation and energy of many sacred places. The harmonic oscillation we spoke of earlier allows such mineralogical harmonics to be the fount of vibrational connection between these sites. Such harmonics occur not just in the mineralogy but also by means of geometry and light quotient.*

*We will say that Skellig Michael is not the original entry point of the 'Michael' leyline, but it now appears to be so, because the line no longer is fully connected to its full compliment. You see, it once encircled the planet. It will again in the future, but that is not yet completed nor is it the time. We will say that its strongest portion extends from Ireland, through Britain, across Europe and forks into the lands of ancient Judea, Israel and Egypt. Does it surprise you to know that it connects to Mecca in Saudi Arabia? It should not surprise you to know that most of you have had lifetimes in every race and every religion. Truth has a way of evolving within the hearts of all who truly seek God, despite the limitations of patriarchal or any other restrictive dogma, you see. All of you are of the family of man, and are truly and deeply beloved."*

… and so it is.

61

# Iona and Staffa ~ Portals of the Hebrides

Lying off the western coast of Scotland are the islands of Iona and Staffa. They are part of the Scottish Hebrides and claim an ancient and interesting heritage. The Isle of Iona became an important missionary center for Scotland and Northern England during the Middle Ages. The celebrated Book of Kells was written and illuminated on Iona during the middle of the 8th century.

But the draw of Iona is not because of its history, rather its history is because of its draw. Iona is an ancient sacred portal that channels a stream of radiant, divine energy. One of the most serene and beautiful places in the world, the island is a harmonic blend of sea and earth. Iona beams like a precious gem. Vibrant with an energetic presence of positive elementals, it is a powerful third eye center, intimately linked to the crystalline basalt Staffa Isle.

## First Christian Monastery

Called the Holy Island, Iona is the site of the first Christian monastery on the British Isles, founded in 563 AD by St. Columba, who recognized its sacred aura and reported that God led him there through visions. He told his followers he had found in Iona the promised holy land from which he would begin his life's mission: "This island God has set apart, a refuge of his divine heart whose understanding and peace is yielded freely to those who truly seek God on earth."

Under the leadership of St. Columba, Iona Abbey became a thriving training center of Christianity and a pilgrimage site for seekers of the early Christian faith. The abbey remained active for three centuries, until invading Vikings ravaged the island in the late 800s and murdered 77 monks at Martyrs Bay. Some monks escaped to Ireland, and a Benedictine Order reestablished the monastery

a few years later, whereupon it remained active until the Reformation in 1560. Subsequently it was abandoned and fell into ruin.

A spirit-led group under the tutelage of Lord McLeod reconstructed the Iona Abbey with the original stones some three decades ago. This led to the resettling of a spiritual religious community on the island, fulfilling a prophecy by founding patron St. Columba. Affiliated with the Church of Scotland, the group is simply called The Iona Community, and Christian services are held in the Abbey nightly at 9 p.m.

Iona is reached by ferry from the highland city of Oban on the western coast of Scotland. The ferry ride is a pleasant one-hour trip to the Island of Mull, from which a bus or car takes you some 37 miles to the small port of Fionnphort. From there, boarding a smaller ferry for the 15-minute crossing to Iona is required, as cars are not permitted on Iona except for permanent residents.

Celtic Druids held Iona sacred long before Christianity appeared on the island with the arrival of Saint Columba. In fact, Iona's Gaelic name, *Innisnam Druidbneach* means 'Island of Druids.' The Druids occupied Iona and used nearby Staffa Island (known for its massive crystallized pillars of hexagonal basalt) as a site of mystical initiation rites for high priests.

## Staffa Island: Crystal Generator

Staffa Island is, in itself, a unique and very powerful energy center, a pulsing generator of white crystalline energy charging all around it. Staffa energizes and protects Iona and is a key benefactor of Iona's vibrational quality. The varying lengths of hexagonal crystalline basalt pillars are like musically tuned windpipes on a massive organ, creating a pure symphonic frequency in concert with all seven chakras. Its generated energy is musical, crystalline and penetrating. It energizes and affects the area like an enormous Tibetan bell, charging and vitalizing the sea. A visit to Iona should also include a visit to Staffa, and especially Fingal's Cave.

I had the marvelous opportunity to spend six hours alone on Staffa Island, half of which was spent in Fingal's Cave, inspiration for Mendelssohn's *Hebrides Overture*, honoring the energetic generator island. Sir Walter Scott referred to the crystalline cave as: "A naturally adorned cathedral where one touches the spirit of God." Jules Verne visited the island and was equally inspired to write of Fingal's Cave in his book *The Green Ray*.

The cave is a pillared sea grotto on Staffa's eastern face, running 227 feet in length, approximately 75 feet wide with a tapered roof and curved basalt pillars extending 100 feet high. Its symmetry is stunning and remarkably shaped like the inside of a great cathedral, complete with buttresses. It is, in fact, an inclusionary crack of the crystalline island. It was said to be so sacred to the Druids that they only entered the consecrated aperture for spiritual rites of the highest order.

The Fingal's Cave fissure contains an inlet of aqua green sea for its entire length. The synergistic relationship of the cave's crystal matrix and the perpetual wave motion inside create a virtual piston of compressed energy. The gentle frolic and splash of sea against the sides releases ionic energy that charges the cave and the tiny island itself. This is further amplified by the potent electromagnetic field of the crystallized basalt.

The cave faces the rising sun and is dancing with energy in the morning hours. Angled beams of sunlight illuminate the entire cave through the high triangular entrance. The rays are rhythmically reflected across the walls and ceiling in a hypnotic strobe-light effect. Even as the sun

moves overhead and the cave becomes shadowed, it somehow retains brightness, as if lit from the waters below. There is an unmistakable inspiring, angelic presence that exudes joy and well being.

Basalt columns thankfully form a relatively safe 10-foot walkway on all sides, some 20 feet above the water level. Including Fingal's, there are six major sea caves on Staffa, even though it is less than a mile in length and a half-mile wide – less than 80 acres.

The basalt crystals vary in diameter from six inches to five feet and vary in length from two feet to one hundred feet. This size variance allows Staffa's crystals to ecstatically sing in every key and octave. The powerful crescendo is an omniscient chant, empowering all around it. Fear cannot exist in such a pure energy, and I was lofted to my higher self almost immediately. The sensation was one of deep joyous belonging, and I was made clearly aware that Staffa is an intimate part of Iona's vibration, as an energy line connects the two.

Staffa is a revered temple, pure kundalini. We are allowed to visit but not to stay, as the island is protected by an angelic host to carry out its generator role, charging and clearing all that is around and channeling pure energy to Iona.

**Iona Isle: Sacred Gem Portal**

While there are no standing stones or stone circles on Iona, evidence of ancient fortresses remain, and standing stones across the Iona Sound at the Ross of Mull are aligned to Iona, as if to guide pilgrims to the departure point to the island.

Iona has a striking panorama of astounding beauty. It shines like a polished jewel, literally emitting a visible indigo energy. I felt an immediate spirit-tug signifying deep recognition of the 'home' vibration, and the rare sacredness of this living cathedral struck a deep chord within me. I could physically see the energy waves blurring parts of the island, like summer heat rising off asphalt. The air sparkled and would occasionally burst with small pinpoints of light – a phenomenon I have seen only in very high-energy points.

The island is 3.4 miles long and 1.7 miles wide, rugged, with jagged rock outcroppings and rounded mounds of ancient granitic gneiss. The glens are magic faerielands of lush grass in which one can feel the faeries happily attending the flora. Green fields are painted with yellow and lilac bouquets of flowers, and the fragrance of sweet grass, lavender and sea make for an intoxicating aromatic cocktail. Groves of purple heather line the highlands and frame the stone mounds. One easily lapses into a meditative alpha state, entranced by the visual beauty and natural perfumes of Iona.

### The Magnetism of Iona

Although the island of Iona is a mere two miles from the island of Mull, there are remarkable geological differences between the two. I was astonished to learn that the island of Iona is a rare upthrust of one of the oldest rock formations on earth. The 2.9 billion-year-old Lewisian granitic gneiss dominates three quarters of the island (the Earth is approximately 4.4 billion years old), whereas the island of Mull is predominantly younger 300 million-year-old pink granite. This is in part an explanation for the differentiating vibration that led both Druids and St. Columba to recognize Iona (and not Mull), as a sacred place for worship.

This surfacing of the ancient, deeply bedded Lewisian gneiss rock strata on Iona is quite a geological feat in which ancient, embedded strata are compacted under enormous pressure that metamorphically transforms the rock to dense, crystalline structure. All crystalline structures have an electromagnetic field, and the greater the density, the stronger the field. The aura of balance and peace that blankets Iona is in part due to the unique qualities of this ancient metamorphic stone – the granitic Lewisian gneiss.

In addition, the strata upthrust and sharp hairpin folding of earth layers that pushed the Lewisian gneiss onto the surface also results in a magnetic energy release that 'thins the veil' between planes. Science has documented the relationship between magnetic anomalies and psychic phenomena and experiences. (The French scientist Mesmer used magnets to put subjects into deep clairvoyant states, and in fact, the term 'mesmerize' originated from his work.)

The metamorphic nature of the granitic Lewisian gneiss, combined with earth-fold telluric magnetic fields, creates a crystalline lattice energy that is very condensed and acts as a receptor to the charged harmonic projections emitted from Staffa. The energy frequencies that bombard Iona segregate in certain pockets of pristine frequencies that correlate to pure musical notes and, accordingly, to the chakras.

### Chakric Complex

The harmonic resonance points on Iona that resonate with pure notes are chakra centers. These combine to make Iona a full spectrum chakric complex. The denoted hills and land areas mentioned below can be found easily on a topographic map of Iona. These are:
- Dun I Mound (cairn on top) – Crown (7th) chakra
- Gneiss Slab (12 x 6 foot slab in field on immediate north side of Abbey) – Third Eye (6th) chakra
- Signal Hill – Throat (5th) chakra
- Angel Hill – Heart (4th) chakra
- Hill of Lambs – Emotional (3rd) chakra

- Back to Ireland Cairn – Creative (2nd) chakra
- Columba Bay (standing rock just before the beach) – Base (1st) chakra

The crown vortex is centered on the stone cairn atop Dun I, the highest point on the island, just to the north of the Abbey. I experienced the Dun I mound to absolutely be the strongest energy vortex on Iona. It takes a 15-minute hike to reach the top, up somewhat slippery trails, but the reward is immediate. I sensed an angelic presence atop the mound. This guardian spirit seems to anchor the portal and radiate joyous love energy into the site. The Dun I mound itself spirals sacred Earth energy in a fountain spray cascade atop the summit. There are several powerful places near the cairn to sit and meditate or pray. I found my chakras literally tingling in the presence of the angelic energy. My emotions were purged, and tears flowed in joyous release. Prayers here are quickened and quickly manifested. Dun I is a place of emergence, clearing and vision. All seven chakras are tuned and healed in this area. It is beneficial to have visited the other vortex sites before making the trip atop Dun I but is not required. Depending on available time on the island, Dun I, Back to Ireland Cairn, Columba Bay and Angel Hill are the principal sites I rate respectively in order of strength.

Beyond the seven centers mentioned above, the entire island is full of lovely moors, rocky hills and glens that are all magic in their own right. In a true sense, Iona is one large batholith stone, aware of itself, complete with seven chakras. Its overriding frequency is the third eye (6th chakra), but it heals and enhances the whole being. The connection of Staffa to Iona has the resonance of six, with Iona as a third eye, or sixth chakra center, and Staffa composed of crystalline hexagonal, six-sided basalt, six miles from Iona.

Britain is an ancient living land, teeming with powerful sacred energies. Glastonbury, dear to my heart, is one of the most wonderful and spiritual centers in the world and is a radiant of the heart energy. Yet Glastonbury, like most mega-power centers I have visited, holds the presence of the duality. The dark side also exists there and is tangible in certain areas. The balance of many power centers allows for, and magnetically requires, the presence of both negative and positive, in achieving its balanced electrical integrity.

Iona is one of the few power spots that does *not* contain this light duality. It is purely positive. The dark presence cannot find a pocket to dwell, which is unique and an anomaly. Its remote position, sparse population and connection to Staffa keeps Iona in the purest frequencies.

Several websites offer information on local hotels and B & B accommodations. You will need rain gear and waterproof hiking boots, because the abundance of rain makes for muddy trekking. The best times to visit are between May and October, but book in advance. Whilst the Iona community are kind, open-minded, spiritual people, they are not all 'New Age' aligned, so while they acknowledge the sacredness of the island and that the 'veil' is thin, the residents tend to follow more traditional Christian dogma and belief. There are no New Age shops or maps of power sites.

When flying into London, the easiest route to Iona is to fly onward (or take a train) to Glasgow, and whence take a bus or train to Oban (the ride is under two hours). I do not recommend renting a car, as cars are not allowed on Iona.

Iona and Staffa are quite unique, the latter is the wind beneath the wings of the former. Iona is a diamond, the white dove of peace. It is a haven of gentle serenity that allows for profound inner unity. Its portal is imbued with a high frequency of pristine celestial light, an energy that feeds the planet as we approach the Ascension.

**Tyberonn Channel**

*"Greetings, Beloved! Now, we are asked to speak of Iona. Dear Ones, we tell you that there is greater life that circles about and above this holy isle. And this energy is now flowing into your planet and is available to enter your field of awareness. It is light of a subtle nature.*

*It is not the light of expectation, it does not hold logic, rather it is the light of wellness and indeed carries the energy of 'home' of the angelic realm. We will say to you upon this special sanctuary, that all who come to Iona and allow this light to enter their sphere of influence, their field of consciousness, will immediately find themselves blessed in spirit and glowing in divine serenity. This energy is quiet, it is reconciling, it connects all of your chakras with your celestial home.*

*Iona is a place of healing and wellness. You humans do not always seek to include wellness in your search for understanding, but all should, as it is complimentary to truth, and all parts of your trinity being cry out for it.*

*The channel spoke of seven chakra points upon this island, we tell you there are twelve. Now, as we have said, in truth all power points on your planet can balance all of the human chakras, depending on the needs of the individual. What occurs on Iona is more of the pure musical note frequency, and there are indeed pockets of energy here that are of singular clarity, twelve in fact. These are indeed generated from the crystal pillars of Staffa and received at node points within the lattice of Iona. These collate in undiluted reverberation and flow into the symphonic amalgam that is Iona. It is the song of life, why else were composers and writers drawn to Staffa and Iona.*

*Now, the channel spoke of the dark not being present on Iona. That is not entirely accurate but is perhaps a misunderstanding of the term. Darkness is the absence of light, not a property of it, you see. As such, Iona does indeed carry the full spectrum of light, and even beyond the visible range, just as it carries pure music notes that are beyond the current human sonic capacity. Light and sound are connected, are they not. Both represent what you might term colors within your perception. The resonance of these on Iona are remarkably refined, remarkably clear and in benevolent harmony. Such harmony is very healing.*

*Now, particularly within this healing harmonic of Iona, within the deep refrain of subtle calm, one finds it easier to understand the true purpose of being. And here it is divine wellness, self love. Love of self as love of source, you see. Does that clarity not bring peace and true well being. Indeed it does. Many, such as the channel, experienced that prioritization here, for here it is easily accessed. There are other sacred portals upon the Earth that provide peace, but here especially that peace is for clearing the mind and illuminating deeper truth, deeper understanding. The divinity here is aligned with the law of creation.*

*That law is alignment with source. Making known what is not always understood. Making known the unknown. You are not put here upon the Earth to live your life in obligation to others. Your obligation is to source, and you are source. Love of self must be first. That is a misunderstanding by many who have spent numerous lives in the 'cloth' of priesthood, in the dogma belief of original sin, you see. You are source, you are the divine. This must be understood. All aspects you create in your life are mirrors of you and source. If you will live your life by obligation, then you obligate yourself in essence to another life, you see. If you live your life thinking you are here to serve others before the self, then you misunderstand the nature of love and purpose. That is the message that Iona helps clarify. Love of self and obligation to self as source can be found here. When we truly love self, we project a balance that radiates the correct balance of divinity to others. This is the gift of Iona.*

*Now, we speak of Staffa Island. This is indeed a generator. This is a receiver and transmitter of unique function. The entire island is noted as a geological wonder, because it is entirely a crystallized volcanic rock. A giant crystal, or hexagonal basalt. The channel described it as a pipe organ, and that is an accurate comparison, although we would describe it as an electrical pipe organ. This portal-vortex complex sends, receives and transmits pure frequencial resonance into a vast area.*

*Now, your planet is undergoing many changes at present, and these are appropriate. All are designed to clean, clear and upshift the vibrations of the planet. Many humans feel the phenomena of global warming is to be feared and stopped. This is not the case. The melting of the polar ice caps and such is appropriate, it is necessary. Global warming brings about the very evolution. It receives the energies of the Sun, melting the ice caps, as it were, releasing that which has been encoded, traveling through the waters and the fields of energy of the Earth, attaching and activating all that touches upon it as well. In this way, even evolution, consciousness and such begins to move forward.*

*Many fear that the warming, the volcanics, the quaking, the magnetic shifts will create a global cataclysm. We tell you that for now it will be more gradual depending somewhat on the reaction of humanity, whether it be with fear or with a recognized restructuring. This is what will determine whether there is to be a great cataclysm or small localized cataclysms. Make no mistake, the changes will and must continue,*

*and if mankind were to be appropriately educated into comprehension of the purpose, appropriate changes could be made with less burden, and sooner rather than later.*

*Many are those who wish to 'save the planet,' in your terms. So the channel asks, what is the nature of man's relationship to the living planet. It would be best if the relationships were to be synchronistic, and be aware that a dialogue takes place now between the Earth's sentience and yours. The difficulty with those that wish to assist is that in many ways they know not how. They believe that to prevent the change or to move it elsewhere is appropriate, better there than here, you see? Not all who wish to assist truly understand the divine purpose and as such are conflicted, torn with fear. Some simply understand fear, but to dissolve fear is not the same as understanding the fear and therefore transmuting it, recreating it with peaceful cognizance. To dissolve or to dissipate change is not necessarily of benefit, not to the Earth and not to humanity. The difficulty with those who wish to assist is that they believe they know better. They do not understand or see the perfection in what takes place, because there is great difficulty for those in misunderstanding or misdirection to realize that all is in perfection, that all is in scheduled order. As such, they do not lubricate the machinery of evolution. Rather, they try to prevent the inevitable and become immobilized in trepidation. So the necessary changes become that much more difficult, you see? Always, fear is the great culprit.*

*Now, one of the very important frequency upshift mechanisms taking place on your planet are the super hurricanes. These are greatly misunderstood and greatly feared. Again, the fear. These are truly intended to charge the oceans with magnificent energies. They are not intended to be drawn to the lands. But it is as if the entire world becomes focused on where it will land, what destruction it will cause, and the experts predict where it will come to shore. And so with such global focus, indeed the hurricane is pulled into shore as expected by the humans who watch in fascination and fear.*

*The true purpose of these storms is to increase the energy of the waters and to allow it to electrically expand. If these remain at sea, then the electrical energy is simply conducted as gentle current waves to great proportions of the planet. As such, it is conducted to the land and peoples, not by wind and waves, but by its energy current, so that it may reach that many more beings. There is a perfection to it, you see? There is what is called the perfect storm in some ways, but the perfect storm is that which is the harmonic blend of electromagnetic currents. As these then move through the fields of humanity, they are of benefit for the frequencial ascension of the planet and to the entirety of mankind.*

*In kind, there have been coronal mass ejections, solar storms creating what is called solar winds, that have been greater and greater and greater in intensity, some of the largest ever recorded. So you ask, what is the role of the solar winds, or the coronal mass ejections, on the ascension of the planet? We tell you these are changing the vibration that affects the earth. They change the frequencies at which humanity's minds operate. They provide the interface to higher dimensional access.*

*How does this work? Is it fair to say that the energy that comes from the coronal mass ejections is being absorbed into the tectonic plates of the Earth and, in a sense, increasing the vibratory resonance of the Earth through that method. These work particularly with certain power points and sacred sites. Particularly those of geometric crystalline overlay, such as Staffa.*

*These then move through the entire node system of the Earth. If such coronal mass ejections create such a vibration, then the entire electromagnetic flow of the Earth is affected. The tides are affected, the tectonic plates, the mind of humanity is affected, how humanity creates the reality in which it lives, the illusion it believes, how it feels toward its own life. All of this is affected by that which comes from the Sun, that which comes from the solar wind. The Sun is indeed conscious and sentient, and it is the great regulator of this solar system in which you live. Indeed, there are myriad other energy sources that are having a great effect upon the ascension beyond coronal mass ejections. It is best to say that the Sun coordinates all the others as well. When there are other rays of influence, even these are absorbed, coordinated and reflected by the Sun.*

*Now, the other celestial bodies, other planets also effect and influence your planet. This has long been known, but greatly misunderstood, greatly discounted. The channel asks, how, exactly, do the gravitational influences from other celestial bodies affect the Earth? We tell you they move outward in rings of intention that are then carried by celestial intent toward the Earth. Some of these are magnetic, some electromagnetic, others of a more subtle matter, that of zero field energy. Others of light beyond your visible spectrum.*

*Now, the greatest mechanism of these energetic and frequencial distributions are what you term power points. Particularly, as mentioned, those of geometric overlay. Staffa Island is one of the greatest of these. It is the crystallization, the sacred geometric matrix that both receives, refines and distributes these harmonics. This planetary node system of sacred sites, grid points and power points is greatly involved in the ascension process. Both for the planet and for mankind, you see. Know that all is in perfect order. You are beloved."*

… and so it is.

# Enchanted Rock ~ The Ascension Portal in Texas

In the southwest 'hill country' region of Texas lies the powerful and sacred dome of Enchanted Rock. Visible for miles around, the impressive dome rises some 450 feet vertically above base (1,850 feet above sea level). Revered by the Plains Indians for centuries, it spirals a potent electrical vortex. It is called the 'Ayers Rock of America.' Enchanted Rock is indeed one of the most powerful points in the southwest, and it holds a special relationship to Sedona, Stone Mountain and indeed Ayers Rock itself.

The hill country region is in itself a very unique area in the 'heart' of south central Texas. A relatively small triangulated region about 180 miles on each side, the hill country has a remarkably condensed energy field, notably higher in frequency than the surrounding area, which creates a sense of well being. Energetically fed by a webbing of hydrolines and a major telluric ley line, this energetic field is roughly triangulated by Austin, Llano and San Antonio. It encompasses Kerrville, Luckenbach, Gruene, New Braunfels, Wemberley, San Marcos and Fredericksburg.

The energy field is directly related to the higher quality of life and sense of well being that has drawn a number of intellectuals, artists and free thinkers to this area. For example, the hill country hosts the four largest universities in Texas, the state capital and a remarkable wine-growing region near Fredericksburg. Nearby Austin is continually ranked as one of the top five quality-of-life cities in the country and is home to a sizeable artistic community of musicians, writers and sculptors. The harmonic frequency of this energy field is uniquely conducive to creativity, especially music. Many recording artists make their home in Austin.

The Edwards aquifer is contained within the triangulated region. As such, an intricate underground network of rivers undulate their way beneath filtering limestone, spouting to the surface as crystalline waters and 'charged' healing springs. Granite and quartz outcroppings mark the rolling landscape between Austin, San Antonio and Fredericksburg, and they act as conduits for the ley line that surfaces in the hill country from its source in the Yucatan. Several energetic centers exist within this charged triangle, the spiritual apex of which is Enchanted Rock.

The Plains Indians of southwest Texas held the lavender granite rock in awe. Its name, translated from the Tonkawa dialect, is 'Glowing, Singing Rock'. The dome does indeed make audible whale-sounding moans at night, a phenomenon explained by the condensing of the rock layers which cool rapidly after the warming sunlight fades into night.

In direct sunlight, the surface of Enchanted Rock does appear to emanate visible energy waves due to the heat mirage effect. Even more fascinating is the green-bluish halo that seems to surround the dome in the brief twilight of sunset. This eerie glow, extending from one to five meters above the granite surface immediately after sunset is not folklore. The phenomenon is easily and regularly observed. The luminous effect is brief, diminishing quickly as the rock cools. Scientists explain the glow as a solar heat radiation from the slightly radioactive granite. In other words, the rock is a giant solar battery, transforming absorbed solar energy into light as it is released.

Enchanted Rock is actually the obtrusive portion of a massive, ancient lava (magma) flow. The greatest part of Enchanted Rock is actually below the surface. And when magma is held under, it solidifies more slowly into coarse-grained rocks with larger, visible crystals. These are intrusive, or plutonic, rocks of which granite is the most common example. Some of the finest examples of crystals, such as quartz, topaz and tourmaline are formed from chemicals that have been dissolved in solutions within rock cavities. Here, they have both space and time to grow. Enchanted Rock is, in a sense, a massive grouping of crystals, and it most certainly contains hollow pockets of prolific quartz crystals. Archeological evidence indicates human visitation at the rock going back at least 11,000 years. Folklore of the local Native American tribes reverently ascribes mystical and spiritual powers to the rock, hence the name magical or 'Enchanted Rock'. Because of its unusual geological features and archeological significance, the U.S. Department of the Interior designated Enchanted Rock as a National Natural Landmark in 1971. The rock was in private hands until 1978 when it was purchased by the Nature Conservancy. The State of Texas acquired it in 1979 and after adding facilities opened it as a state park in 1984. It was included in the National Register of Historic Places on August 29, 1984.

## Formation

Enchanted Rock appears as three domes. The three are not just connected but are part of the same rock. The geological name for this is 'batholith,' or an underground igneous rock formation, revealed by erosion. The granitite domes are some of the oldest rock on earth; this ancient landmark began taking shape more than a billion years ago. Geologists know that from the earth's molten core, underground rivers and plumes of magma (molten rock) swelled upward with an incredible pressurized force that squeezed lakes of magma into the upper crust. This magma congealed into solid rock before penetrating the surface. Amidst eons of time, massive telluric forces played out, and cataclysmic metamorphisms occurred. Colliding tectonic plates conscribed upheavals of great mountains. Oceans came and went. Volcanoes burst and spewed. Rampaging storms deluged the land. Roaring rivers

formed and slowly subsided, creating the deep canyons and valleys of the Texas hill country. This erosion uncovered the pink granite dome of Enchanted Rock.

## Holy Ground

The first known indigenous people to revere the rock were the Tonkawa Indians, who may have been descended from the Mayan and Anasazi. The Apache and Comanche displaced the Tonkawa at Enchanted Rock about 300 years ago. Through the Comanche and Apache wisdom and legends, we get a more complete picture of Native American beliefs as they relate to the sacred nature of Enchanted Rock.

According to the Southwest Indians, the Creator, Wanka Tanka, sent the 'Wanbli Luta', or Red Eagle Spirit, to offer vision and wisdom and to cure them of the illnesses that kept them from the true path. The allegorical narrative states that these benevolent and powerful spirits chose to live in sacred mountains, where they live forever and can be sought in ceremony for guidance, wisdom and protection. It is clear that Enchanted Rock was the sacred site for both the ritual spirit dance of the Apache and for the vision quest ceremony of the Tejas Comanche. Early German settlers reported seeing stone circles and stone alters directionally aligned atop the domes.

Spanish explorers and German settlers postulated that the Native Americans feared Enchanted Rock, and that only tribal medicine men could enter its perimeter without being struck down by the rock's powerful spirit. The lore further asserts that the Apache were forbidden from launching spears or arrows in its direction for fear of retribution. But it was not fear. Truly, it was a profound recognition and respect for the deity of hallowed ground. The Indians viewed Enchanted Rock as a living cathedral, and rightly so. Only their Holy men lived there as guardians, but sacred quests and ceremonial religious rites clearly were conducted there.

## The Batholithic Park

The Enchanted Rock batholith covers 100 square miles, or some 1,650 acres. It is the second largest natural dome formation in the United States, the largest being Atlanta's Stone Mountain which is considerably taller.

Texans, accepting second status to none, have found a way to give it top billing. They retort with a humor as dry as an armadillo, that, "Enchanted Rock is the largest dome in the United States that doesn't have dead confederate soldiers carved in its side!" One Park Ranger exudes," Enchanted Rock is geologically exquisite regardless of its comparative mass … and besides, size doesn't matter!"

## Trails

Two major trails wind their way up to the summit of Enchanted Rock. One base trail winds four miles around most of the entire base within the park grounds. The other trail goes steeply to the summit. The two are quite different in feel, but both categorically are enchanting walks and merit the effort.

The summit trail is a 45-minute hike from trailhead to apex. It begins at the campground map pavilion. Mesquite trees and cacti grow in huddled bunches along the flower-sprinkled trailside up to the base of the smooth granite matrix. There, the trail leaves laterite and climbs steeply inclined igneous rock. Extreme caution must be exercised when traversing this arduous portion of the upward trek. The precipitous slope of the rock dome has erosion polished surfaces; smooth granite is slippery even when dry and is extremely treacherous when wet.

## The Granite Domes

The half-sphere geometry of the dome is conducive to the spiraling energy pattern. Granite domes do appear in other areas of the USA (and the world), and, without exception, they create a potent energetic field. In most cases, they have been recognized and worshiped by the ancients.

Enchanted Rock's three domes have characteristics unique unto themselves, but all three are components of the one circulating energy. The largest dome, Enchanted Rock, is considered feminine in energetic aspect. She is the mother, the nurturer. She feeds energy to the other two domes, which balance and anchor her. The combined energies blend and swirl in a clockwise pattern. The two lateral domes – Little Dome to the west and Freshman Dome to the east – are both male in frequency and triangulate with the mother to form a powerful electrical vortex.

The energy of Enchanted Rock resonates to the 5th center, the throat chakra – fitting for the spiritual-called 'Singing Rock.' The batholith is part of the Llano Uplift; at 1.1 billion years old, it is one of the oldest granites in the world! A portion of it is metamorphic and holds a condensed crystallized pattern.

The fact that the dome is composed of granite is quite significant. Granite both stores and radiates energies. Granite is composed primarily of feldspars, mica and quartz and is significantly traced with potent pegmatite. Pegmatites are veins of crystallized minerals that form during the cooling of the magma. They are usually lined with crystallized stones such as quartz, but often contain other varieties including tourmaline, topaz, beryl, amethyst and citrine. The pegmatites of the Llano Uplift have housed some of the most unique crystals and rare earth minerals known to man. Burnetts Hill, located nearby within the granite of the Llano Uplift, has been found to

71

'glow' green, due to rare radioactive minerals such as gadolite. Enchanted Rock contains veins of crystallized quartz in several varieties that contain significant quartz crystal clusters. Larger crystal points have been found along the surface veins, but unfortunately most were broken off by visitors. Enchanted Rock contains significant fluorite and beryl formations within the pegmatites, and traces of gold and silver are commonly found in the granite. Certainly, the energetic properties of these powerful gems and metals add tremendously to the aura of this site.

## Spirit of Place

Enchanted Rock is now a popular spot for those seeking commune with nature and for quiet time for mediation. The park is so popular with rock-climbers, hikers and campers, especially on weekends, that it occasionally fills to capacity and has to be closed. The tops of the three domes are quite spacious, perfect for finding quiet isolated spots for prayer and meditation. I have spent many 'contemplative' moments on Enchanted Rock and found the 'Spirit of Place' to be very peaceful and comforting. Many have connected with the spiritual entourage that abides there. Legends abound about the 'Guardian of the Rock', an indigenous Holy man called Windsong.

Sensitives can recognize his presence on the apex of the mother dome. He stays to balance influx of human energies and to offer protection to those as they walk up and down the steep dome. His presence is that of a robust, vital energy and is deeply compassionate.

Another powerful presence is found in the cave on the northwest face of the dome. An older, more ancient guardian spirit resides in this energy. The cave is the root center of the site and houses a raw, primordial energy … a fire energy, kundalini. It is a powerful, intense enclosure. The cave is said to lead inward to a crystal cave

in the center of the dome with massive crystals of many varieties. It has been the site of initiations and ceremonial rites. A portion of the spiraling vortex energy re-enters the dome through the cave and is spiraled up and outward at the top of the mother dome.

## Energy Dynamics

The principal portion of energy flows into Enchanted Rock from underground, via the telluric energy flow of the Mayan ley line. This energy is spiraled upward into all three domes. The primary conduit and receiver is the perfectly shaped mother dome of Enchanted Rock. The telluric energy is combined with the solar energy stored into the granite, and it is amplified further by the quartz and pegmatite crystals. Once the energy is sprayed atop the domes, it enters the vortex cycle and gradually diffuses outward on all sides. The perimeters of the 'electrical' vortex are then incorporated into the 'hydroline' 'water' energies from the surrounding streams, springs, aquifer and lake.

The dome is bordered on the south and west by a small, clear stream that forks and cascades in shallow silver ribbons over the granite base rock. A small spring-fed lake lies at the western face. The stream is lovely, and it forks into three smaller brooks depending on the amount of rainfall. There are several magnificent faerie dens created along the brooks' paths as they bubble their way between jagged boulders at the base of the domes. In springtime, the grounds are awash with bright Texas wildflowers. Bluebonnets, red indian-paintbrush, orange pots and bouquets of yellow coreopsis blanket the campgrounds, trails and stream sides in vibrant colors. The site literally becomes a canvas of southwest art – bright flowers among red laterite, green cactus, gnarled mesquite trees and powder blue skies.

All three domes hold magical energies and

pockets of condensed ionic fields. A variety of focal points are created by crevices, crystal veins and overhangs that are an absolute pleasure to experience. Huge rectangular monoliths, broken off by lateral cleavage and erosion, stand like giant guardians and Stonehenge replicas. All are very inviting and very special. A beautiful variety of orange lichen covers portions of the rock. 'Moon pools' of trapped rainwater create beautiful floral gardens in sections of the top. A tiny, rare brine shrimp, a relic from ancient times when this area was covered by ocean, comes to life when these garden pools occur.

Depending on your available time at Enchanted Rock, there are many power places to explore and visit. The focused energies are tangible and can be discovered throughout the park. However, the single most powerful energy is found on the 'summit' of the Enchanted Rock dome. The energy here is a virtual fountain of electricity.

The flat summit is pitted, stark, pink granite, a 'Marscape' the size of two football fields. Somehow a lone tree manages to grow out of bare rock in the center. This is the apex. The tree is sacred, sustained by the fertile energies pulsing from the dome. Any spot within 30 meters of the tree is in the powerful fountainhead, a tingling, invigorating flow of gushing, blue-white energy in the ley-fed outflowing vortex. Extreme meditative states are easily reached, physical stamina and vitality are heightened, the chakras are balanced and hearts are healed.

While the entire area abounds in special energetic sites, which correlate to all the major chakra centers, none matches the pure power and energetic healing of the summit apex. In fact, I found the summit to correlate simultaneously to the crown, third eye and throat centers, depending on the exact spot chosen as well as the time of day. The innermost portion is the crown, within 10 meters of the apex tree. Moving outward over the next 15 meters, the third eye is stimulated. From 25 meters out to virtually the curving sides of the dome, the fifth chakra resonates.

I also discovered that sunlight activates certain portions of the dome when it shines directly on its curved, indented surface. Certain pockets on the summit are creviced and scooped into perfect little reclining chairs, complete with granite backrests. The energy within these indentations is concentrated and allows your body to be immersed into an energy bath.

Enchanted Rock is now becoming recognized as a major emerging energy site in the ascension of the new Earth. Lightworkers, such as Lakota master Adam Yellowbird, have been drawn there in recent years to anchor in the energy of the ascension portal that now flows into the vortex. Enchanted Rock is connected to the energy of Ayers Rock through this portal. Enchanted Rock is connected to Sedona through the triangulation of the Mayan ley line that emerges from the Yucatan Peninsula, undulating in and above the ground up to Monterey, Mexico. There, the energy splits, with the main body continuing upward to Sedona, and the other portion coming up through San Antonio into the hill country. The Mayan line in the hill country has fissure lines from the main body that feed Austin, Wimberley, New Braunfels and Fredericksburg. The two lines converge again at Monument Valley.

The aquifer energy of the hill country also has a complex synergy with the ley energy. The hydraulic energy from the aquifer has a strong, benevolent effect on the overall energy field of the region. The two energies, hydro and ley, form a six-pointed star, evidence of sacred geometry in the living landscape. The principal points of the hydro energy lines are the Aquarena Springs in San Marcos, Founders Park Springs in New Braunfels, and Barton Springs in Austin.

Enchanted Rock is a one-hour drive from Austin. It is located 18 miles north of the wine region and resort town of Fredericksburg, along Ranch Road 965. The entrance fee to the State Park is $5, and over 50 campsites are available. The park is normally full on weekends, and the summit can be quite busy. I recommend carrying earplugs, (for meditation privacy) and an extra jacket and water when going to the summit. The top is almost always windy, and the hike up is quite tiring. In the summer, heat is a factor too. The times best for meditation are sunset and or sunrise. The top is less frequented at these times, and solitude is not interrupted. Also, some spectacular colors and energies emerge at both sunrise and sunset, colors and lights that resonate well with the enchantment to be found on this magical rock.

A unique characteristic of the dome is the 'glowing' phenomena of the quartz, which can be experienced after sunset on a sunny day. I have had some deep and wonderful experiences meditating atop Enchanted Rock from sunset into moonrise. The Indians believe the mountain spirits live, that their profound message can still be heard today. The stories of humans can be lost, but the spirit of the mountain lives forever. Its voice is as ancient as stone.

Enchanted Rock's summit under a full moon is simply magical, but be sure to descend slowly, and carry a flashlight. Windsong will help you down.

**Tyberonn Channel**

*"All sacred sites and power points are living and conscious, and have what is termed a 'Spirit of Place'. The Spirit of Place is an awareness and sensitivity that the seeker should acknowledge and honor before entering. The indigenous always recognized the consciousness of the elements, the directions and of Living Earth. They conducted ceremony to honor them, and we tell you that it was correct to do so. And we tell you that it is still appropriate. The Earth responds in kind. Honor her, and she will nurture you. This has especially been the heritage of Enchanted Rock and is the manner in which to enter her uniquely fertile field. This location emits a very joyful energy 'pulse,' and those who visit can experience an emotional and spiritual recharging.*

*Now, the electrics you refer to as ley energy, (leylines) are a great part of the dynamic of Enchanted Rock. There are three such flows that converge, intersect and encircle these powerful domes. The manner in which they are absorbed, amplified and conducted is determined to a great degree by the mineralogy and shape of the physiographic.*

*Granite, as the channel has explained, contains a high concentration of quartz. This mineral compound is quite unique and is known to be a transmitter, receiver, amplifier and conductor of current. Very few materials can match the energy transmission of vitreous quartz, especially in the ultra-violet and infrared ranges. We tell you that quartz also stores energy and high dimensional light. Quartz is capable of converting energy to electricity. Your scientists have long been aware of the property of piezo-electricity displayed by quartz ... the ability to release voltage under applied mechanical stress. When pressure is applied to quartz crystals, the crystal lattice becomes temporarily deformed. The positive silicon ions move to one side of the crystal, while the negative oxygen ions move to the other side. This results in the opposite faces developing different and powerful electrical charges. Granite domes, conical and pyramidal shaped mountains also have this property. The shape determines the manner in which the energy is conducted. Now, the differentiating characteristic of Enchanted Rock is that it is a natural capacitor. Granite enhances this ability. The domed shape of this living stone allows the dual charges and integrates them in microbalance. It is capable of infusing beneficial electromagnetic and light energy to all who go there. This transference occurs in very low amperage, suitable for human physiology in such a way that the body physical is balanced and restored. This charging is congruous, evenly distributed throughout the body physical. The etheric body, the chakric system, is also balanced and robustly so. Many such energy locations that blend ley energy, electromagnetic, mineralogy and hydro energy can actually create an overload, depending on the time spent within the energetic differential. This is not the case with Enchanted Rock. Its energy has a soothing, gentle effect, specifically because of the low level of 'amperage' that is extremely compatible for human biology. Many who go there simply to climb the mountain are surprised at how invigorated they feel after exerting such physical effort. You see, the energy level spent is quickly replenished. It is this same energy that allows trees and plants to thrive on solid rock surfaces, even when water and nutrients are seemingly sparse.*

*The aquifer beneath much of this area adds considerably to the creative frequency here. This water is exceptionally ionic and carries an electromagnetic charge that is very beneficial for the body. The aquifer charging zones, or springs, found in New Braunfels and Austin are exceptionally powerful. Aquifer waters of this frequency also occur in regions of the Yucatan, southern California and Arkansas. The body physical will benefit greatly from bathing in these waters.*

*Indeed, your crystal talismans can also be well charged in these waters.*

*The geometrics of this area are spherical, thus the balance, but a tetrahedron and hexagonal matrix are enclosed within the sphere. The vortex in this area is disseminated throughout the region for a distance of about 100 miles in radius, but its energy is triangulated.*

*There is indeed an entourage of benevolent spiritual guardians in place that were formed through the worship of the 'Spirit of Place' by the indigenous peoples over millennia. Higher thoughts are creative, and pure and religious thought will manifest itself into mass conscious forms that are sovereign in their own right.*

*This region of the United States particularly benefits from this vortex. It is emerging into greater potency in preparation for the planetary ascension. This vortex portal has the role of bringing higher dimensional feminine energy into an area that has had an imbalance over the past 150 years. It will in time connect to the emerging vortex forming on Galveston Island and to the Crystalline Vortex of Arkansas. This can be referred to as the 'Return of the Dove', bringing a softer higher frequency energy to an area that requires such an influx for balance. You are beloved."*

… and so it is.

That the infamous Butch Cassidy would choose the mystical altiplano of Bolivia to hide is less ironic than fated. The pristine Andean high plane is a 'crucible,' where hidden truth implodes to discovery … precisely the sort of place where souls may run, but cannot hide. It cannot have been otherwise, Butch.

Bolivia was a pilgrimage I had yearned to undertake for decades.

## Sacred Altiplano

Bolivia's altiplano is home to some of the planet's most sacred energies. Containing numerous power points and pilgrimage sites, Bolivia is dotted with towering volcanoes, spectacular jagged mountains, mystical high planes, a massive snow-white salt desert (with a hotel and chapel made of salt blocks), pre Colombian and Incan ruins, jungles and the highest lake in the world. And what a lake!

Lake Titicaca is globally recognized as a potent sacred energy and has long been a pilgrimage site. It hosts an incredible mega vortex, with an effective diameter of between 120 and 175 kilometers. This vortex is balanced by several powerful and pristine portals contained within its fluctuating perimeters. One of the most powerful and unique is the ruins of the ancient city of Tiahuanaco … Bolivia's Machu Picchu!

Tiahuanaco, like many of the planet's 'sacred ruins' is located on a major grid point. Its energy field is tangible … and the fabric of life around it is indelibly affected. Located a few miles south of Lake Titicaca, the ruins of ancient Tiahuanaco contain a massive pyramid, beautiful stone temples, monoliths and a wealth of indigenous legends of a mystical underground city beneath its temples.

Incan and pre Colombian legends claim that Tiahuanaco is an entrance to a vast underground labyrinth, connecting the city to other sacred sites. Incan prophecy tells of an upper world and two stages of underworlds, dimensional realities existing in both physical and etheric form. Several places in the Andes Mountains are considered gateways to these realms and doorways where emergence and entrance are possible. The Temple complex of Tiahuanaco is said to be a primary gateway to all three.

## Tyb's Journal: Arrival

March 2, 2003: The morning I arrived in La Paz, it was cold and rainy. Thick clouds hid the magnificent snow-capped volcano called Illuminati that towers 20,000 feet over the city. I was still a bit stiff from a fitful sleep on the plane as I exited the terminal building and surveyed the horizons. I waved down a radio taxi at the airport and crawled inside. Then the elevation took effect. The international airport in La Paz is the highest airport in the world, higher than Nepal, located at an elevation of more than 13,400 feet! The resulting lightheadedness was something I would experience for several days.

We drove to the inner city, and after checking into my room I lay down for a two-hour nap. I awoke in the early afternoon to find the sun beaming. The view of the volcano from my hotel room was splendid. Illuminati was magnificent. The indigenous people held it sacred, and folklore deemed 'her' the protective Goddess of La Paz. Located in the base of a caldron at an elevation of some 13,000 feet, La Paz is the capital city of Bolivia. At this elevation there is significantly less oxygen available, and the altitude 'adjustment' created a slight dizziness. I had to gasp for air about every thirty feet, as I walked down the steps from my hotel room to reception. I spoke to the clerk and made arrangements for a trip by car to Tiahuanaco and Lake Titicaca. We would depart the the next day at 7 a.m.

## The Tibet of South America

The following morning I felt refreshed. After a delicious breakfast of fresh papaya, I made my way to the hotel exit and the waiting car I had arranged. I greeted the driver and stuffed my frame into the small taxi, then watched the waking city roll past. The next few days would pass inside the Titicaca vortex.

After twenty minutes we exited bustling La Paz to enter soft rolling hill tundra, with tall blue peaks in the distant horizons. Twin spines of the mighty Bolivian Andes towered up to 25,000 feet on either side. The 'cordilleras' stood like jagged blue teeth of a massive saw blade. Our road paralleled both columns, a symmetrical seam that lay like a gray ribbon between the splendid ridges.

Bolivia is often called the Tibet of South America, and indeed this countryside could easily have fit into the wind swept steppes of the Himalayas. While the countryside was beautiful, there was a great tugging intensity to the energy. Everything inside me, every feeling and emotion felt amplified, something I call the 'crucible effect.' Whatever issues one has, they will surface here. A few days in the altiplano is like an emotional sauna! Perfect for pilgrimages.

## Tiahuanaco and the 3-3-3

My taxi driver was a very humble and endearing gentleman named Edalio. He was an indigenous Incan descendent and a tribesman of the Ayamara Indians. He had the swarthy leather complexion and high olive cheekbones typical of Bolivians of indigenous ancestry. I liked him immediately. He was in his mid fifties but had an athletic gait and huge energy field about him. He projected sincerity and honesty.

We began speaking about the sacred sites in Bolivia and eventually about the sacred portal of the 3-3-3. I was delighted to discover he was quite aware of Living Earth energies. I was even more surprised to learn that he was aware that the 3-3-3 was locally being recognized as a day of prayer.

Edalio told me of a sacred spring, reputed to give health and protection to all that drank from it. It was outside a small mountain village not too far off our path. I needed a rest stop, so we decided to head there. The road veered closer to the mountains, and jagged granite outcroppings were popping up on both sides. The spring was lovely. It was a small 'cenote,' a sunken artesian well, similar to those found in the Yucatan. The water was crystal clear. The energy around the fountain was amassed, as is typical of springs, with the concentrated energy of released anionic particles. The 'energy pool' was refreshing. As we rested, I looked at the powder blue sky. Gliding silently overhead, three condors sailed down a few thousand feet from the thermals they had been riding, wanting a closer look. Their massive seven-foot wingspans looked like black fingers. They weaved through one another in an amazing spiral pattern. I was mesmerized by their grace and presence. Condors and red eagles are not uncommon in this area of the Andes. However, each sighting would be a grand joy for me.

I relaxed and watched the magnificent birds for several minutes until they drifted away from sight. We both smiled as we climbed back into the taxi and began rumbling and bouncing downhill on the rocky earthen road to the smoother paved tarmac. Onward to Tiahuanaco!

## Energy of Place

I began to sense the energy of Tiahuanaco as soon as we entered the 'bowl' that encapsulated its energy. It felt very unique, very ancient, and very separate from the energies I had felt at Machu Picchu. Local tourist companies bill Tiahuanaco as the Machu Picchu of Bolivia, but that is a monumental misnomer, excuse the pun. While both hold very sacred energies, their fields and roles are very different.

Machu Picchu is built on the summit of an awesome telluric energy generator, virtually the top of a pyramidal mountain, and that is much of why it was chosen and remains such a vital power point. Tiahuanaco is much older and feels very different. It is one of two balanced male energy centers of the Titicaca vortex, which is balanced male and female energies. It was, and is, an entrance to a vast tunneled underground world that operates on a multidimensional level. It is connected to many sacred sites, among them Egypt's Karnac Temple, Easter Island and the San Francisco Peaks of Arizona. All of which have legends of underworld entrances.

The original site of Tiahuanaco is believed by some to have been on the shores of Lake Titicaca, but now the waters of the sacred lake lie some 12 miles away. Others contend that the city was built before there was a lake at all. The discovery of 'lost cities' under the waters of Lake Titicaca a decade ago confirmed many mythical legends of an ancient civilization built before the lake was formed to its current massive volume. It also confirms some sort of cataclysmic earth movement, and perhaps even the infamous flood that resulted from the final sinking of Atlantis.

### Entering the Sacred Grounds

Ninety minutes out of La Paz, we arrived at the Tiahuanaco ruins. As we neared, Edalio slowed and turned smoothly onto the pebbled road that was the entrance way. In front was an impressive, modern visitor center à la museum. We pulled into the parking area and went inside to purchase our tickets. A photo gallery with exhibits of statues and monuments are housed inside, along with a walking tour explaining the various

phases of the ancient city.

According to information in the museum, ancient Tiahuanaco 'province' was populated by some 300,000 residents in its heyday. One third lived in the capital and 'suburbs,' with the remaining two thirds engaged in farming, herding and fishing within a 50 kilometer radius of the core of Tiahuanaco.

The Temple core of the city was said to be a sacred center, surrounded by waters flowing in a stone canal. The inner core of pyramids and temples were home to the elite. Priests had exclusive access to certain sections of the Temple complex, similar to the Egyptians' Holy of Holies. The artists' depictions revealed a city plan similar in many respects to the Temple of Karnac in Egypt, with pyramids, monoliths and sacred lakes. I would sense connections throughout the day to Karnac, Easter Island and San Francisco Peaks.

### Kachina Man and the 'Huacas'

There was one display that depicted pictographs of small hump-backed men that looked strikingly like the underground 'Kachina' man of Hopi Indian lore (said to live inside San Francisco Peaks Volcano near Flagstaff, Arizona). The local indigenous people call the underground men in Tiahuanaco legend 'huacas.'

They are elusive, mythical residents of the vast underground city below Tiahuanaco. Local legends speak of sightings of small men, usually crouched or hunchbacked in posture, that appear throughout the Temple complex of Tiahuanaco. Small relic carvings of the 'huacas' are sold on the grounds by the indigenous artisans.

When asked, the artisans explain that these men are caretakers of the tunnels. Miners and excavators, they have been included in folklore for millennia. The lore of subterranean cities, tunnels and wispy gnomish caretakers is backed by adamant eye witness accounts among the residents of Tiahuanaco. Edalio claimed that he heard stories of elders allowed to enter the subterranean passageways years ago, although he had not met anyone who had, nor had he heard these stories first hand. "They may be just stories," he admitted humbly. But the stories claim that massive hidden doors to the tunnels open from the sunken temple floor when those pure in heart 'sing the sacred songs of the Gods.'

## Major Energy Points

As I left the museum and entered the fenced grounds of the ancient city, I felt a unique, layered concentration of energies. Similar to the 'zipped space' phenomena I have felt in other power points of multi dimensional grid overlays.

There are four major energy points within Tiahuanaco itself. These are the Akapana Pyramid, the Sun Gate, the Sunken Temple and the entrance to the Kalasasaya Temple.

I became very aware of energy emanations from the Akapana Pyramid almost immediately as I entered the gated grounds. I stopped to realign my energy. I looked around to fully survey the ruins.

The actual site is on level ground, with a visible ridge line in three directions. The terrain is grassy tundra, with a few trees scattered about, growing at wind swept angles. Parts of monoliths, block-carved stones and statues dotted the grounds, where cataloguing and archeological digs are ongoing.

It is important to understand that Tiahuanaco was really only discovered in the early 1900's and was largely undeveloped and still covered in mud and silt until the 1960's. Much of its complex, including the Puma Pyramid, is still buried in earth. In its prime, it was a regal, flowing Atlantean-Egyptian-esque energetic complex of earth, water and light.

## Directional Orientation

The largest terraced step pyramid of the city, the Akapana, is aligned perfectly with the cardinal directions, facing east for the sunrise. It is energetically paired with another pyramid, called the 'Puma Panku,' also aligned directionally and facing east. There is a clockwise energy pattern flowing in ovaline vortex motion that forms an effective magnetic membrane around the inner core of Tiahuanaco. The flow contains the major energy points. Tiahuanaco is in essence a solar/telluric battery. The complex design uses natural energies to generate and amplify a light and magnetic pattern via the architectural and landscaped template. It utilizes the basic mechanics employed at stone circles, such as Stonehenge and Avebury, and progresses them a step further by employing solar energies and sacred geometric energies, as in the pyramidal structures. By placing such a complex on a natural telluric vortex and grid point, the force is amplified and utilized to anchor a portal of immense proportion.

The core of the template was surrounded by a carefully constructed stone canal, flowing and cascading waters from Lake Titicaca (which at that time contained salinity).

## The Akapana Pyramid

The Akapana Pyramid is the largest structure on the ruins. It has seven terraces rising to 70 feet and is just under 700 feet in length on its longest wall. The pyramid terraces are quite impressive, and they are similar in appearance to those at Machu Picchu. The construction was done without mortar, and the stones are perfectly fitted. They have an interesting 'glazed' appearance in places, a characteristic common to many pre Colombian and Incan ruins. The summit floor, according to author Helmut Settl in *Tiahuanaco and the Deluge,* was embedded with copper ore. (Which I believe was to enhance amplification of electric and magnetic energies.) A sunken court, perhaps for meditation or preserved as a sacred pool, crowned the center summit. I found the energy around the sunken court the most potent. The energy seems to circulate upward in a spiral around the perimeter of Akapana, creating a sort of cone peak apex. It seemed to reenter the center of the pyramid at the sunken court on the summit. The pattern repeated itself in a cycle. Each of the major points had there own concentric circulating pattern within the ova-line vortex of the complex.

The energy pattern was fascinating. It seemed similar to Avebury Stone Circle in England, in the sense that there is a weaving of energetic strands. The structures seemed to be able to generate pristine telluric and solar energies, and then isolate, circulate, amplify and weave them into amazing blends and patterns.

A second massive pyramid duplicating Akapana, Puma Punku, was built in the energy flow sequence. It represents the feminine energies to balance the male of Akapana.

The Kalasasaya Temple complex is to the northeast of Akapana. It is raised and appears like a massive, walled football field. It is 130 meters by 120 meters and is raised about 3 meters from ground level.

The Subterranean Temple is located next to the Akapana, just south of Kalasasaya. The axis of this entire complex is aligned to the east/west, the sunrise and sunset.

## Puma Pyramid

The female Pyramid, Puma Punka, is still in a state of excavation, yet the energy flows between the two are still very potent. The purpose of this structure is a counter balance amplifier, a twin platform mound *coupled* with Akapana.

The placement of the mounds do suggest they were used for ceremonial purposes at different timings of the solar calendar and of the day. Sun, moon and elemental worship is very prominent in Andean spirituality. The Puma Pyramid would also have had a lunar utilization ceremonially, the Akapana a solar … female-male, yin-yang.

Per researcher and author Helmut Settl, the granite monoliths atop Akapana direct compass needles away from magnetic north toward the west, directly to Puma Punku. Another point of interest is that the stone structures and temples of Puma Punku were connected with metallic clamps.

## Gateway of the Sun

Built in a rectangular fashion, the massive ten-ton 'Gateway of the Sun' is carved from a single block of granite. Its upper portion is deeply carved with beautiful and intricate designs, including a human figure, condors, elephants and some geometric symbols. Directly in the center of the gate is the so-called 'Sun-god,' Viroacocha. The placement of the carvings seems to align, with astronomical precision, the course of the annual solar cycle. European researcher and author Dr. Arthur Posnansky in *Tiahuanaco, the Cradle of American Man* used this alignment and that of the Subterranean Temple, to help defend the 15,000 BC time line.

The Sun Gate stands in the northwest corner of the Kalasasaya complex. It emits a very special vibration, especially powerful when the sun is angled in mid morning and mid afternoon. The alignment of the Sun Gate with the rising and setting sun plays a key vibrational frequency role in the opening of the dimensional 'underworld,' which is pivoted below Tiahuanaco.

## Scaling the Top

The Akapana Pyramid is the first structure one passes after entering the fenced perimeter. I felt two tangible walls of energy as I entered. The first was the line of the circulating inner vortex, which has a diameter of about 1,000 meters, the second was the inner spinning vortex surrounding the Akapana.

An interesting silence pervaded the area, despite the fact that some four or five dozen visitors were combing the large grounds. I noticed suddenly that all noise seemed very muffled. I seemed to be in an area of almost total silence. Voices, that a hundred meters back at the entrance were being carried with amplified echoes from the area of the pyramids and Sun Gate, were totally inaudible here as I reached the base of the pyramid.

The silence had a low-pitched 'white' hum. The hum was felt more than heard and had a tranquilizing quality, a telltale effect I often experience within the core of multi dimensional portals.

I struggled for breath as I climbed the steep sides of the large central pyramid. The pyramid had seven distinct levels and a flat, terraced summit. Each level seemed to have a unique frequency that flowed in circulating energy belts. These increased in frequency as I approached the flat summit. The summit was a cornucopia of light, electrical energy. The pattern around it is clockwise, and it spirals to the summit, re-enters in the Sunken Temple then exits along a subterranean canal to the Puma Pyramid to the west. I found an inviting space strewn with double piled pieces of cut limestone that had once been part of the retaining wall overlooking the Sunken Temple and sacred pool atop the pyramid. I sat on an interesting trapezoidal shaped block, with another block tidily stacked sideways to allow me a perfect back rest.

As I sat, my head begin to swim. The elevation was certainly taxing and effecting my perceptions. Light sparkles were everywhere as I breathed deeply after the steep climb. Energy swirled through me. I

felt tired, detached but also fully focused.

The sun warmed my face. I closed my eyes to face the warm sunlight. Looking into the sun, with eyes closed, a kaleidoscope of geometric shapes and colors danced visually in front of me. The shapes were rectangular that formed into eight pointed stars, effectively forming a 'Star of David' style formation, except using two squares instead of two triangles. I found this quite interesting and perhaps significant. I wondered if this amazing array was symbolic of the energy of place. The eight-pointed star seemed to represent the area geometrically for me. The synergy of elevation (lack of oxygen at 13,500 feet), the energy of the pyramid and the dimensional portal combined in a very potent fashion. This was a 'sungate,' a pristine masculine energy portal.

I required a few moments to adjust. I regained my ballast after a few minutes, and my breathing stabilized. Aspects of the effects lingered as I drifted into a deep state. I sincerely feel this enhanced access to altered states was the result of a synergy of the elevation and the pyramidal grid-vortex of this sacred space. There was little to no veil. I was in a multi dimensional vacuum. This was a higher form of lucid dream state, and a very active one, yet cognizant retention of what occurred in this state seemed somewhat more difficult. I felt I was traveling back in time. I could have fallen into a sleep very easily … but fought the impulse. I knew intuitively this was a different dimensional experience, and I worked at keeping aware, as I tried to navigate within this unique dimensional frequency. I had a series of flashing sensory images of what the area looked like in the days of Atlantis and an awareness of the vast expanses of space that were zipped into this concentrated area.

**Clockwise Energy Pattern**

I ambled slowly, still feeling quite lofty, to

the edge of the Pyramid's summit and sensed the energy points of the Kalasasaya Temple and the Sun Gate, both of which are on the Kalasasaya Mound (which is the size of two football fields). I walked to the Sun Gate, which was my first stop in flowing with the clockwise pattern from the pyramids. After arriving at the Sun Gate, I felt compelled to circle it seven times. Interestingly, I recalled Kryon once saying that the great Titicaca vortex was the counterbalance to Sedona. Vortex patterns north of the equator tend to flow counterclockwise, and south of the equator clockwise. I felt compelled to walk in a clockwise circle around the Sun Gate and temples.

I found an area to sit and meditate, facing east. I visualized energy connections between Tiahuanaco and several global sacred sites. I then sat for a prearranged 3-3-3 grid mediation, coordinated with several friends. The experience was powerful for me. I placed several special stones and quartz points around the Sun Gate, and would do the same at the Sunken Temple.

**The Sunken Temple**

My last hour was spent in the incredible Sunken Temple. The energy within this subterranean complex was very unique. It was here that I sensed the greatest dimensional focus and the inward fulcrum of the heliocentric labyrinth. There seemed to be a dimensional gate overlap that allowed the inner and outer worlds to coexist and transport.

To enter, one goes down a series of steps to a depth of about ten feet. It literally feels like entering another world, not unlike the feel of the lower chamber at Rosslyn. The amazingly intricate granite walls around it are adorned with stone carved guardian 'heads' and seem to lock in the energy. In its center is a tall well preserved statue, aligned perfectly with the Pyramid and Kalasasaya Temples. This was absolutely the epicenter. I sat

in a timeless bubble for a long time. I watched 'energies circulate and swirl' inward with great detachment. I meditated and went again through the geometric swirl into a deep state. I opened my eyes in what felt like about an hour. I was surprised to find only 15 minutes had passed, and again I experienced the strange sensation of having been in another dimension for a long period. But I was unable to retract memory of what had occurred. Like waking from an intense vivid dream, and losing recall in dimensional drift the instant of waking.

**Closing**

As the sun began to drop below the ridgeline of the Andes, the sky became a Van Gogh of stark gold and orange that was slowly absorbed into the velvety blue of night sky. A deep emotion of melancholy fell over me, and I felt a tremendous connection to this place. I glanced to the north and saw a small red eagle flying toward the great lake. Soon I would join him. I stood up slowly and headed back to the entrance. I said my goodbyes for the evening to Tiahuanaco, flowing with emotions. I felt a mixture of joy and sadness that would stay with me throughout my time in Bolivia, experiencing both sides of the emotional coin at once.

The time I spent here at Tiahuanaco had taken on an unreal quality. It felt like days but, in truth, was only a few hours. I knew I had just touched the tip of an iceberg. There was far more beneath the surface … much more.

**Tyberonn Channel**

*"Greetings, Beloved! And so the channel finds himself again in the very interesting area of the Lake Titcaca vortex. In the land once called Og. It is as if he is drawn here, you see, because many of his lives were spent here in this region. Particularly those immediately after the fall of*

*Atlantis, before his sojourns in Egypt. Thus the feelings of sadness, you see, particularly in the area you call Tiahuanco, for it was immediately after Atlantis, where the channel began the current cycle of physicality.*

*As Tyberonn, the channel was not Atlantean. In that time, you must know that you were not of the Earth. We tell you that many in the first phase of Atlantis were of extraterrestrial origin, and their beingness was manifested into full consciousness, sometimes in full physicality, sometimes not. These beings had the ability to come and go in that way, you see. The channel found such great interest then, as he does now, with all that is relative to the grids. Tyberonn, in those long series of life manifestations, was in many, many scientific aspects of the ley systems, crystalline energy systems, and even was consulted in the design of the Pyramids of Giza. But not truly as man, in current form, rather as manifested consciousness. Tyberonn carried an understanding for interpreting the energetic system, as an information keeper and in making this knowledge useful to the Atlanteans. You see, Tyberonn spent great periods of time in etheric non-physical state in order to have the direct knowledge of the Mastery.*

*In the third phase of Atlantis, Tyberonn became more and more drawn to the experience and chose a selective form of what we will term physical birth, once the physical rejuvenation technology achieved a level that allowed very long lifetimes. In the process of physical birth incarnation, much had to be relearned each time. Then, as now, much is hidden by overlay in each new incarnation and must be relearned by seeking. But through prearrangement, we will say, Tyberonn was recognized by those adepts that were still in physical body, much as is done in Tibet even now, and his exact time and place of birth were known, and he was given special training from an early age to allow for the*

*remembering, in order to achieve the purpose of his chosen physical life. The technologies were available for greatly renewing the physical body and allowing for long physical lifetimes, some of which exceeded 1,000 years in your current measurement.*

*So in time, Tyberonn became captive to that grid and in some ways became captive to the Earth. He was called upon to experience physically what he need not have experienced physically.*

*After the fall of Atlantis, the channel found himself in the Atlantean colony near Tiahuanco. In that lifetime, he became aware of what had happened and knew no way back home other than to align himself with the highest peoples, the highest points that he could discover upon the Earth and thereby accept and experience full cycle of reincarnation. And that is how you became aligned with this place and with this land and these people. But we will add that, as Tyberonn in Atlantis, you visited Og, Yucatan and Egypt many times in scientific endeavor.*

*You see, Tyberonn, your root soul, is now, as then, an Ascended Master of Light, yet when the decision was made to manifest into physical life cycle, in physical body, your true identity and true nature are hidden from you, somewhat. So as with all humans who become ingrained deeply in reincarnational pattern, he became somewhat separated from the source Tyberonn. His incarnations became slowly less aware of that root essence. You see, after Atlantis humanity fell greatly in terms of knowledge and technology standards.*

*You had a series of lifetimes in Tiahuanco. At first you were disoriented and wandered a bit as if lost, sensing the recent cataclysm, as did many souls after the fall. Many were initially confused, as they discovered the lifetimes of the Earth were much shorter than had been expereinced in Atlantis.*

*There still remained pockets of learning and awareness, here and there, especially in the Andes, Yucatan and in Egypt, and you were drawn to these academics. At that time, your name was Culnerah. In Og, you became what one would consider a vulcanologist. You learned how to utilize such energies and were among those who participated in the sonic lifting of stone blocks, by manifesting them in higher dimensions and stepping them down into physicality. Thus, the Pyramids of Tiahuanco would feel very familiar to you, and you would also sense a strange sadness according to that sojourn amongst the 'lost people' after Atlantis.*

*Now, we are asked to speak of the energy of Tiahuanco. Tiahuanaco became populated as a LeMurian colony in the land called Og and eventually became Atlantean after the demise of Mu. It was one of the major colonial centers of civilization during the final Atlantean periods, although much of Og was devastated by the Atlantean tsunami. Only those regions of elevation above 6,000 feet survived relatively intact. But it was here that other beings, an extraterrestrial race, participated upon the Earth, temporarily assisting and sharing themselves and departing after that. This race of beings interacted with the LeMurians and Atlanteans in Tiahuanco and with the Egyptians, in order to assist for a period after the demise of both.*

*The energy harmonic of this ancient place is very complex, and aspects of its energetic structure functionally occur in several dimensions beyond the three. This is the phenomenon the channel refers to as 'zipped' space, a condensed and concentric folding of the various dimensional grid fibers. This enhances the ability to coexist within several realms of dimensionality at once. It is similar to what many call passing though the*

*veil, yet that is not a totally accurate description. It is more akin to entering a hologram of five dimensions in which all are experienced at once, without actually leaving the dimensionality in which you normally function. Therefore there is not a 'passing through,' but an overlapping coexistence of dimensional membranes. This happens in many areas of concentrated energies.*

*Below Tiahuanaco are vast chambers and geometrical inserts (holgrams) under the Earth that are connected by intricate tunnel systems to many other grid points and sacred sites. These include the areas of Machu Picchu, Egypt, the Glastonbury Tor, Easter Island and San Francisco Peaks in Arizona. The great subterranean labyrinth of what is termed fourth dimensional leys connects all of these.*

*Directly below the entrance is a vast, spacious underground temple, as large as a small city. A magnificent temple still exists there; there is an inverted pyramid that corresponds to the Akapana Pyramid above. This completes an energy pattern of the octahedron. Entrance to the vast subterranean chambers is achieved through obtaining a vibration of high frequency. Few souls in biology have the ability to achieve this entry. There are few in biology on the planet that retain this ability and knowledge, although that number is beginning to increase. As we have told you, there are thousands of crystal harmonic children on the planet now who have the potential to achieve this frequency.*

*These subterranean gateways contain energetic amplifiers and refineries that were once used both in the subterranean and atmospheric levels of the planet. And, among other uses, they projected an energetic field that was connected to the Earth's magnetic core. This field is still somewhat projected, but with far less scope and utility. This is an energy operated through what you term the gravity grid. These are still maintained somewhat* by extraterrestrials, particularly those of Sirius B, primarily for a revamping of portions of the fourth dimensional ley system.

It is also the same energy that was 'tapped' sonically for the anti-gravity aspect, used by the post LeMurian and post Atlantean adepts of this area. It was used for the lifting in place of the enormous stone blocks for the precision engineering and construction of the Pre Incan and Incan Temples in this region of ancient Og and as well with the Mayan civilizations of Mexico. Scientist-Priests, who were very advanced in their technical knowledge of frequencies, telluric and light energies, held the knowledge. The priest-scientist in those times, before the deluge and for a period afterward, were trained for intense periods of about 20 years, both in scientific and mental development, thus to combine the science with the psychic or spiritual aspects of living energy.

A process, involving a correlation of energies received by solar and cosmic rays, amplified at certain refraction angles with crystals and frequencial thought, created sonic light projections of antimatter and antigravity.

A different application of frequencial technology was utilized to open and operate the harmonic byways of the labyrinth leys, again, with the integral wisdom of spiritual science. Great ceremonies were held as a method of fine-tuning this energetic network. Like the ley systems, this energetic labyrinth is but a remnant of its Atlantean utility.

Many pyramids were once connected to this labyrinth network and were used as multidimensional wormholes in the fabric of the planetary and universal grids. Many natural power sites were incorporated into this vast network. These leyways were initially developed in the third Atlantean period from about 28,000 BC and functioned with great enhancement utilizing extraterrestrial technology, until the demise of Atlantis and for a short period afterward. The tunnels were laid in many instances, but not all, along existing leyline paths utilizing a hyper dimensional technology. The leys were amplified and used for travel, communication and energy grid relay. The tunnels likewise were used to connect underground chambers and, in some circumstances, for mining.

Some of the subterranean chambers held the functions of receiving, storing, amplifying and projecting certain refined energies that were aligned with the Earth's molten core. These were for many uses, including planetary balance and for pooling and concentrating certain forces of energy for use in projecting fields. The projection process is similar in nature to the nozzled jet stream effect, or hydro jacuzzi force as you term it, although the energy was of a electromagnetic nature, and contained in a sophisticated refined matrix of opposing electromagnetic fields. This process utilized science and knowledge of planetary and universal energies such as mineralogy, tectonics and astrological gravities.

Some of the subterranean chambers were inhabited by man. These evolved into what we will term fourth dimensional beings.

The chambers below Tiahuanco, Peru and Yucatan resonate to specific frequencies of light and sound. These resonances could enhance human consciousness, not unlike the chambers of cathedrals but on an enormous scale, hyper dimensionally. The refined energy accumulations were incredibly potent and capable of being converted into many utilities. It could be brought closer to the surface of the world in places like Tiahuanaco for the purpose of group experience and individual participation. People are still drawn to these sites in the act of receiving from the Living Earth."

… and so it is.

# Lake Titicaca ~ Vortex of the Condor

Most people go to cathedrals to obtain holy water. The Andeans of Peru and Bolivia go to Lake Titicaca.

The stunningly beautiful site of this holy lake is simply breathtaking, literally! At an elevation of 12,700 feet, Titicaca is the highest navigable lake on the planet and the second largest lake in South America; its elevation alone is capable of creating altered states. Some say it is one of the most sacred places on the planet. I have been there five times and wholeheartedly agree.

Titicaca lies between majestic jagged spines of the Andes Mountains in a vast basin of about 22,400 square miles in area that comprises most of the altiplano of the northern Bolivian Andes. In the snow-covered Cordillera Real on the northeastern shore of the lake, some of the highest peaks in the Bolivian Andes rise to heights of more than 22,300 feet. The scenery is visually stirring, and the energy is magic.

**Vortex of the Condor**

Lake Titicaca is in fact the largest vortex portal in South America, and it performs a unique role. The complex vortex of Lake Titicaca is, per Kryon, in unique synchronicity with the Sedona Vortex in Arizona, but spinning in the opposite direction. Sedona is counterclockwise, Titicaca is clockwise. This unparagoned counterbalance effect puts the two in an exceptional synergetic interchange and holds a direct communication portal gate, that indigenous Elders from the Mayan and Hopi have referred to as the 'Gateway of the Condor and the Eagle.' Both areas are activation centers, both Sedona and Titicaca are part of ancient LeMuria. What is now Bolivia and Peru was in ancient times called the land of Og, and was a LeMurian colony.

The importance of the Titicaca Vortex cannot be understated. Its pristine vitality has been recognized and honored by guardians for millennia, on both sides of the veil. The indigenous Earth-Keepers and Lightworkers are being called to participate in the 'Activation' of Titicaca and its important alignment to Sedona. This is an aspect of the Hopi prophecy termed the 'Eagle and the Condor'. In essence, the alignment of Titicaca to Sedona allows the balance of Sedona to be restored.

Lake Titicaca is an enormous planetary vortex, the largest this writer has ever experienced. It is, in fact, a vortex that contains numerous portals and unique interdimensional gateways. It contains smaller vortexes within its mega swirl and is triangulated with the vortex/portal of Sedona and Diamante, Brazil. Titicaca is fed by Salar de Uyuni and contains several stargates and underworld gateways within its majestic matrix. It is connected by energetic artery or ley to 12 other major planetary meridians. Titicaca also contains an ancient resonant energy device called the Solar Golden Disc.

Many state that Titicaca carries a feminine energy. Indeed it does, but it also carries the masculine. It is an exemplary marriage of both. In fact it is Titicaca's perfectly heterogeneous balance of male and female that attracts so many to the healing terraqueous energy colloid. The holy lake does receive and blend enormous inflows of the female energy so necessary for our planet to achieve balance, but it is the female/male balance that Gaia ultimately seeks to project, not a predominantly male or female field. However, the ongoing influx of female energy is required to achieve planetary neutrality with the male energy that has predominated since the sinking of Mu.

## Salar de Uyuni: The Great Salt

The primary telluric source of concentrate female energy (anionic charge) that feeds into the Lake is from a little known power site several hundred miles south of Titicaca called Salar de Uyuni, located in remote southern Bolivia near the border of Chile. It is not a journey for the weak-spirited. It takes a four-hour bus trip, an eight-hour train trip and then a two-hour SUV trip. But the end result is beyond serendipity; it is profound beyond measure. Salar de Uyuni is an amazing (protected) UNESCO site of the largest complex salt field on the planet. The salt flat is a pristine alabaster white, often surface crystallized into an exquisite hexagonally tiled mosaic. It glows. It is white beyond white; its is crystalline. The Uyuni salt flat is enormous, measuring approximately 70 miles by 25 miles, with the halite and kyolite salt reaching as deep as 250 feet. It is stunning to see and even more stunning to experience. It is in this writer's opinion, the most potent location of mineralogical female energy on the planet's surface. The salt flats refract sunlight such that the surface emanates incredible refraction mirages, and one cannot discern where the salt horizon ends and the skyscape begins. Two potent burnt orange stratocone volcanoes are aligned on opposite sides of Uyuni. The result is an intertwined energetic cocktail that atmospherically tri-helixes with the energy of Lake Titicaca.

The massive anionic plasma of the pure salt creates, in essence, a telluric battery that is incredibly cleansing. One's chakras are aligned, and one's energy field is balanced and charged. Auric fields of the human body become crystallized into merkabic stars within this energy. I spent three remarkable days in an adobe hut with indigenous resident hosts there in 2002. There is a hotel, no longer functional, in the center of Salar de Uyuni built entirely of salt blocks, including the beds, tables and chairs. A church built of salt lies on its edge. It is located in the center of a snow-white world, and is a focal temple of plasma and light.

Salar de Uyuni is a dried salt sea and is the underpinning 'wind beneath the wings' of the Titicaca vortex. It is one of the most powerful and pristine energy generators on the planet.

## The Golden Disc

As a result, the waters of Titicaca are indeed holy, robustly sanctified with a plasmic colloid of cationic solar photons, anionic electrons and a rich array of trace minerals … ah but there's more … the Golden Disc of ancient LeMuria!

There is more to this than legend. Scientific explorations have determined that Tiahuanaco is believed to be at least 15,000 years old. Further evidence of a pre flood colony was discovered six years ago, when a European expedition of anthropologists discovered a massive Pre-Colombian ancient temple and road below the waters of Lake Titicaca, near the Island of the Sun. Edgar Cayce refers to the areas of Bolivia, Peru and Ecuador as having been a colony of LeMuria, (and later of Atlantis) called Og.

Peruvian and Bolivian legends speak of a sacred LeMurian Golden Solar Disc having been placed in Cusco, in the Temple of the Sun, just before the sinking of Mu. It is said to have been placed in the waters of Lake Titicaca, just off of the Island of the Sun (in the etheric city of light said to exist below the clear waters of the translucent green lake), before the Spanish Conquistadors ravaged the Incan civilization.

## The Sacred 'Stone Puma'

The Andeans of Bolivia and Peru inherited a rich, spiritual culture. The Andeans are a humble yet proud people, very much in touch with the living energies of the planet. There are four very

87

sacred animals in the indigenous spiritual tradition of the Andes: the Condor, the Llama, the Anaconda and the Puma or Jaguar. The Condor represents the upper world, the element of Air. The Llama the sustenance of the Earth. The Anaconda (snake) represents the underworld, the element of fire, Vulcan. The Puma represents the female energy of water, the Lake. In fact, the origin of the word 'Titicaca' is believed to have come from the ancient Ayamara and Quechua tongue, and is believed to mean 'Stone Puma' ... El Rocque.

The Lake and surrounding area is a massive vortex containing many, many sacred energies. The two most potent points within the 'Sacred Puma' waters are the 'Island of the Sun' and the 'Island of the Moon.' The etheric city beneath the waters is said to have been guarded by a society of warrior priests on the Island of the Sun. Andean legends claim that the first two-leggeds, the 'Adam and Eve' of the Incans, M'anko Qapak and Mama Oqllo, were created on the Island of the Sun from deep within the Living Earth, Pachamama, at a powerful point called 'El Rocque,' the 'Holy of Holies.' It is located at a high point on the Isla del Sol near the Incan ruins of the guardian Priest monastery.

## Tyb's Journal

I arrived in the Bolivian lake port of Copacabana, after spending two marvelous days exploring the Pyramid city of Tiahuanaco, the 'Machu Pichu of Bolivia.' The four-hour drive from Tiahuanaco had been tiring. The combination of elevation and being cramped in the small taxi I had hired for the excursion left me stiff and thick headed. My taxi had rolled along a beautiful verdant expanse of road surrounded by high snow capped mountains, reaching as high as 21,000 feet. Open tundra fields waved in the wind like velvet chartreuse. Between the cordilleras of the Andean mountains, we drove past a myriad of high elevation landscapes that varied from lush to

moonscape. Finally we reached our turning point, and our destination came into distant view. As we began our descent, Copacabana sparkled on the horizon like a jewel at the bottom of the descending serpentine road. Beautiful eucalyptus trees lined the road and the lakeshore. Titicaca glowed like a fluid aquamarine, contained between the majestic snowcapped peaks of the Andean sierra. The vista is simply surreal. My first impression was that it looked like and felt like Lake Como in the Italian Alps. The tranquility and sense of well being was ambrosial.

I found the city of Copacabana delightfully pleasant: cobbled streets, shops with open doors hanging a variety of bright wares, for locals and tourist alike. Quite a festive change from the rather ominous allure of the remote and mystical Tiahuanaco ruins. Artisans offered handicrafts of every description. Bright splashes of fabrics, alpaca ponchos, hats, leather goods, fruits and vegetables adorned the plaza shop's tables and high portiere displays. I felt uplifted and happy as I strolled the plaza, amongst bolo hatted vendors and backpacking tourists.

An amazing Cathedral dominated the city plaza, and it captured my awe with its beautiful white stucco and splendid domed and spired architecture. Local lore of many healings within the Cathedral abounds which made the Cathedral a pilgrimage point for the Catholic population. Built by Spanish missionaries in the post-Inca era of the late 1500s and early 1600s, it is an impressive Moorish-influenced structure, with whitewashed stone walls and domes decorated with deep blue tiles. Inside, worshipers were gathering for evening Mass. My heart smiled in comprehension that the immaculately constructed Cathedral was built on a healing telluric current.

A light mist rain began to fall as we strolled down the cobbled street to the water's edge. I pulled on my new water resistant alpaca poncho and glimpsed the panorama of colorful boats, lined up along clapboard piers, spot-moored in the clear blue green waters. There were boats of all sizes and types, brightly painted and flagged, most wooden and rough-hewn. A gentle breeze, piquant with the sparkling sweet perfume of lake mist wafted past, and I became mesmerized by the tranquil rhythm of soft waves sweeping the pebbled shoreline. I was magically entranced, and for a brief resplendent moment I was back in my boyhood, reminiscent of my summers spent on the crystalline lakes of central Arkansas. I sat in silence on the rickety boardwalk, and after twenty minutes, decided to find accommodations for the night.

**Lonely Planet**

There were dozens of hostels and several stucco hotels. Copacabana is a popular destination for foreign travelers, primarily students doing the 'Lonely Planet' bus trek. The hostels and internet cafes were full of happy European, Australian and North American backpackers, thumbing through travel guidebooks and pocket English-Spanish dictionaries. It took me back to Europe in the 60's and 70's … I liked the vibe.

Touting a population of 5,000, Copacabana is a picturesque cluster of low-rise adobe structures with red-tile roofs, extending upward from the edge of the water to the sloped sides of the altiplano mountains. Along the stunning lakefront camino, shawled Andino women were smoking fish and sausage on small cast iron grills. The smell made me famished! Restaurants and shops were neatly arranged in a sequential waterfront enclave. The exteriors were strung neatly with multi colored lights, creating a warm convivial ambiance. I chose an open air eatery with thatched palm roofing and savored an exquisite meal of lemon garnished lake trout, black beans, roasted yucca and fresh mango juice – comeda tipico. It was 'gustoso,' quite delicious!

I found a small hotel with a reasonable bed and private shower, and slept with the window open. The fresh cool breeze from Titicaca gently filled my sleep, with an aromatic bouquet of eucalyptus and sweetgrass.

I woke early, and to my dismay, a heavy torrential rain began as I sipped a small cup of aromatic café andino. I overheard several trekkers saying that the tour boats would not make the 90-minute boat trip to the Island of the Sun. The regular excursion boats had cancelled the trip for the day due to inclement weather.

My taxilero had slept in his car and offered to help me hire a private boat through an acquaintance. We drove down to the docks, and in a few minutes a young Ayamara man in his mid twenties approached me with the driver. His name was Luis, and he seemed very pleasant. After a few negotiations we mutually agreed on a private charter rate. I made arrangements to be taken to the Islands of the Sun and the Moon, despite the torrential rain. I chartered a 30-foot 'covered tour boat' for the day for less than 50 dollars. After a brief but thorough inspection of the rather rickety appearing vessel, the 'Graca Maria,' I was reasonably convinced she was 'seaworthy.'

I made arrangements with my taxi to be waiting for me on my return and climbed aboard the boat. I was the lone passenger and sat under the roofed shelter taking one of a dozen seats, as we departed across the choppy rain pelted waters toward the sacred island. The morning sky was an ominous gray. Heavy rain hammered the wooden roof, as streams of water rolled off the top into the open hull in the back. The battered looking Johnson 150 outboard puttered and belched an occasional plume of white-gray smoke as Carlos and Miguel, Luis' younger brothers, used coffee cans to bail out rain water that gathered in pools along the hull's gutter. That issue concerned me, but my Andino marineros did not seem worried.

After an hour, the rain slowed to a drizzle and then stopped. Yes! The canopy of dark clouds blew open to reveal patches of sky and a beaming mid morning sun. The water became as smooth as glass. What a different view! I ventured out of the covered area and took a seat on the roof à la sundeck of the 'Graca Maria.'

The last of the rain clouds drifted westward and within a few minutes were replaced by a powder blue sky and a few puffy white cumulous clouds. The sky and lake transformed into a picture of beauty. The sun was brilliant, and the visibility was crystal clear. The panorama around me was in high definition, the colors were simply mesmerizing.

It is an interesting point, but certain places I have visited within exceptionally high-energy centers seem to have a higher lucidity of apperception. A greater amassing, if you will, of visage pixel, photon concentrate. Coagulated light! It is a phenomenon I have observed in parts of Scotland, yet nothing can quite compare to the quality of light over Titicaca on a clear day.

Indeed at Titicaca, the pristine air at this exceptionally high altitude seems to combine with the fast-moving air, water and light to create a constantly shifting theatrical display of such a deep blue that the visible spectral panorama often looks as if it is being viewed through a high definition photo filter. The rays of the sun seemed individually defined and etched in silver and blue as they danced on the turquoise water. Visibility burst the paradigm of mere length, width and height, and became a ballet of exquisitely complex multidimensionality.

The water was remarkably clear, refracting the sunlight into translucent green in shimmering geometric beams, with the towering Andes peaks on all sides animated like giant snow beings. I found myself in a state of pure joy, fully drinking in the magic of this NOW moment, sun and wind on my face. What an amazing magical place. What an incredible lake. I gave thanks for being here and for the clearing weather that would now allow me to fulfill my strong desire to explore the spiritual depths of this mystical place. I had to pinch myself!

At last I was nearing the shores of the Island of the Sun on Lake Titicaca. The Island of the Sun is so called because the Incas believed it to be the Sun's birthplace. Perhaps there is more to that legend that meets the eye, for it is truly a place of variegated, complex geometric light.

## The Island of the Sun

After 90 minutes, the Isla del Sol loomed in front of us. It looked a bit like a massive sleeping sphinx, terraced in the symmetrical farm shelving of the Incans. It loomed high above the water and emitted a powerful pulsing energy that was exciting and tangible. The island is about 12 miles in length and has some 2,500 permanent residents, primarily Ayamara farmers.

Isla del Sol is Titicaca's largest and most important island. A religious shrine for local tribes as long ago as A.D. 350, it was transformed by the Incas into a major pilgrimage destination in the 15th century. Perhaps coinciding with the placement of the Solar Disc. In fact, 'the Rock Sanctuary' on the island has been recognized as a major stargate since the time of Mu, in the ancient land of Og. A mystery school of LeMurian priests had been here since the beginning. The Incans carried that tradition forward, and the remains of their Incan monastery are but a hundred meters from the hallowed Puma Rock, the 'Creation Zero-Point,' where Incan folklore says the Sun emerged and manifested the first humans.

The island sloped up to a prominent steep back peak, with jutting granite and sandstone domes forming the head and shoulders of the island's sphinx shape. It was easy to see where the energy was most potently centered. I asked Luis if it looked like a sphinx to the locals. He didn't quite understand what a sphinx was, so I explained that it was like a lion. He smiled and said, "Leon no, Puma si!" Puma, of course, claro que si! With the terraced farms, it looked like a puma with cornrows!

My guide was full-blooded Bolivian Ayamara. I told him I wanted to go to the holiest place, El Roque, offer blessings and do a prayer ceremony in the Lakota modality. That seemed to please him, and he enthusiastically agreed to take me and to participate in the ceremony. I gathered my 'chenupa' bundle, and we began our trek to El Roque, perhaps the most powerful point of the Titicaca portal complex.

Luis explained to me that El Roque was also called 'El Sanctuario' and Stone Puma. "We believe it is a place of great power," he added, "and we come here when we want receive strength and guidance. It is the most sacred place of the Inca."

I felt invigorated, and I imagined the sense of reverence from the thousands of Incan and Pre Columbian pilgrims who had made this pilgrimage over past centuries. Perhaps their religious fervor had been imprinted here in the fiber of the energetic matrix. I wondered how many modern day tourists truly understood the massive energy that this place magnetically pulsed.

We hiked upward along a steep stone paved trail, past terraces of maize and fields of grazing sheep. Along the way, Luis told me the history of the Incan site and the traditions of the Incan pilgrimages. Women in bolo hats herded gaunt looking cattle into stone walled pens, while children dressed in brightly colored clothes laughed innocently. They darted and ran freely, peering at

us from behind boulders, their round brown eyes a mix of bashfulness and curiosity. Soon we were on a high ridge, away from the village and above the coastal loam. After climbing five hundred feet, the terrain expeditiously transformed from lush pasture into an arid laterite, impervious with cactus and flowering sage. Flocks of small black birds with yellow striped wings would occasionally thrust upward frantically from one sage bush to another, making a succinct whirring sound as their wings fluttered busily. Apart from the birds, we had the trail to ourselves.

## Path of the Golden Light

Luis told me that he was an apprentice of the 'Camino de Luz d'Oro' (Path of the Golden Light). To my delight, he added that 'most' of the local residents followed the ancient wisdom teachings of the Indigenous traditions and took part in annual ceremonial pilgrimages to the island.

Incan pilgrimages to El Rocque were highly ritualized. The pilgrims passed through three initiation tests, or gates, before being allowed to the Puma Stone, El Sanctuario. Few Incan pilgrims made it through the third gate on their first pilgrimage. In essence, it was a journey of succession, of learning the disciplines and mysteries and of evolving into the status of an Elder. I was very pleased to know that these traditions were continuing.

## Ceremony of the Ancient Pilgrimage

In ancient days, per Luis' teaching, there were numerous rituals and ceremonies at El Rocque. Each ceremony was designated for special dates, such as the equinox, solstices and moon phases. The most important pilgrimage was the camino (path) of the 'Shaman-Warrior,' which he referred to as the 'Golden Light.' I wondered if that specific term had been coined in connection to the legend of the 'Golden Solar Disc.'

The pilgrimage to the Island of the Sun began on the south of the island, and the pilgrims walked along the high spine ridge on a stone path that is still intact. Each pilgrim passed through three sacred gateways, after first purifying themselves in the 'Fountain of the Inca,' an amazing spring that gushes pure water from a deep spring along the south ridge of Isla del Sol. To this day, locals go there to drink the healing waters and for purification rites.

Elder Shamanic Priests presided at the three gateways and determined the merit of each pilgrim, either blessing their passage or disallowing them from further advancement. To be granted access through the three doorways was a great honor, one that was earned. One imagines that this trek was akin to the Islamic Hodge (holy pilgrimage to Mecca) as an enormously important Holy rite that defines one's life.

The first 'Holy Gate' was called Pumapunku, meaning 'the arch of the Sacred Puma' because an etheric Puma guarded it. Puma was said to have emerged from the Waters as a Stone being and represented strength and nurturing.

The second, Kentipunku, 'the arch of the Humming Bird,' was covered in Incan times with the iridescent green-blue feathers of the 'messenger' bird. Hummingbirds were felt to be emissaries of the higher worlds and able to exist in other dimensions. They represented purity and the ability to 'fly' in other realms.

The final gateway, Pillcopunku, 'the door of Joyous Pure Hope,' was covered with the larger green feathers of the pillco bird and blessed with incense, with wing feathers of the mighty Condor. This was the final blessing and archway. The passing through this arch required that the pilgrim had met his death and recognized his immortality as a being of light. Only those souls who had achieved impeccability could enter to El Roque as

pure Warriors of Light. These were the elite, the symbology apparent.

**The Trek**

I considered my own worthiness, as I huffed up the path to El Rocque. Luis had given me sacred coca leaves to offer as blessings at specific points along the walk. I mixed these with small prayer ties of tobacco, as was the Lakota way. I acknowledged the 'Spirit of Place' and the powerful spiritual energy that abounded. I respectfully asked permission to proceed.

Although we had climbed only a thousand feet or so above the lake, it felt much higher. The elevation was nearing 13,500 feet, and the sheer exertion required in the rarified air created little starbursts that appeared in my field of vision. These were physical, due to fatigue and the lack of oxygen, but nonetheless gave me the sensation of being in another dimension, and part of me knew that indeed I was. The perspective down to the water's edge seemed greater than its measured distance and gave the illusion that I was walking on top of the world. The sun had risen to the mid-point, the lake's surface looked like a blue green mirror, and at some points it glowed an incandescent white. Was it the Sun Disc?

Looking down at the vast panorama of the lake and its surrounding peaks was a study of blue; every possible hue and nuance of blue seemed to dance from the lake, patchworked into the massive surface below. The areas near the shoreline were a beautiful Caribbean turquoise that evolved into larimar, lapis and even a fiery amethyst. Even the snow capping the enormous spine of the Andes had an indigo violet tint.

As we began to approach the Sacred Rock, I could not help but recognize certain elements of how perfect the energetic blend of this point was. Each feature of the landscape now started to be dramatized with great pulsing intensity. 'El Rocque' was a jutting section of natural rock that seemed to be sliced into a half dome, like an enormous ball sliced in half. It was situated atop the island, perfectly centered, with a view on three sides of the Lake below. The open face of the Holy Rock had a wall built in front of it that served as an alter and was laden with offerings: feathers, fruit, coca leaves, small ribbons and crosses. About 50 meters in front of the Holy Rock was an enormous stone table, looking like an Irish dolman, set on three smaller stones. It was circled, by 12 chiseled stone monoliths, about two and a half feet in height and about eighteen inches in diameter, and again circled by a larger diameter circle. These were more recent additions, placed there within the last decade, but served the energy well. The placement was correct and looked like a smaller version of the inner circle of Avebury. One circle flows with clockwise energy, the other spins counterclockwise.

Luis and I approached El Rocque in reverence, stopping at three points to offer coca leaves. We then went forward to the rock and knelt individually in prayer. After an appropriate time, we moved to the alter and walked the stone circle counterclockwise, then clockwise on the inner circle, before kneeling at the table alter. I unrolled my bundle, and we prepared a pipe prayer ceremony in the Lakota way. Luis, offered coca leaves to each direction and to each element in the local Incan tradition. After our prayers, we each found a stone within the circle and went into meditative silence. I sat for well over an hour and then walked to the nearby Incan Monastery ruins. I gazed over the turquoise waters in awe.

## Center of the Earth

Incan folklore and Ayamara legends speak of an ancient forgotten time in which Pachamama decided to cover herself in water in order to purify her body. The entire body of the Mother Earth was covered with devastating tsunamis and floods. All of the known regions of Earth were covered in darkness, and icy winds blew for countless ages. Most of mankind was erased from the land of Og.

In time, Pachamama felt clean and allowed the purifying waters to recede. The remaining waters of purification remained cupped in a high sacred part of the Earth ... and formed a Holy Lake. From here, creator God Viracocha arose from the depths of the sanctified waters of Lake Titicaca. Journeying to the islands of Sol, Luna and Amantani, Viracocha commanded the sun (Inti), the moon (Mama-Kilya) and the stars to rise. Next, going to the island of Tiahuanaco, he fashioned new men and women out of stones, and sending them to the four quarters, began the repopulation of the world. Titicaca became, and has remained to this day, the sacred purification cradle of man and the gateway of the Gods.

As I began my descent, I felt drained and pure ... perhaps reborn is a more fitting term. I had a brief vision of a great condor arising from the purity of the great salt desert, circling the holy Island of the Sun. And in a graceful sweep, drinking the water of life from the sacred lake. Soaring upward in grace, in strength, to the direction of the eagle.

## Tyberonn Channel

*"This powerful prophesy from the Hopi care-takers is sourced in the energy of what is termed Star Nation, those wise and peaceful beings descended from the LeMurian red race, that you now call indigenous. In what the Hopi refer to as the 'Eagle and the Condor,' the Eagle represents the energies of the North, and the Condor, the energies of Latin America. Both were once as one, and the prophecy states that when the Eagle and the Condor agan fly together, it will signify the return of wisdom and balance.*

The meaning is that without the Condor, the Eagle cannot fly. You see, it is the sacred wisdom of the Condor, the indigenous of South America, that has not been as scattered, we might say. The ancient wisdom of the Condor must go north, and that of the Eagle south. It is to heal the Eagle. That is why those Earth-Keepers and Lightworkers of the North are drawn to the Land of the Sacred Lake, and those of the Condor are drawn to the North at this time.

Now, the Eagle will fly, and much is being done by Lightworkers, by true seekers in the United States. The Harmonic is rising. The United States has many spiritual pockets, and these are growing in greater inertia. It is the masses of the people there who are incased, we might say, in their own cages of misunderstanding. Few have true sovereignty. Americans are enslaved by debt, manipulated by media and intoxicated by quantity. America is a corporation, based on profit, and many are now working to change this. There are indeed those in South America, primarily of the Star Seed, the indigenous wisdom and medicine keepers, who are assisting in the healing and awakening experience. Certain sacred plant modalities, shamanic journeys, ancient wisdom ceremonies and quests that allow for multi dimensional clearing and understanding are available in the land of the Condor, and no longer in the land of the Eagle.

Certain of the key power point portals in North America are clouded, and this is a prime piece of the Eagle and Condor. The key power points that are aligned to the United States from South America are assisting in this vital balance. Beloved, a great connection has always existed between Sedona and Titicaca, but that ancient energetic ley route has become less effective and is now to be repaved and retread, as 2012 nears. That portal, which is Titicaca, is much more intact and more capable of feeding and healing the other.

Some of the once potent centers in the North are diluted, surrounded by commercial interests, and much of the ancient indigenous knowledge and wisdom regarding the Living Earth and her centers of power have been disregarded or lost. It still remains, but only on reservations, in small enclaves in the North. As such, clearings and revitalizations need to occur, and many new portals are emerging. Do you recall the biblical allegory of Jesus casting out the merchants from the Temple? You see, portals and celestial points are living Cathedrals because of their natural magnetics and alignments, and were never meant to be areas of commerce and housing. That is why indigenous caretakers designated certain sites as Hallowed Earth, and only adepts were able to live within the energies on a permanent basis. That is why many of the potent vortex/portals in the United States, such as Monument Valley, Grand Canyon, Sedona and Mount Shasta were designated to the care of certain Indigenous Tribes. In later years others were protected through divine guidance of inspired human beings into reserves you call National and State Parks.

Many of the key sites in Europe became Cathedrals, lest they become villages and shops. The Templars who chose these Cathedral locations were guided and inspired to do so not as dogmatic Christians, Muslims or Jews but as Earth-Keepers who did what was required to protect the integrity of the grid-portal. An inner circle of those holy men who devoted themselves there received inner purpose, intuitive guidance and inner understanding of their protective roles.

Cathedrals, Monasteries and Chapels, such as Rosslyn, Chartres and Montserrat in Europe, are major stellar grid points that still function! The human element within these major 'natural vortex points,' such as Sedona, Montserrat, Rosslyn and Titicaca, when not properly attuned can create a frequency disturbance akin to what you might call a 'computer virus.' The virus does not

Figure 00.1 Sacred Geometry is the fabric of the Cosmos. The Platonic solids are the building blocks of the fabric of reality.

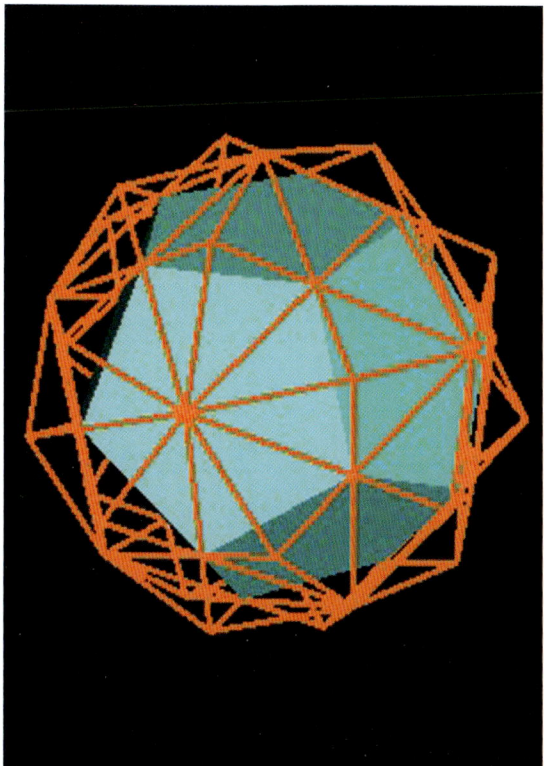

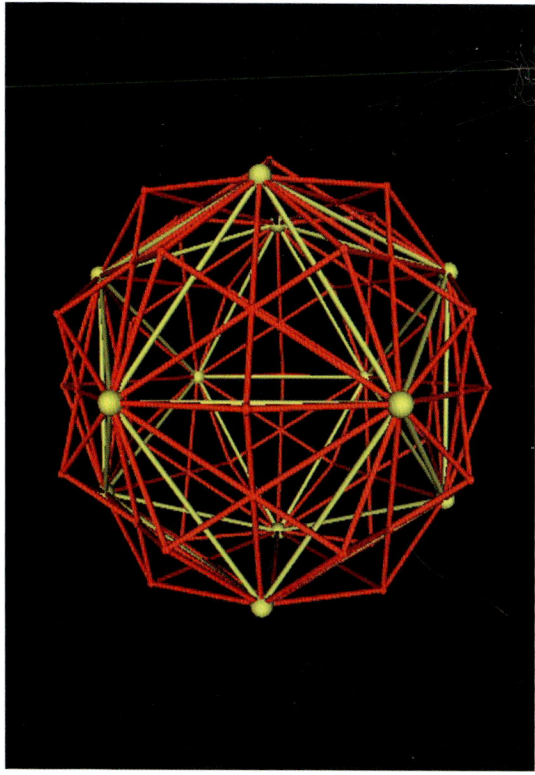

Figure 00.2 The 144 Grid, the double penta dodeca-hedron, is the catalyst of the planetary Ascension. The frequency of this Grid covers dimensions 4-9.

Figure 00.3 The 120 Polyhedron is the grid lattice from the 10th to the 12th dimensional fields.

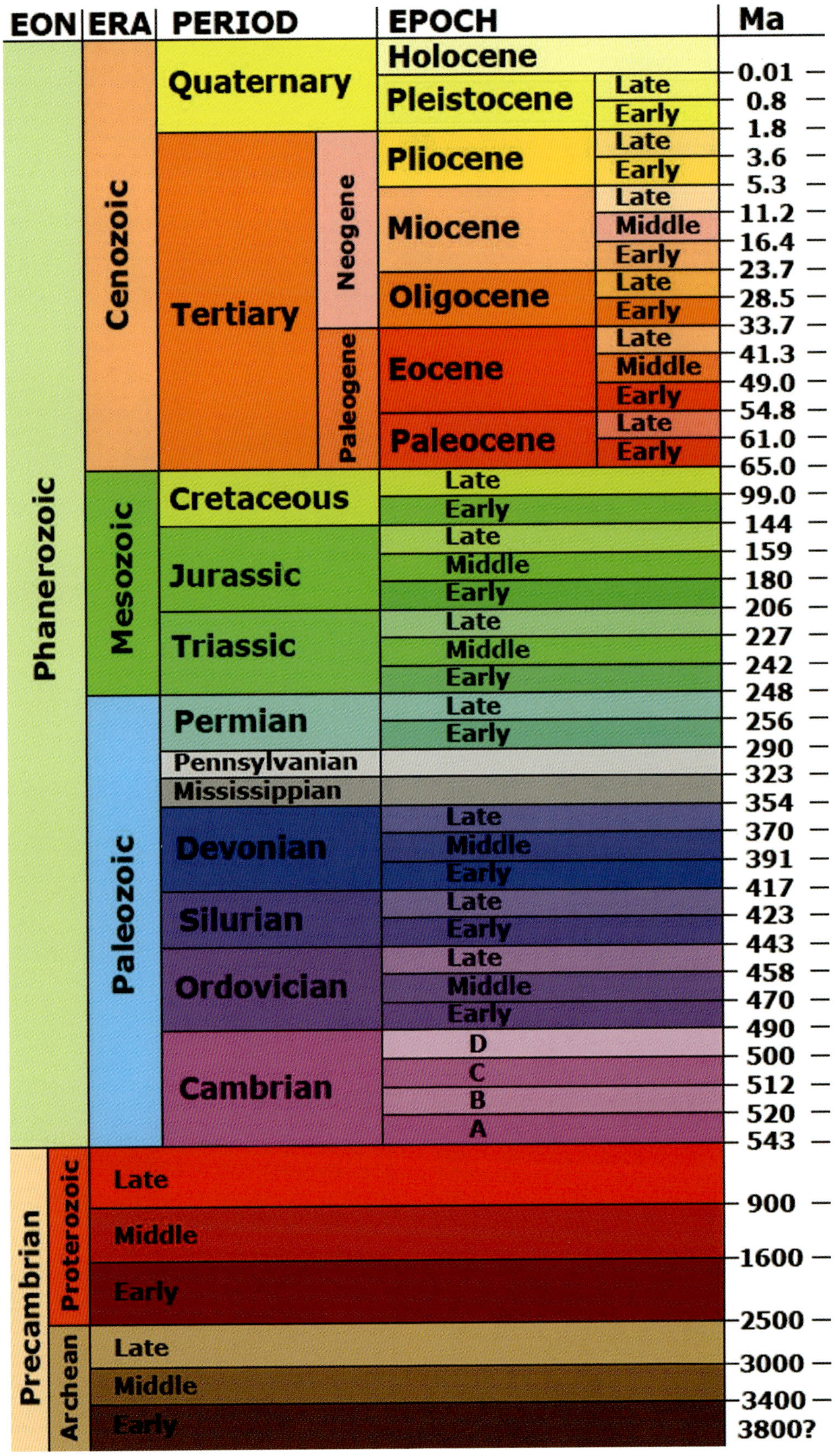

| EON | ERA | PERIOD | | EPOCH | | Ma |
|-----|-----|--------|--|-------|--|-----|
| Phanerozoic | Cenozoic | Quaternary | | Holocene | | 0.01 |
| | | | | Pleistocene | Late | 0.8 |
| | | | | | Early | 1.8 |
| | | Tertiary | Neogene | Pliocene | Late | 3.6 |
| | | | | | Early | 5.3 |
| | | | | Miocene | Late | 11.2 |
| | | | | | Middle | 16.4 |
| | | | | | Early | 23.7 |
| | | | | Oligocene | Late | 28.5 |
| | | | | | Early | 33.7 |
| | | | Paleogene | Eocene | Late | 41.3 |
| | | | | | Middle | 49.0 |
| | | | | | Early | 54.8 |
| | | | | Paleocene | Late | 61.0 |
| | | | | | Early | 65.0 |
| | Mesozoic | Cretaceous | | Late | | 99.0 |
| | | | | Early | | 144 |
| | | Jurassic | | Late | | 159 |
| | | | | Middle | | 180 |
| | | | | Early | | 206 |
| | | Triassic | | Late | | 227 |
| | | | | Middle | | 242 |
| | | | | Early | | 248 |
| | Paleozoic | Permian | | Late | | 256 |
| | | | | Early | | 290 |
| | | Pennsylvanian | | | | 323 |
| | | Mississippian | | | | 354 |
| | | Devonian | | Late | | 370 |
| | | | | Middle | | 391 |
| | | | | Early | | 417 |
| | | Silurian | | Late | | 423 |
| | | | | Early | | 443 |
| | | Ordovician | | Late | | 458 |
| | | | | Middle | | 470 |
| | | | | Early | | 490 |
| | | Cambrian | | D | | 500 |
| | | | | C | | 512 |
| | | | | B | | 520 |
| | | | | A | | 543 |
| Precambrian | Proterozoic | Late | | | | 900 |
| | | Middle | | | | 1600 |
| | | Early | | | | 2500 |
| | Archean | Late | | | | 3000 |
| | | Middle | | | | 3400 |
| | | Early | | | | 3800? |

Diagram 00.4 Earth Strata Timeline: Geologists have determined our planet to be approximately 4.5 billion years old. Metamorphic and igneous rock emit the strongest electromagnetic fields.

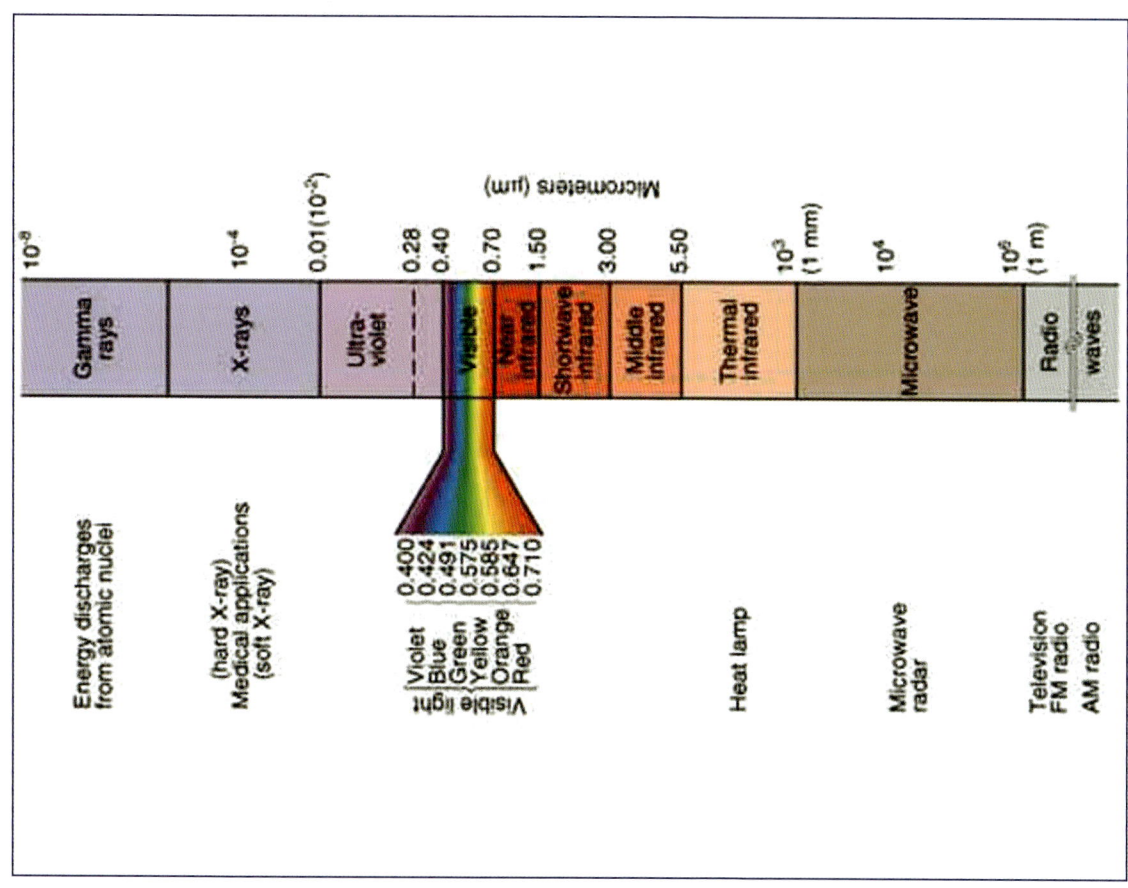

Figure 00.6 The Light Spectrum: Electromagnetic wave lengths determine the llayers of dimensional fields.

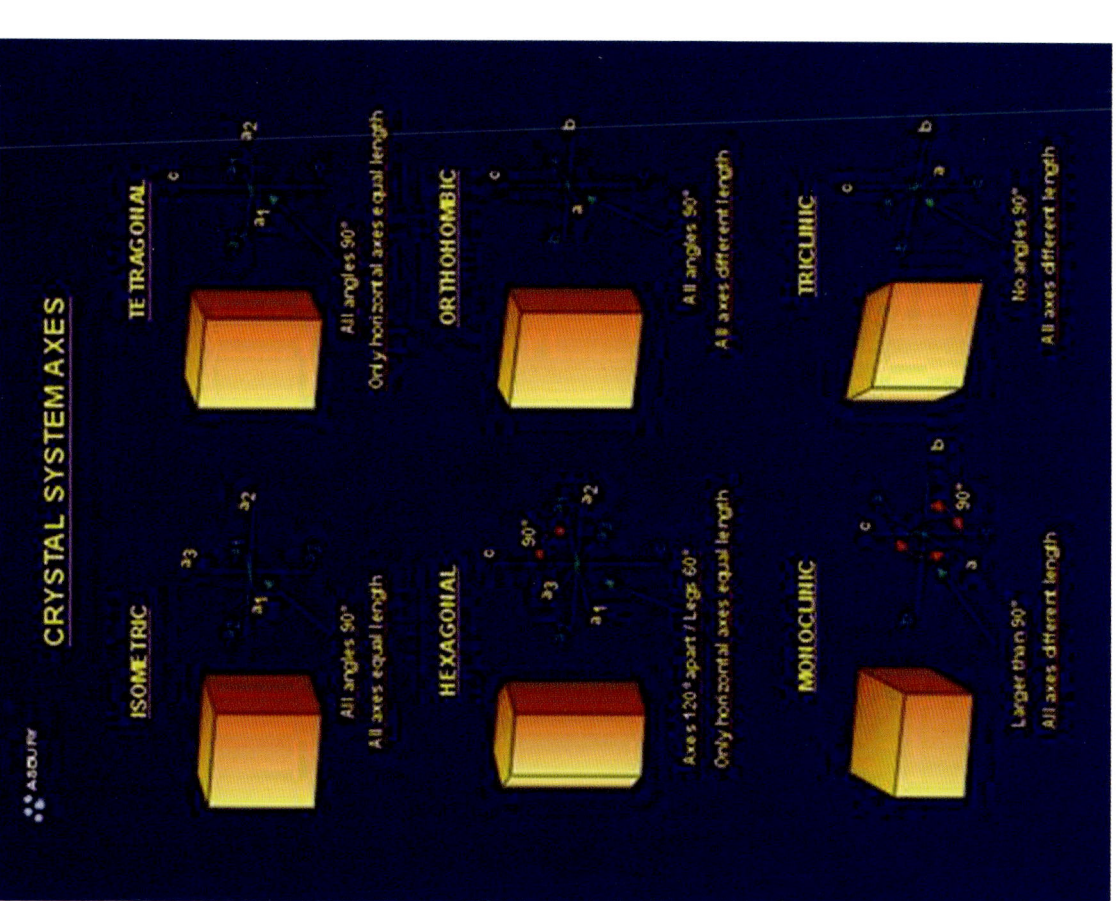

Figure 00.5 Crystal Systems: The manner of crystallization influences the beneficial energy fields of gems. All crystalline gems form in one of six geometric crytsalline stuctures: tetrahedron, hexahedron, octahedron and dodecahedron.

Figure 01.1   The Buffalo River Wilderness in the Ozark Mountains of Arkansas is a pristine, magical area.

Figure 01.2   The Talimena Ridge in the Ouachita Mountains of western Arkansas contain crystal beds and magnetic iron lode stones, a potent combination.

Figure 01.4 Cavern Falls, Ozarks: Arkansas is dotted with limestone caverns, many of which are said to connect to the hollow earth.

Figure 01.3 The thermal springs in Hot Springs, Arkansas are used for healing baths. The therapeutic waters contain trace minerals and radioactive elements only found in one other area, Banff, Canada.

Figure 02.1 Lake Moraine, in the Michael Vortex of Canada, is another of the crystal-water lakes within the spectacular energy of the Canadian Rockies.

Throat Center

Figure 02.1 Emerald Lake is part of the Michael Vortex in western Canada. The turquoise color of these lakes is created by crystalline silicates. Mount Michael is shown in the background.

Brow Center

Figure 02.3 Lake O'Hara in Yoho National Park in Canada is connected with the Michael Vortex crystalline lakes: Lake Louise, Lake Moraine, Emerald Lake and Peyto Lake. Lake O'Hara is the crown. *CROWN center*

*(Heart center)*          *(EMOTIONAL center)*

Figure 02.4 Lake Louise is the heart center for the Michael Vortex in Canada. Its spectacular beauty is stunning.

*Heart center*

Figure 03.1  Torres del Paine in Patagonia, Chile is a Michael Vortex and is connected to the energies of Lake Louise and Lake O'Hara in Canada.

Figure 03.2  Horseback treks to Los Torres del Paine and Los Cuervos in Chile takes one through magical lakes and valleys.

Figure 03.3 Ascension Portal: Autuna Mountain in the remote sourtheast frontier of Venezuela is a 12th dimension portal. It is amazingly potent.

Figure 03.4 Los Torres del Paine, Chile: The three blue towers are granite monoliths and are generators of crown energy.

Figure 03.5 Mineas Gerais, Brazil contains the largest quartz crystal fields on the planet, as well as topaz, diamonds and aquamarine.

Figure 04.1 The Pyramids at Giza are perhaps the most powerful portal vortex complex on the planet.

Figure 04.3 Mount Sinai in northeast Egypt is one of the most powerful holy mountains on the planet, anchoring leys and gridpoints.

Figure 04.2 The King's Chamber is the energetic center of the Pyramidal vortex, the most powerful place on the planet.

Figure 04.4 The summit of Mount Sinai has a serene depth and multi dimensional overlay that is very, very potent.

Figure 04.5  Both the Temples of Greece and the Pyramids were built with sacred geometry, utilizing the golden mean phi and spiral.  As such they become portals of light energy.

Figure 04.6  The Kings Chamber of the Great Pyramid, is the energetic center of the Pyramid vortex. It is activated by sound toning.

Figure 04.7  The Temple of Karnac in Luxor is along the Nile leyline.  It contains obelisks and sacred lakes.  Amazing energies in the Temples.

Figure 05.1 The Inca Trail traverses the Sacred Valley of Peru at heights of over 13,000 feet. It is the prerequisite path for pilgrims to approach Machu Picchu.

Figure 05.2 The Sacseyhuaman temple at Cusco is one of the holy Temples in Peru and radiates a regenerative magnetic field..

Figure 05.3 The crown summit of Huayna Picchu, the pyramidal mountain of Machu Picchu, is the most potent energy point of the Temple complex.

Figure 05.4 Machu Picchu is a major contributor to the massive chakric vortex of Lake Titicaca. It exudes heart energy.

Figure 06.1 Skellig Michael is a pyramidal mountain off the coast of western Ireland. It is composed almost entirely of purple granite and is the entry anchor for the Michael leyline.

Figure 06.2 The ancient domed monastic hives on the summit of Skellig Michael glow with energy. How the monks built them is a mystery; no mortar or cement was used.

Figure 07.1 St. Columba Abbey on the Isle of Iona. Iona is a vortex portal of great tranquility. The island is a rare uplift of one of the oldest metamorphic rocks of the planet, over 4 billion years old.

Figure 07.2 Staffa Island is located seven miles from Iona and is composed of hexagonal columns of crystal basalt. It energizes Iona. Fingal's cave is shown in the photo.

Figure 08.1  Artist Cathy Whitewolf's channeled portrait of Medicine Bear after my shamanic journey at Panther Meadows atop Mt. Shasta.

Figure 08.2  Medicine Wheel ceremony and sweat-lodge at Mount Shasta.

Figure 08.3  Ronna, Tyb and family anchoring the reshel grid of the Moody Pyramids in Galveston, Texas. The Moody Pyramids are the anchor point for the emerging 'balance' portal of Galveston-Houston.

Figure 08.4 Enchanted Rock in the hill country of Texas was considered sacred by the Native Americans for millenia.

Figure 08.5 The lavendar granite dome of Enchnated Rock contains massive amounts of quartz and pegmatite crystals. It is a very powerful vortex-portal.

Figure 09.1  Illimani, sacred volcano towers 19,000 feet above LaPaz, Bolivia.

Figure 09.2  The Sun Gate - Tiahuanaco, Bolivia is theorized to have been built over 15,000 years ago.  It was once part of the Atlantean colony called Og.

Figure 09.4 The alignment from the Sunken temple is perfectly framed to the Kala-sasaya Entry temple. Each of the Temples are aligned to the cardinal directions.

Figure 09.3 The construction of Tiahuanaco was without mortar, and reveals a remarkable precision of construction..

Figure 10.1 The sacred Samaipata Mountains of northern Bolivia are triangulated with Salar de Uyuni and Lake Titicaca.

Figure 10.2 Spectacular Lake Titicaca is the largest vortex-portal complex on the planet and is in counterbalance alignment with Sedona.

Figure 10.4 The sacred Incan Priest Temple next to El Rocque on Island of the Sun. The Golden Disc of Mu is said to be in the waters pictured, just off the island.

Figure 10.3 El Rocque, on the Island of the Sun, is the most sacred place on Lake Titicaca. It anchors the vortex portal and is a sacred ceremonialRich black

Figure 10.5  El Fuerte in Samaipata Bolivia is a powerful and sacred energy point.  It is an entrance to the Atlantean underground labyrinth system, connected to Tiajuanaco, Bolivia and to Diamantina, Brazil.

Figure 10.6  Shaman's Eye: Spirit Mountain in Samaipata Bolivia is a potent vortex with red sandstone similar to that of Sedona.

Figure 10.7 The 'Grandmother' volcano of the western perimeter of the salt desert of Salar de Uyuni in southern Bolivia is considered a living deity by the local indigenous people.

Figure 10.8 On the slopes of Grandmother volcano, the background shows the massive crystallized salt of Salar de Uyuni. These snow-white crystalline salts supply the femine energies to Lake Titicaca. This is one of the most powerful places in South America.

Figure 11.1  Shaman's Dome is in the Red Rock National Forest near Sedona, Arizona.  It was the site of my third vision quest.

Figure 11.2  Atop Shaman's Dome after ceremony with Adam Yellowbird, after 5 day prayer fast and vision quest.

Figure 11.4 The womb of Gaia: Grand Canyon, Arizona. Hiking the bottom -- the energy at the base of the Grand Canyon is pristine and incredibly intense.

Figure 11.3 Shaman's Cave - stargate window.

Figure 12.1  Rosslyn Chapel in Scotland sits atop a powerful vortex-portal and houses a stargate.

Figure 12.2  Rosslyn Glen is the generator of Roslyn Chapel.  The North Esk River Canyon has sandstone cliffs and Neolithic spirals carved into its walls.  It lies next to the chapel.

Figure 13.1  The Tor of Glastonbury, Scotland has a seven tiered labyrinth along its rim.  Both the Michael and Mary leylines cross the Tor.

Figure 13.2  The Glastonbury Abbey Ruins, near the Tor, project a very sacred energy.  The site has a marker claiming King Arthur to be buried here.

Figure 14.1 Spring thaw at Lake Baikal in eastern Siberia. Lake Baikal is the most powerful energy vortex and generator of Russia.

Figure 14.2 Buryat Shamans have been honoring Lake Baikal for millennia. Buryat ceremonies and beliefs are similar to that of Native Americans.

Figure 14.3 The Golden Temple of 'Christ the Redeemer' in Moscow is the center of the Golden Ring Vortex.

Figure 14.4 Statue of Saint Basil in the Red Square - Moscow, Russia

Figure 15.2  The Red and White Springs of Stewart Mineral Springs near Mount Shasta are very sacred and aligned to the Chalice Wells of Glastonbury.

Figure 15.4  Mount Fuji Japan, shown in this photo, is aligned in purpose with Mount Shasta.

Figure 15.1  Mount Shasta, California

Figure 15.3  Ceremonial site on the big island of Hawaii.  The energy of LeMuria is anchored here.

Figure 15.5 Borobudar Temple, Indonesia - Living Mandala.

Figure 15.6 The ancient Hindu Temples of Java, Indonesia are over 900 years old and contain amazing harmonic chambers inside them.

Figure 15.7 The Borobudar Buddhist Temple is a living mandala. Built on the sacred volcanic island of Java, it is surrounded by four active volcanoes.

Figure 15.8 Shown here are the "Guardians' of Montserrat. Montserrat in Spain is a grid anchor point.

Figure 15.9  This site in the Caucus Mountains near the Caspian Sea of Azerbaijan is called the 'Praying Hands of Allah.'  It has been a pilgrimage site for centuries and projects a potent energy.

Figure 15.10  Sacred tree at the Buddhist Shrine at the base of Mount Fuji, Japan

Figure 15.11  The Hindu Temple of Divine Wisdom on slopes of a volcano on the sacred island of Bali.

Figure 15.12   Chitzen Itza, in the Yucatan of Mexico is one of the most potent pyramids in the Americas.

Figure 15.13   The Mayan Temple Complex at Altun-Ha Belize on the Atlantis Reunion Tour with Steve Rother and Ronna Herman. The Mayan Pyramids were built with the Atlantean technology of sonic manifestation.

# Sedona ~ Shaman's Dome nad Cave

Shaman's Dome is perhaps the least 'known' vortex in Sedona. It is isolated in a magnificent, rolling valley of the Red Rock National Forest, just south of Sedona. It is a perfect dome of rose sandstone quartz, soaring 750 feet above base. A powerful cave, known as Shaman's Cave, is carved into its upper portion. Known to indigenous holy men for centuries, it is an inter-dimensional portal, a stargate.

Shaman's Cave is a protected site. Local legends claim it is used by Starseed, extraterrestrials who taught and lived among the Indians. It is the most pristine, if not the most powerful, energy portal in the Sedona vortex.

In December 2001, I had the wonderful opportunity to do a five-day vision quest in the magnificent energy of Shaman's Dome.

**Tyb's Journal: Quest, Day Four**

The fourth day of my quest brought a profound vision, but it was not what I expected. I had awakened at dawn from an endless night of tossing and turning, feeling glad the long cold night was over. Sleeping on the ground is hard enough without freezing temperatures. I repositioned myself inside my sleeping bag and blankets to watch the emerging sunrise. I was 'in the effect' of four days of fasting.

Still early and still freezing cold, I sat up, lightheaded. I rubbed my eyes and gazed at the amazing Sedona landscape from inside my prayer-tie circle deep in the Red Rock National Forest, 300 meters from Shaman's Dome. Dawn bathed the silhouetted cliffs in pink. I closed my eyes momentarily, not quite awake but not asleep.

**Vision of Red Feather**

Then it happened. I felt a tap on my shoulder and turned to see a regal looking Native American with jet-black hair. His raven mane was adorned with a small red feather in the back. He pointed to the feather, and I knew that was his name – Red Feather. He had a huge mountain lion with him, a sleek magnificent creature! He kneeled in front of me and pointed to Shaman's Dome, and I knew I had to go there. Timeless moments passed, and Red Feather came again. I sensed a great integrity in him and felt humbled by his presence. I got the same message again … go to the Dome. Suddenly I jolted up, eyes wide open, as though I'd seen a ghost which, of course, I had.

Visions do not come easily to me; in fact, I had never experienced one before in ceremony, and this was my third 5-day vision quest in as many years. I was not sure at this point if it had been one. I hadn't been asleep and was cognizant of observing an unusual scene with my eyes closed … but I *had* felt that tap on my shoulder, and I *did* feel his presence … and when I opened my eyes, he was still there for a few fleeting seconds before he evaporated into the morning fog.

Both excited and uncertain of what had just occurred, I sat and stared at the Dome. I gathered my energy and stood up, still lightheaded. Little stars burst all around my field of vision, a result of the physical exertion and the fasting. I balanced my stance and evaluated the walk, decent and climb in front of me. I wondered if I should chance it alone. It was a steep hike, and ice was everywhere. Red Feather's presence suddenly reappeared to tell me it would be okay. He would guide me.

I smiled in disbelief. The light-headedness was gone. Energy was pulsing through me as my numb fingers fumbled to tie the laces of my hiking boots. With appropriate ceremony, I opened the prayer-tie circle and left, not waiting for Yellowbird.

I should explain that Adam Yellowbird was the elder and facilitator for my vision quest. He is a man of great integrity and humility. A keeper of the Earth, he has an incredible affinity with earth, sky, elements and all life. He conducts quests in the Lakota tradition. This is my third under his tutelage. He kept an anchor fire for me at his camp in Cornville and made daily visits to council me, sage my site and sing vision songs.

I headed for the dome without him.

## Shaman's Dome

I really don't know how I got to the top so easily. I crunched through frozen grass and snow, down a steep arroyo and up an icy switchback trail, the last 150 feet of which was darn close to vertical. When I reached the top, the morning colors were dancing. It was like a peyote dream with little crystal explosions popping all around, and I had to sit down. Though winded and a bit lightheaded, I felt remarkably aware.

An icy wind whipped across the top of the dome, but I was well wrapped, and the sun was warming despite the frigid gale. I felt a sense of joyous well-being. I was totally in the NOW of this lucid moment. The adrenaline energy returned, and I scampered over the summit of the dome. I saw four distinct energy springs, small electrical (out-flowing) vortexes, spiraling purple light. As I sat right on top of one, the vital earth current flowed upward through me. With legs gangling over the edge, I shifted until I fit comfortably in a small dip near a ledge. It offered a perfect back support, and I closed my eyes. The feeling was delicious – completely alive, so in spirit, so melded into the dome.

With eyes closed, I faced the beaming sun, and everything appeared red through my closed lids. Geometric patterns danced in my head in a vibrant kaleidoscope of color, and I drifted into vision.

Red Feather took my hand, and we flew effortlessly over the valley. What a sensation of euphoria! Visionary experience is vivid, so real, yet always with the knowledge that this was a lucid dream. The rare joy of flying in that brisk, icy air was exquisite. Even now, I wonder if I was actually out-of-body. The flying sensation lasted for ten minutes or so, and then the vision shifted. I went deeper and higher … as if sleeping. I came into a place of great silence. I sat at the feet of my Godhead and asked questions, but I knew the answers before I heard them. I had the rare experience of knowing I was having a vision, and knowing I was watching it, and still not losing it with that realization (as is normally the case with dreams). Then more visuals began, this time animals. I saw a rattlesnake on the ground, and then the huge lioness. I was in curious awe of her, but not afraid. She walked into a cave and lay down. An hour passed.

A noise. I opened my eyes to see Yellowbird's green truck whining up the steep rocky track. He stopped thirty meters from my vision quest site. I stood and waved, then called to him. He saw me, and I motioned for him to climb up the Dome, which he did.

Thirty minutes later he arrived, so I shared my vision and spoke of the energy fountains. We built stone cairns denoting the spirals' locations. We connected the four to Ayers Rock, where he had been earlier in the year, and then to Machu Picchu, Enchanted Rock and Mount Shasta … places I had been.

We then made the precarious walk along the outer dome rim to the 'CAVE.'

Shaman's Cave was everything I anticipated and more, much more. The symmetry was beautiful. The cave featured an arched, semicircular entrance and a colonnaded buttress on the eastern side, with a stunning 360-degree circular window.

Not a cave it the traditional sense, it is a sandstone erosion overhang, 40 feet deep, 70 feet long and 25 feet high, with the back carved into sandstone. It had a stone alter, with floors and walls of wind-polished quartz.

As we walked into the magical entrance, I felt an immediate energy shift. My eyes were first drawn to a pictograph on the cave wall. I walked forty feet to the back wall and saw, with a wave of validation, that it was the face of a lion! The lioness of my vision!

## Inter Dimensional Portal

A condensed energy sphere pulsated inside, just below the pictograph. A lateral portal flowed through an amazing circular window. Electro-magnetic ley energy was focused inside the center aperture of the cave, like the fulcrum point of an hourglass. Three separate lines of energy met at the center, and the entire cave held an inter-dimensional portal, which can be opened with the appropriate intent.

Yellowbird and I did a pipe ceremony and circled with white sage. He sang a vision song of the Lakota tradition, made offerings, and we positioned for prayer and meditation. Two hours later, we knew it was time to leave. I knew I would return.

## Quest: Day Five

During another cold but beautiful night, I watched billions of stars in the clear night for an hour, as the occasional meteor streaked across the black velvet fabric of sky. My sleep was embellished with dreams.

## Transition Team

The sunrise was another study in pink and violet. After full sunrise, I was joined by Rainbow Spirit Woman, who lives in the Dakotas and is a guardian of the Earth. A degreed attorney, she works only now in spirit callings, working as a channeller, healer and facilitator. She came to the vision quest to assist in my 'transition', something that she felt compelled to do. She brought prayer ties, and she had prayed at the entrance of the National Forest over a mile away for the last two days. Her presence was a gift.

After her arrival I left the prayer tie area, and we trekked easily to Shaman's Cave for day five of my fast. The dome and cave were vibrant on that December 20, the potent eve of the Winter Solstice. Blessings were offered and permission received to enter the cave. A small stone fireplace was built in an earthen covering of the cave, so we gathered a few pieces of dried wood and built a small fire. With the aroma of burning cedar filling the cave, we offered blessings with prayer and sage.

## Shaman's Cave: Transitional Portal

After the appropriate ceremony, we went into meditation, and the vibration grew higher and higher over the next half-hour. Then, in the whiteness, two light beings appeared, and the energy was so overpowering that tears welled in my eyes, and my heart and spirit were laid open. I absorbed every vibration of the sacred moment. I was in awe of the holy light beings, who gifted us with an energetic transformation, a knowledge implant and a light code. A separate entourage made adjustments to my knee, nervous system and sensory capacities. I was told this would enable me to better receive and interpret terrestrial and celestial energies.

The whole experience was very clear, very personal and empowering. Rainbow Spirit Woman and I received simultaneously, with her vocally channeling what we both sensed. Our combined meditations and prayers opened a special portal that allowed an activation to occur. Despite a cold gusting wind and temperatures in the 40s, the cave felt warm. After 90 minutes, in symbolic ritual I felt compelled to pass in and out of the magical circular window in the 18-inch thick sandstone walls. The window itself was amazing, facing easterly directly onto an electromagnetic vortex called the 'Seven Chimneys.' The window is a rebirth portal, the womb of the Goddess. After my last passing through the window, I knew my quest was complete.

**Symbols and Meaning**

After doing vision quests for three consecutive years each December, each for five days , I had at last had a vision. It had not come easily; gifts of spirit rarely do. My vision was in essence, a lucid dream. Such visions do occur more readily for me now. I am still 'downloading' much of what was given. I obtained three new guides and now know that learning is an unending climb. In fact, I am not sure that we ever truly 'arrive.' There is always more, and always the responsibility to treat the gifts of awareness and knowledge with great respect. The Goddess, represented by the Lioness, teaches that ego, greed, and 'masculine' power struggles cannot mix with love, service and humility ... which are traits of true strength. Gifts of spirit are never 'taken away,' but they are often lost, because they simply cannot exist when negative traits resurface.

The metaphoric meaning of Jesus on the cross is his choosing love over power. He could have led an army. Which choice took greater strength?

When Yellowbird joined me in the afternoon, he came carrying a gift. Despite snow on the grounds and fluffy snow blowing in from the west on gray clouds, a rattlesnake had come out of hibernation and slithered under his truck tires, just 100 meters from my vision quest site. He could not avoid running over it. He recognized the symbol and gift. The snake represents transition, and he presented the rattles to me, wrapped in cloth cured in sage and cedar, at the Sweat Lodge ceremony that evening, the ceremony to ritually end the vision quest. In the native vernacular: AHO!

**My Take on the Sedona Vortex**

Now, to change directions slightly, let's make just a few comments regarding Sedona. Energy centers are crystalline in many respects and amplify the energies brought into them. There is no doubt that the Earth energies around Sedona are magnificent and powerful, but Sedona was never meant to be a metropolis. The Native Americans recognized the natural energy cathedral it was, and it was respected accordingly. Villages were kept in outlying areas, but few lived inside the principal vortex itself. Shamans recognized, understood and worked appropriately with the amplifiers and portals of Sedona.

**One Major Vortex: Hundreds of Fountains**

My take on Sedona is that there is one enormous vortex, circulating above the area. This vortex has a pulsating diameter of between 18 and 35 miles, depending on lunar, solar and telluric energy cycles. Within this diameter are literally hundreds of energy fountain vortexes, not just the eight shown on the touristy vortex maps. The vortex fountains all contribute to the mega-vortex of Sedona, which has a counterclockwise spin and is principally an outward flow vortex, although, there are dozens of areas with lateral energy flows and inward (magnetic) pulls within the Sedona energy field diameter. Many of the more potent vortex sites are also succinct inter-dimensional light portals and stargates. These are both functions of the light grid, whereas vortexes and tellurics relate to the gravitational and electromagnetic grids.

The 'Sedona vortexes' printed on maps and

offered on tours are: Boynton Canyon, Bell Rock, Airport Mesa, Cathedral Rock, Red Rock Crossing, Oak Creek Canyon, Coffee Pot Rock and Court House Butte. I have visited all of these, and I feel the site with the most pristine, sacred energy isn't even listed – the Chapel of the Holy Cross site.

## Closing Comments

One cannot quantitatively compare vortex sites. Power sites within the umbrella of a central vortex such as Sedona, Glastonbury or Titicaca are often tuned to specific chakras in order to work in specialized focal sequence.

Shaman's Dome and Cave, while both remote and 'protected,' are meant to be used. They are not 'off limits' or secret; the only requirement is respect of place and knowledge of purpose. Opening or 'fine-tuning' into the portal is a different matter. That is a process of intent, preparation and prayer. I was taken there just once, before sunrise. I departed days later in a heightened state. But it did not come easily to an old bear like me. After three years, I achieved a vision, and a portal was opened!

I remain humbly grateful for that experience, especially to Yellowbird and Rainbow. I have since learned that Red Feather has served as guide to at least two other writers (both published) regarding earth energies. That was a wonderful validation for me, always the doubter. And he is with me still.

I continued the following June with my fourth vision quest, and was blessed with several lucid dreams and vision -- a gift of intent, perseverance, growth and ceremony. I have continued to do ceremonial fasting and dance once each year. Each has been profound, each has been humbly treasured … but my first at Shaman's Dome opened a window of knowledge that I will forever remember with special reverence and gratitude.

## Tyberonn Channel

*"We greet you, Beloved! Now, Sedona is a most sacred and ancient land and was recognized since the days of LeMuria. It has been, and remains, a powerful vortex system, with many energetic pools being generated from the Earth. Much is misunderstood at present regarding the mechanics and vitality of the vortex systems. There are those that say this or that system is in need of repair, or in need of alignment. We tell you that the vortex of Sedona is a powerful complex and has always been so. It will continue to be so, you see, it is geo-physically triggered by the forces of the Earth herself.*

*Now, the channel has asked for the defining of what is termed a sacred site, or a point of power. We tell you quite simply that a power point is many things. It is that which is of relevant importance to both the Earth and to humanity, to within and to without the Earth, to the celestial heavens and to the celestial body itself. It is that which empowers, it is that which evolves, it is that which affects conscious evolution, it is that which is destined to remain a part of humanity's cellular existence.*

*A portal is that which allows one source of energy or beingness to transfer its energy from one source to another, from one world to another, such as physical or non-physical. It allows that which is a transmission, transition of energies for purpose, some portals through dimensions, some through space, some through time, some through all of these. Some portals align to specific star groups, others to specific planets. Some are set to receive energetic feeds of light and of more complex higher dimensional energies. The adept can determine which ones are which type. The channel is well on his way to rediscovering that ability within himself. Such knowledge he has had* in previous experiences, and it is being activated by his travels to and from, here and there across the continents.

Now, there are many forms of conscious energies that attach themselves to the structure of power sites. This is enabled by the energetic nature and multi dimensional overlay of such locations.

When these living Cathedrals are so recognized, the very reverence that they attract from humankind is imbued upon them. The accumulation of such high vibratory emotions collates and forms the energies of what you call 'guardian spirits.' This is different from what is called the 'Spirit of Place' and from the energies of the angelic realm, devic and elemental kingdoms. Know that all of these exist more tangibly in power points.

Now, we will say that within Sedona exist all of these. What can be termed as a collective consciousness of spirit guardians is currently drawn primarily from the imbued reverence of the Indigenous peoples who honored this area for millennia. Such was their recognition and understanding that the major vortexes of Sedona were ceremonially utilized and inhabited only for that purpose. So there is an energetic code that has shifted somewhat when the area became inhabited, roads and buildings constructed and venues of commerce eventuated in this century. You see, such areas reflect and absorb the harmonic of those within its structure. There has been, nonetheless, a significant drawing of reverent seekers to this area in current times, and these are devoted to the sacred guardianship and preservation of the vortex harmonic. The ceremonies of indigenous dance and worship and spiritual understanding have been re-energized and continue to seek the balance. These activities are so appropriate, and, you see, the Earth responds.

While some of the areas within this vortex have shifted, the primary mechanics have not. Vortex-portal points are timeless, and as such, all that has or will occur in space-time continue in the now of such places. The eons of reverence within Sedona coexist with what you term the present and future.

Now, beneath parts of Sedona and the volcanic area of the San Francisco Peaks are a network of tunnels and hollow earth. These are inhabited by what would be considered fourth dimensional beings. Those that were third dimensional of LeMurian descent but have not claimed a fifth dimensional reception. They are those of an in-between nature, quite accustomed to being in the Earth, not yet wanting to allow a body to dissipate, not yet called to the fifth dimensional state, for instance. The realms of the fourth dimension can experience the tangibility of the first three dimensions. It is as if a third dimension plus, you see, all three plus the fourth, not just the fourth. Although the true fourth dimensional state is primarily non-physical, in your terms. And yes, the true fifth dimensional state is also non-physical, an enlightened translucent state, but that does not mean it cannot be sought and realized from a base of physicality. The third dimensional state, then, being the density of a physical state. A third dimensional plus energy would be a little of all of the above, which is why they find themselves within the Earth, then, not completely capable of surfacing, not completely capable of becoming fifth dimensional beings. It is an alternate choice, a parallel reality choice. Once chosen when the beings of LeMuria and her colonies chose to leave the surface world at the time of the deluge, some 30 thousand years ago in your time. There are other such subterranean colonies throughout the Earth. Others of kind in California, Central America, Peru and Bolivia.

Now, the vortex of Sedona is seeking the balance of what is termed the male and female energies. It is the equal balance that is desired, and at present this area of the Americas is in imbalance. The influx of the softer, more subtle feminine energy is being received via the portal and disseminated via the vortex engine. The description of vortex portal energies, and specifically the attempt to label them accordingly to chakras and experience, is somewhat misunderstood. All vortexes can and do effect all chakras. The resulting experience varies with the individual, according to their light quotient, their integrity, their needs and what qualities are in the inner self. Vortex energy resonates with, and strengthens the Inner Being of, each person who comes within it. This resonance occurs because the vortex energy is harmonically in tune to the subtle energy of the chakric system. The very potency of geo magnetic and geo electric forces within the vortex system of Sedona are capable of creating an initial imbalance in those that visit there. You see, it amplifies that which is within in order to allow energetic observation for purification. The indigenous understood this, and accordingly only their teachers and adepts resided full time within the vortex. That is why some of the residents of Sedona may appear to be eccentric or imbalanced. The electro magnetic frequencial in power sites can in itself create what we will term an energetic pressure differential with the human EMF or auric field. In the period of equalization, auric fissures can occur, until such time as the balance is recreated. As such, there are times when it is prudent for the human to not overstay in power sites, until their auric energy is better adjusted to the harmonic. Those who choose to live in such sites will in time either gain the equilibrium or experience imbalance.

Now, within Sedona there are also several extraterrestrial bases. Those of Sirius B and the Pleiades have at varies times involved themselves in the maintenance of the ley system and energetic matrix of the portal complex. Those beings, called Starseed, that have worked with the spiritual indigenous peoples in this area, were from an aspect of the Pleades that we call Star Nation. One of several primary stargates in the area is focused at Shaman's Cave, as the channel has described. Although, these points shift and are not as fixed as one might believe.

Sedona is indeed aligned with the vortex of Lake Titicaca. The two might be said to be hemispheric counterbalances, one in clockwise vector, the other in counterclockwise. The communication between the two is immense and is connected to the purpose of what the Hopi termed, 'The Eagle and the Condor.' Many are drawn to the two in contract with this energetic blending. We will say that at this time the more potent, the more balanced, the more vital of these vortexes is Lake Titcaca. You see, at this time, Lake Titicaca is providing an energetic assistance to Sedona, and in the past there were times when Sedona provided such assistance to the south. But now, on your Earth, it is the southern portal that provides energy to the northern, and as such, much of the feminine is so drawn.

The geometry of Sedona is complex, consisting of the tetrahedron and hexahedron, and these two are enclosed within the octahedron. The tetrahedron represents the aspect of humankind, the hexahedron his search for understanding and knowledge, and the octahedron the connection to the celestial beingness. The octahedron is the I AM of 'as below- so above.' It is the emergence. You are beloved."

... and so it is.

135

# Rosslyn Chapel and Glen ~ Uncoding DaVinci

That Rosslyn Chapel was featured as the final scene of the infamous 'DaVinci Code' has its downside. The enigmatic stone rubik is now a pop-trend tourist site, and quiet reverence is much harder to find there. You see, to the seeker the biggest mystery in Scotland was never Loch Ness, it has always been Rosslyn.

Let's start at the beginning …

**Mystery**

The famed mystery Chapel looks the part. Rosslyn adorns the summit of a rugged mound in the verdant rolling hills of southeast Scotland, looking somewhat like a spired crown.

It lies on a ley, the Roseline, thus the name. But much of Rosslyn's lore comes from its over embellished decor, specifically the stone carvings. Appropriately called a tapestry in stone, many of these carvings relate to the symbolism of the Christian Bible, the mysticism of Freemasonry, the Knights Templar, Gnosticism and even the Hopi-Mayans.

These stone carvings as historic art are among the finest period works in Europe on that basis alone. There are dozens of books written about what these unique carvings represent. Yet it is the tangible presence of something greater that tugs deeply at the visiting seeker's heart and defines Rosslyn. That was, indeed, this writer's experience.

**History and Legend**

The mysterious Rosslyn Chapel is an extraordinarily beautiful 'Cathedral in miniature.' Renowned for its elaborate construction, the Chapel was built in 1446 by Sir William St. Clair. It is located seven miles outside Scotland's capital city of Edinburgh, amid flaxen rolling hills and jagged granite outcroppings.

The Chapel is rich in both historic fact and legend. Supposition regarding religious artifacts stored in its hidden vaults has inspired academics and mystics for centuries. There are bodies of factual evidence pieced together with intricate theories that cover a wide spectrum of interest. Reputed devotees contend that some incredible relics, including the fabled Holy Grail, sacred gospel texts, secret dossiers, Solomon's treasure and the Arc of the Covenant are housed in the Chapel's sealed underground vaults.

However, the 'spirit of place' at the geographical location of Rosslyn goes back much further. The core question of the mystery of Rosslyn Chapel is why it was built in the first place. For this writer, one <u>key</u> part of the *why* is the *where*. Rosslyn sits amid an extremely potent telluric vortex and houses one of the most powerful portal-gates on the planet. Rosslyn is a multidimensional stargate.

**Hawthorden: Rosslyn Glen**

Overlooking a hidden river canyon, the 'Rosslyn Glen,' (aka Hawthorden) lies a few hundred meters below. The geology is a rich blend of volcanic and sedimentary strata amid a webbing of fault lines and anticlines.

Worthy of celebrity on its own merit, the enchanting glen is serendipitous to most visitors, unaware of its majestic geological expression and important energetic connection to Rosslyn Chapel. Within the magical depths of Rosslyn Glen, the crystalline River North Esk flows through a walled sandstone canyon that is embellished with Neolithic sacred sites. There are several Druid caves with pictoglyphs of spirals and concentric circles inside the canyon. On the path above the glen is a well-known Neolithic 'bust' of Green Man, the pagan personification of the male aspect of nature, carved into a stone outcropping. Such markings are the ancient pagan denotation of vortex and ley sites, held sacred by earth aware Druids. Rosslyn Glen is the wind beneath the wings, the underpinning generator, of Rosslyn Chapel.

## Tybs Journal

It is mid summer, as I walk the steep path from the Rosslyn Hotel to the sacred Chapel I have traveled so far to see.

Leaden skies frame the silhouette of Rosslyn Chapel, the gothic miniature cathedral, symbol of legend and lore. It is a blustery day and feels more like October than July. Dark clouds loom on the horizon, a fitting backdrop to the mystical aura emitted from the weathered, brown stone of the majestic structure.

Damp winds gust steadily through the spires and buttresses, whistling through the hollow expanses of metal scaffolding placed around its perimeter for much needed restoration.

Gravel crunches beneath my feet as I enter the courtyard, holy grounds by any standard. I make my way to one of several benches in the churchyard and sit quietly for a few moments to drink in the energy of place. The grounds are tidily manicured, the vibrant green garden adorned with rose bushes, fragrant with heady perfume.

After an appropriate half hour, I rise and carefully walk around the chapel. It is intricately carved in the finest Gothic tradition, with gargoyles and flying buttresses. Each conical spire is individually sculpted into a unique symbolic note that choruses an enigmatic symphony. Even without foreknowledge of its mystical lore, its coded

ambiance is a tangible force that is immediately provocative. There is a 'feeling,' undeniable, that there is more to Rosslyn than just a chapel. Much more.

There are two entrances to the Chapel, and after circling precariously, I was curiously conscious of selecting the south entrance to go inside. Being one who is prone to expect a depth of sensitivity in sacred places, I was not surprised by the powerful emotions that met me at the doorway. I was instantly overwhelmed. Few structures have affected me with the degree of immediate sacredness that I felt here. I literally tingled, as my eyes took in the sights in the subdued light of the interior. The light inside was filtered through stained glass of gold and purple, and seemed to float in mesmerizing pockets of color. Every inch of wall, ceiling and pillar was intricately carved.

Rosslyn has been aptly described as a 'tapestry in stone.' The three renowned pillars were bathed in soft candleglow, aligned along the back of the alter. One senses immediately that a message is being offered, juxtaposed in time release to those who would be dedicated to the consuming task of unlocking the complex riddle.

The inner dimensions of the Chapel are somewhat deceptive. Measuring perhaps 60 meters by 30 meters, it has a larger sense of space than its actual area. Its entry level gives way to a subterranean chamber that preexisted the more ornate construction of the ground floor.

Soon after entering, I circled the expanse of the Chapel, observing the detail of each carving and pillar as one might view art works in a gallery. The energy and sense of space shifted dramatically as I moved about the miniature cathedral. Each corner and facet curiously projected a very different energy and, again, felt much larger than it measured. I had the sense of being in a labyrinth. The very tangible 'spirit of place' is quite stirring, and one feels driven to understand the juxtaposed message of the sacred puzzle within the ambience.

## Zipped Space

Rosslyn Chapel is said to be centered over a dimensional gateway, and certainly the perception of 'zipped' condensed space had been apparent to me. There are several parts of the chapel that had an energetic hum, but this description does not entirely fit the bill, as it was more felt than heard. Two were especially apparent, one in front of the alter, another behind the famed Apprentice Pillar.

The subterranean room had a serene energy, quite different from the upper floor. It felt far more ancient and very pagan. While a sense of well being is felt throughout, in no place was it more soothing than the cool darkness of the lower chamber.

## Peaceful

When I returned to the vestibule, I went to the center alter. The vaulted ceiling is in a barrel curve from organ loft to alter and is embellished with cubed rows of stars and flowers, each one slightly different. Despite a steady stream of visitors, I was able to find deep solitude as I sat contemplatively in one of the heavy oak pews aligned for church services. Most of the visitors seem to explore in respective silence and, like me, felt compelled to meditate in the sacred presence that permeates the chamber with a sense of peaceful timelessness. An energy of discernable silence, perhaps due to the geomantic pulses, seemed to white out sound waves. I found I was able to drift into deep states quite readily.

## Symbolism

The mixture of spiritual symbols is beyond the expected adornments of Christianity. The array of biblical characters and Masonic symbols share space with carvings of the devic Green Man, maize corn and aloe cacti. Here the mystery deepens. The corn and cacti, sacred symbols to the advanced spiritual tribes of Native Americans, were chiseled into the walls of Rosslyn Chapel four decades before the acknowledged discovery of America.

How could the builders have known of the sacred corn and cacti? The Chapel was built by Sir William St. Clair of Orkney Island, off the northwest coast of Scotland. His grandfather, Henry St. Clair, first Prince of Orkney, is claimed to have sailed to America in 1398, a full century before Columbus. While the claim is highly controversial, Native American folklore does provide some support to this theory. It occurred to me that perhaps the knowledge of the 'New World' carvings of cacti and maize, may have been gained through metaphysical transport, within the dimensional gate of Rosslyn. Yet, Inuit carvings dated from the 14th century depict a robed man with flowing hair, wearing a Templar cross.

The St. Clair's have owned the Chapel and their namesake Castle since its foundation. The 7th Earl of Rosslyn owns it still. The St. Clair's arrived with William the Conqueror, and the barony of Rosslyn was granted to them in the 12th century.

While the royal St. Clair family was powerful and wealthy, they were also metaphysically aware.

## Orkney Island: Home of the St. Clair's

The rugged and remote island of Orkney is a uniquely potent grid site. Legends claim an Atlantean Temple, and later a monastic school of an ancient secretive order, was placed there precisely because of its remote site and powerful energies. Certainly Sir William was aware of geomancy in his selection of the precise location for the Rosslyn Chapel. It crowns a telluric generator and borders the 'Rose' leyline connecting Orkney to the Compostela de la Santiago in Spain. Rosslyn Chapel was the final location of a seven-site pilgrimage that included cathedrals in France and Spain.

## The Seven Planetary Oracles

The seven sacred sites of Christian pilgrimage in sequence were Compostela de la Santiago (Spain), followed by five sites in France and one in Scotland: Notre Dame de Dalbade in Toulouse, Orleans Cathedral, Chartres Cathedral, Notre Dame de Paris, Amiens Cathedral and Rosslyn Chapel. Researcher Trevor Ravenscroft writes that these sites were all specifically ancient Druidic 'power' sites that were dedicated to planetary oracles. Each site possessed powerful 'earth magnetic pulses' combined with specific planetary alignments.

Sir William St. Clair is said to have been in at least two secretive orders of enlightened mystics that studied Gnostic belief and achieved spiritual mastery. One senses his energy and glimpses of his intent throughout the Chapel. Building Rosslyn became his obsession, and no expense was spared. The fruit of his labor is so over expressed that Rosslyn is more encoded message than chapel, more metaphysical than orthodox. It is, however, multifaceted, softened to be both, as was often the case during times of theo-political instability.

Perhaps the most celebrated of St. Clair's interior embellishments are the famed pillars. The Mason's Pillar and the ornate Apprentice Pillar, for which Rosslyn is renowned worldwide, are said to represent the pillars of Joachim and Boaz, which stood inside Solomon's Temple in Jerusalem. Indeed many scholars speculate that

Rosslyn Chapel is a reproduction of that temple, and that crusading Knights Templar had in fact unearthed Solomon's treasure centuries before from beneath the ruins of the dilapidated temple while seeking to recover sacred relics. Solomon's treasure was theorized to be the mysterious source of the Knights Templars' enormous wealth, taken to France and later to Scotland. Among the relics, the Arc of the Covenant and Holy Grail. It is a fact that sealed vaults are located beneath the Chapel, and it has long been speculated that recovered relics such as the Grail and Arc may have been placed there.

Interestingly, Prince William St. Clair is recorded as having personally overseen each construction and carving with meticulous control. Vaults and chambers were built beneath the structure and carefully sealed. The finest materials, craftsmen and stone sculptors were brought in from Europe. The village of Rosslyn was formed in the forty-year construction process of the Chapel. It ended before completion of the full plan, with Sir William's death and with the theo-political upheavals of the era. Yet even so, the centerpiece completed is fully sufficient to superbly tap and employ the vortex engine of the volcanic land into a mega portal and accessible dimensional stargate to those seekers who are sufficiently advanced in such metaphysical sciences to tap into the energy window at Rosslyn. The Chapel pulls in, stores and amplifies pristine telluric and grid energies with its sacred geometric structure and key geomantic placement.

The vortex energies here certainly predate the Chapel, by countless millennia. St. Clair brilliantly recognized them and constructed around them, as was done with many cathedrals of the era. Yet none were done with such multi tiered message, that goes well beyond the somewhat narrow constraints of theo-political Roman Christianity. As such, it would be limiting for the seeker to visit Rosslyn Chapel without spending time in the accompanying glen canyon. The former feeds the latter. The Chapel refines, stores and makes available the high frequency energy. The two are intricately connected, braided together into a singular higher purpose.

## The Glen

I was very fortunate to have booked a tour of Rosslyn with Jackie Queally of Celtic Tours. Jackie met me in the Chapel as I was completing a long meditation. We walked about the Chapel as she explained its history and meanings.

She told me about the importance of Rosslyn Glen, and about its powerful energies. We exited the Chapel and walked a steep wooded path that began at the north perimeter of the Chapel fence. The day contained all four seasons, and at this moment the sky opened to a clear blue, dotted with fluffy clouds … and, to paraphrase Scottish poet laureate Robert Burns, "To know a clear day in Scotland is to feel the smile of God."

After walking some 300 meters along housing parallel to the Glen, we exited the path and entered a lush, elfin forest. The devic presence was apparent and beautifully expressed in the ancient growth woods. All of the trees and plants were vibrant. We headed to two ancient and sacred Oak trees. The first view of them was adorned with an immediate sense of their noble presence. They stood in front of us, past a crumbling stone wall, like deities. These incredible trees dominated the forest. Estimated to be at least 700 years in age, their energy fields were regal. The trunks at base were easily nine feet in diameter. Their huge root banks were gnarled above ground into elfin looking domes, curling in serpentine undulations. One felt compelled to address them, sit in their presence, lean against their powerful trunks.

Further down, a stand of some two dozen mature Yew trees, also sacred to the Druids, created

a very different and yet equally nurturing energy. The beauty and aura of the trees and plants within this area are quite impressive. Green Man at his finest.

As we cleared the forested trail, the path gently switchbacks downward another 200 meters to the gurgling River North Esk. I was fortunate to have a knowledgeable local guide, as the path forks at several points. There were literally dozens of Neolithic carvings of concentric circles, single, double and triple spirals, and what appeared to be a large eye on the walls of one of several small sandstone caves. I have seen pictoglyphs of this sort in other telluric sites. It is my conjecture that perhaps the spirals were carved to indicate vortex and ley energies, the concentric circles, grid points. The canyon river bottom was full of them. The 90-foot vertical cliffs of bronze sandstone enclosed the energy, and it felt quite invigorating. One senses a spiritual renewal, a 'joie de vivre' walking along the moss covered banks of the clear gurgling waters, cascading gently over half submerged boulders. Colors were vibrant, plants were exquisitely formed.

Everything was bursting with life along the river. As we walked around the gentle curve of the North Esk, (more stream than river), the scenery serendipitously transformed. The golden bluffs were replaced by rolling slopes covered in orange-gold ferns and bright luminescent moss. A faerie garden lay ahead. A living verdant Monet! A natural stone barrier created a soft cascade, with white plumes of water gently cascading into silver pools. The rich loamy earth of the banks had a sweet musk that blended into an aromatic cocktail with the evergreen fragrance of fir that framed the upper canyon. I was intoxicated by the soft beauty of the scene before me. I was in the ornate beauty of nature at its finest, in a Cathedral whose spiritual energy equaled the Chapel above.

I was reluctant to leave there, but there was

more to see. I climbed from the river path onto the rather steep trail. We walked back into the lush enchanted forest trail to a site called lover's leap that contains another energy spring. Carved into the rock is the bust of the Green Man.

We continued to the ruins of Castle Rosslyn. The Castle was built on the overlook bluff of the Hawthorden Canyon (also called Rosslyn Glen). Parts of it have been restored and host special events. The grounds are quite majestic. A magnificent Yew tree adorns the entry. A beautiful stone bridge crosses the river, affording a magnificent view.

Arthur's Seat and the Salisbury Crags are very significant geological sites a few miles from Rosslyn. Some 340 million years ago, Arthur's Seat was an active volcano. It is renowned globally as a geological research site. It is also a powerful magnetic generator that disperses an energy matrix throughout the region.

### Reshel Grid

Through my site guide, I became interested in the amazing work of William Buehler. Buehler introduced me to the advanced technical concept of 'reshel' grids. These are essentially a grid matrix deliberately established through sacred geometry in sacred sites and over larger geodesic areas. These are self generating energy templates that allow for a multitude of frequencial portals. These are also keys to uniting the three major geodesic grids around the planet, as well as astral grids. Rosslyn contains a potent reshel grid within its structure.

### Conclusion

We began with a question. Now, let's end with an answer. Three reasons: 1) the builders had a message, 2) the builders stored something inside and 3) the builders wanted to house a star-

gate portal. The pre existing grid point and energy of place located precisely on the location of the Chapel is perhaps the most powerful point on the planetary geodesic grid, with concentric access to all twelve dimensional overlays.

All day the chilly wind has coiled around the mysterious hill at Rosslyn, drumming the Chapel with an ominous whir. The last of the daylight floats over the glen. The gray clouds lift slightly on the horizon to allow an incredible burning orange sunset. A breathtaking sight. A flock of sparrows thrust up and hover over the Hawthorn trees, like devic spirits, seeking refuge in nooks and turrets. Great gusts of wind sweep down from the hills at Rosslyn and then drive onward. I rise from the ornate iron in the grounds and carefully gaze over the Chapel one more time as I walk to the gate. Rosslyn remains an enigma, and I am ever enthralled.

### Tyberonn Channel

*"Rosslyn is a very special place, indeed, and its energies are an especially potent blend of geomantic and cosmic energies that converge precisely at this point. Here is a rare concentric apex. Because of this, within its structure lies a very ancient energy device that utilizes and refines the energy. It is not a relic from the Christian crusades.*

*The component is well below the structure of Rosslyn chapel. It is a circular vessel, both metallic and crystalline in composition, containing twelve half spheres around the rim of its circumference. It is very ancient. Its source and technology are of extraterrestrial origin. Its base is of a unique metallic alloy, having properties similar to gold and platinum, but with a much stronger magnetic field. The spheres are crystalline, each attuned to a dimensional field and projecting a strong electrical field. The structure facilitates dimensional travel to those adepts capable of achieving sufficiently high vibrational rates.*

*This component may be considered as energyware. It utilizes and refines the energies that culminate at this precise point. Rosslyn is set on a powerful telluric generator and is a major fulcrum point on the Planetary and Stellar Grids. This knowledge has been known in more advanced eras. The device is from Arcturian source, but constructed with Sirian B technology for use in balancing planetary energies in tune with the grid system. Other such devices exist around the planet, including placement below the Giza Pyramid, Lake Baikal and LakeTiticaca. Twelve primary units exist, and each of the 12 have 12 smaller units placed in energy locations in their proximity. All are placed under primary telluric points. These are in harmonic oscillation.*

*The location of Rosslyn Chapel is very specific. St. Clair was in direct communication with an Angelic Host of Ascended Masters, who guided the location selection and every aspect of the coded construction of the Chapel.*

*The Chapel at Rosslyn contains a full spectrum dimensional gate. There is a primary vortex in the center of the structure, in front of the alter. There are five smaller vortexes with unique frequencies surrounding and circulating the major vortex, which contains the portal gate.*

*Rosslyn Chapel is intricately connected to the Rosslyn Glen. The powerful leyline, that runs through the glen along the river, encircles the Chapel but does not intersect it. This provides a double matrix of clockwise and counterclockwise spin around the mound that emits the vortex complex into the Chapel and supports the pattern of the dimensional portal.*

*The Castle nearby is also connected to the energy of the Chapel. It stores the energy of the founding St. Clair and those who protected the*

*site for centuries. The Castle still houses a living, conscious energy of protection, vital to the portal located in Rosslyn Chapel. You see, the energy in a grid-fulcrum vortex, such as Rosslyn, is multidimensional, thus timeless. Its energy of protection is a dimensional insert, a conscious, living hologram.*

*The grid overlay separating dimensional frequencies is particularly translucent, within the unique fountain of electro-magnetic energy at Rosslyn. As such, a dimensional overlap occurs, and the linear space-time continuum is weakened. A space-time window occurs within a specific frequency. The vibrational blending of the electro-magnetic ley, planetary and stellar grids creates this dimensional overlap.*

*The energy within Rosslyn Chapel is generated and directly feeds a series of energy sites in Europe and Britain. The majority of these sites have majestic Cathedrals constructed over them, and they pulse with great energies.*

*Rosslyn also both sends and receives energy from specific global locations, from a pulsed system, a more ancient system. This function was based in part on a solar gridwork. But as the sun continually evolves, it is not now what it was then in aspect, and as such this system is not in exact synchronicity.*

*The channel has asked whether certain portals require guardianship or protection. We say that this is not necessarily the case. At one period in your planet's evolution, it was germane. In current times it is not required. It is appurtenant to see such sites as holy, to see them as great beacons of light, to imbue them with congruous intent. Are they not interactive shrines, are they not of great assistance? Indeed they are, and you must honor them accordingly and see them in that aspect, just as it is equally important to see each one of humanity as such, you see?*

*The channel asks about the nature of what is termed 'reshel grids.' The reshel points are very feminine points of self-directed energy. Because of such, they draw upon all they require. They draw upon the masculine, they draw upon the balance, they draw upon the neutral, they draw upon the past and they draw upon the future. They are that which is in timelessness. They are installations of light. They are permanent to the Earth in essence, and when one recognizes their power, they can harness it for appropriate purpose.*

*This magnanimous system is one that belongs to the polarity of the divine feminine. These operate to maintain the femine aspect, as it is and once was. In areas where it becomes dormant, the reshels assist in resuscitation, in order to achieve the desired balance.*

*Now, there are other systems that belong strictly to the masculine polarity of the planet. Where this falls into disarray or reticence, they will also come forward. Now, it is the reshels that are in prominent activation, in prominent activity. These are in place in both natural and man made structures, such as the great ley point cathedrals and the great points of light. Power points and sacred sites as you term them.*

*Reshels are the frequencial keys that harmonically intertwine and integrate the other grid systems. The Templar, Druid, Egyptian and Mayan understood their purpose. These savants would align them to planetary and stellar systems. As such, the stellar sytsems could align the Earth, and the Earth could align the stars.*

*The terrestrial essence of the reshel is such that it is both electromagnetic and geometric. One creates the other, and the other supports*

*the first, you see? The more that humanity understands its own consciousness, the more the geometry becomes multi dimensional, and so the geometric expression of these will upshift in kind. It will become first one, then the other, just as the Earth is now the 3$^{rd}$ dimension and then the 5$^{th}$. What is it that will move it to the 5$^{th}$? Not simple consciousness but the activation of the consciousness. The activation of the consciousness comes from the understanding of the grid, and the activation of that grid, which in turn compliments the cosmos, and is reflected back again.*

*Reshels are not recognized or understood in most parts of the world. When humanity gains greater understanding of this system, a great quickening will take place, and the quickening will lead to expansion. Once all of these grids are recognized, all of the others will come into a bright global synergy. The entire system will then have more power. There will be a surge both in the spirit of humanity and upon the earth. Reshels are self-generating and self-directed. The human understanding and realization of the grid system in itself will create a resonate harmonic that becomes part of the system, in a manner of speaking. When that occurs, the reshels expand in frequency projection. The reshels attract and pull in brilliant energies of a celestial nature. It is a conscious system, a living system, that calls to itself those that follow. It calls to itself those sacred places, and it is the grid system itself that directs the activity within it. There are many, such as the channel, that are drawn to understand these, and we tell you that the overlay complexity of the grid systems play a pivotal role in the planetary ascension. You are beloved."*

... and so it is.

# Glastonbury ~ Vortex of Avalon

Located in England's southwest corner is the legendary village of Glastonbury. Rich in both myth and history, Glastonbury is one of the most spellbinding places in the world. Recognized as a spiritual center since the Megalithic Age, it is the site of the first Christian church in the British Isles and claimed to be the Avalon of King Arthur.

The small village of Glastonbury itself is lovely and quaint, cradled among a series of velvety, green hills. The tallest of these hills is the famous Glastonbury Tor, an oblong hill formation, with the impressive remains of a church tower on top dedicated to Archangel Michael. At the foot of the Tor is Chalice Well and the spherical dome of Chalice Hill. Below in the town center lie the ruins of the famous Glastonbury Abbey, site of Joseph of Arimathea's church and the gravesite of the legendary King Arthur. On the west entrance to the village is Wearyall Hill, location of the legendary Thorn tree.

Glastonbury was a major religious center long before the time of King Arthur or Joseph of Arimathea. The Druids used the Tor from 2500 BC as an initiation center for priests. Megalithic Age remains dating from 5,000 BC reveals Glastonbury as the site of a massive, astrological calendar atop the Tor, combining a stone circle with solar and lunar alignments, and a land-carved zodiac map ten miles in diameter.

Druid priests and society considered Glastonbury their 'holy Mecca,' and understandably so. Complete with temples, stone circles, fertility sites and a sacred goddess center, Druid high priests and high priestesses were trained, initiated and centered at the Tor and Chalice Well. The Chalice wellspring was considered to be the earth source for the goddess, Gaia. Her red waters were considered sacred and used for healing.

## Glastonbury's Vortex Sites

There are four powerful energy sites within the township, each site activating one of the upper chakras, which is in itself an extremely interesting phenomenon. The Earth currents in the Glastonbury sites are all 'electrical' vortexes, meaning the flow is outward. These four vortex sites work synergistically to balance all four upper chakras and resonate in unison as the World Heart Center. These currently resonate as follows:

- 7th Chakra – Crown: The Tor (Archangel Michael Tower)
- 6th Chakra – Third Eye: The Chalice Well (Kings Court)
- 5th Chakra – Throat : Wearyall Hill (Sacred Thorn Vortex)
- 4th Chakra – Heart: Abbey Ruins (Lady Chapel)

Three of the vortexes listed above – the Tor, Chalice Well and Lady Chapel – are created by the spinning effect as the Michael and Mary ley lines intersect. These sites also contain myriad other energetic sources, but those equally sacred energies are not telluric in nature. The vortex at Wearyall Hill occurs only on the Michael line, as the Mary line is absent. Precisely at the Holy Thorn, an energetic node occurs with a powerful, eight-foot-wide earth-current vortex, spinning upward.

In addition to the primary power points in Glastonbuty, numerous other energy centers occur. The locations in Glastonbury I feel resonate to the first three chakras are:

- 3rd Chakra – Solar Plexus: 'Egg Stone' (northwest side of the Tor slope)
- 2nd Chakra – Creative Center: Chalice Spring Wellhead (Chalice Well Gardens)
- 1st Chakra – Base Center: Whitesprings wellhead (west side of Chilkwell Street)

The combined Glastonbury energies resonate as

a heart center and accordingly vibrate to the number four. Now, I must include the caveat that chakric designations to energy sites are relative to the individual. Perhaps it is more appropriate to say that the area of Glastonbury is a major vortex-portal matrix, and within this complex all chakras are activated and aligned.

## Cradle of Christianity

Local legends claim that the first Christian church in Britain was formed in Glastonbury by Jesus' uncle, Joseph of Arimathea, and that Jesus himself was brought here as a boy to be schooled by esoteric Druid priests. Legends further claim that Glastonbury was temporary home to the 'Holy Grail,' and housed the great 'Ark of the Covenant.' While certain claims are perhaps folklore, others are supported by some credible historical evidence. Although notable historians are divided on these claims, there is ample academic evidence to support the presence of Joseph of Arimathea in Glastonbury, for England was part of the Roman Empire at the time of Christ's birth.

Roman occupation on the British Isles actually began around 55 BC and continued for 400 years. The Romans invaded England to take possession of the burgeoning mining activity in order to supply their vast military needs. At this time, Glastonbury was an inland island, surrounded by a great tidal-fed lake and therefore directly accessible from the sea. While Romans conducted mining operations in nearby areas, Glastonbury Isle served more as a center for religious sects and as a refuge for healing, due to its well-known curative springs. The Romans recognized the healing properties of the spring and are credited with building the original well basin.

The nearby counties of Cornwall and Somerset were the principal sites of Roman mining, where lead and tin were extracted and smelted. Ancient remains of tin mines still remain in several area locations.

According to historians, Joseph of Arimathea, uncle of Jesus and provider of his tomb, was a wealthy tin merchant who had, on numerous occasions, come to the British Isles in his business capacity. Southwest England had active lead, iron, zinc, tin and copper mines from the Bronze Age forward and was the primary supplier of tin and lead to the Roman Empire by 15 BC. (Bronze is an alloy of copper and tin.)

## Jesus in Glastonbury

As a metal trader, Joseph of Arimathea had business dealings in Roman-occupied Somerset and Cornwall, and made numerous trips to Britain on the regular ore transport vessels. Popular legend claims he brought the boy Jesus with him on several of his trips. The Cornish Celts claimed that Joseph of Arimathea left Jesus, by divine order, at the Druidic college at Place-on-the-Roseland peninsula in Cornwall. Several pictographs dated to 500 AD on the arched door of the Saxon and Norman church in the township of Place, Cornwall, depict the scene of a young Jesus arriving and receiving instruction.

After the crucifixion of Christ in 33 AD, Joseph of Arimathea sought refuge in the British Isles with his family and a small entourage of believers. Some claim Saint Mary was among this group. The sacred and powerful Lady Chapel in the Glastonbury Abbey Ruins is named in her honor.

## Wearyall Hill

Joseph of Arimathea reputedly carried with him a staff made from an Israeli Hawthorn tree. The story goes that he thrust his staff into the moist ground at his campsite in Glastonbury Isle on Wearyall Hill, and within days it took root. He interpreted this as a sign from God to stay there and to establish his home and the first Christian church in Glastonbury, which he did in 37 AD. The descendents of the Glastonbury Thorn tree still grow on Wearyall Hill and near the Tor. This particular variety of Hawthorn blossoms twice annually, at Christmas and at Easter, as do varieties of Hawthorn found only in Palestine and Israel. Interestingly, no indigenous English varieties of Hawthorn bloom at Christmas time.

Some 1,500 years ago, like the Tor and Chalice Hill, the oblong Wearyall Hill was an island in the great tidal lake of Avalon. The Michael line flows freely along its base and up to the Holy Thorn. At the Thorn, an impressive spiral of energy fountains upward. Renowned Cornish dowser and author Hamish Miller confirmed both the ley line path and the spiral energy fountain at the Holy Thorn in 1997. Miller traces the ley line across England in his book *The Sun and the Serpent*. He further notes that the ley line turns at a sharp angle toward the Abbey, precisely at the Holy Thorn. I found the energy there to be very invigorating and crisp. The lushness of the hill is similar to the Tor, and meditation comes easily.

Despite the proximity of the entrance road some 350 meters below the Thorn, I could hear only the serene flow of breeze while on the hill. The silence and serenity were unique and somewhat striking. In the perimeter of the Holy Thorn, I was able to lapse into alpha state immediately. Visions and inner voices were enhanced, and the energy fountain was mesmerizing. Wearyall Hill and the Holy Thorn resonate to the fifth chakra.

The ancient remains of a church and chapel have been discovered on Wearyall Hill, and it is thought to be the initial location of Joseph's Waddle church. Sacred Earth, indeed!

**The Holy Grail**

Joseph is said to have brought with him a precious relic that was displayed on the church's altar – the chalice from which Jesus and the 12 disciples drank in the Last Supper, and which Joseph used to collect Christ's blood at the Crucifixion. This chalice became the legendary Holy Grail proliferated in Arthurian legend, symbol of man's eternal quest for perfection. He is said to have buried the grail near the Chalice Well, which caused the well to flow red, signifying the healing blood of Christ.

**The Blue Chalice**

There are fascinating connections between Chalice Well, Glastonbury, the 'Holy Grail' and the Ark of the Covenant. In the early 1900s, a chalice was found in Bridie's Well in Glastonbury and determined by the British museum to be 'consistent with' Syrian or Middle Eastern artifacts from the period of 100 BC - 300 AD. An incredible sequence of events led to the discovery of this so-called Blue Chalice, which received great notoriety and became the topic of global interest and study. Today it is stored in a protected chamber of the St. Michael Retreat House on the grounds of the Chalice Well Gardens. Members of the Chalice Well Trust are able to request appointments to see and, on rare occasions, hold the chalice, under the guidance of the trustees. Many reputed clairvoyants and psychics have lauded the chalice and claim it to be connected to Christ, while others claim it to have extraterrestrial origins. All believe it emits a strong vibratory field. In Spring 2001, I had the great opportunity to have one hour alone with the Blue Chalice, and it had a profound effect on me, as an undeniable pure energy radiated from the precious crystalline vessel. It has an unusual texture and color, and is unlike anything I have ever touched before.

**Isle of Avalon: Camelot**

The Chalice Well and the Holy Grail became center points of the Arthurian legends. The actual site of Camelot is believed to be at Cadbury Mound near Glastonbury. Arthur's birth place is

Tintagel Castle on the nearby rugged Cornwall coast. Arthur's final hours were spent at the Tor, near the Chalice Well, and his body was buried at Glastonbury Abbey. Arthur's gravesite is marked with a plaque at the abbey ruins.

The Arthurian myths are well known, but what is less known is the historic evidence of the actual existence of King Arthur in Glastonbury, Cornwall and eastern Wales. The epic story has been so sensationally projected in print and film that, to the general masses, it is merely a wonderful fable. In fact, it is much more. Arthur lived and was a Christ Consciousness. The written works, coming centuries later, were in a true sense a channeled symbolism of the sojourn and trinity of man in the three-dimensional plane.

Obviously, the actual story lines of King Arthur are symbolic truths and probably not his actual life story. They served as a metaphoric treatise on the struggles of man searching for truth. It is, and was, a repetition of the inserted living hologram of the Man/God passion. The symbology of the Arthurian epic reveals a slightly different aspect of the Christos hologram, a mirror of that of Jesus the Christ. Subtle correlations exist. For example, the 12 knights of the Round Table symbolize the 12 disciples, and Guinevere being tempted with the forbidden fruit symbolizes Eve in the Garden of Eden – just two of literally dozens of correlations that subtly mirror the story of Christ.

## Grid System

Glastonbury is the principal of three portals within the UK. These portals – Iona, Findhorn and Glastonbury – form a triangular energy grid that injects the enclosed ley lines with an infusion of cosmic energy that accelerates Earth's vibratory rate and thus her ascension. These portals are anchored by the intent of resident Lightworkers working with the portal sites.

Glastonbury's placement as a portal makes it a

node in a global triune that extends energy lines to many sacred centers worldwide. Glastonbury is, in fact, one of the 12 sacred global centers. That is, both a planetary and celestial chakra. Its energies are multi-faceted, as a tremendous influx of ley energy, earth currents, anionic plasma and electrical vortexes connect to create an incredible force field. The energetic cocktail can be overwhelming, and it extends about 3.5 miles out from the town center.

The template for our Earth contains three grids. The three become the one. The emerging crystalline gird, or 'ascension grid,' is composed of a lattice of triangulated pentagons and covers the Earth in a geodesic matrix. This pattern of 3-D and 5-D pentagonal shapes interlock to create a multi-dimensional geodome sphere over the planet. In truth, it extends to 12 dimensions. The connecting apexes of these triangles and pentagons are points of energy focus. The grid lines joining these apexes conduct an energy flow which can be regulated. Glastonbury is a primary apex that functions in all three Earth grids and, as such, becomes a portal-vortex.

An interesting side note to the triangulation of apex energy points is that indigenous people such as the Hopi, Lakota and Aborigines have said for centuries that sacred sites always come in threes.

## Ley Lines

The Druid Masters were keenly in tune with Earth energies and carefully identified and tracked the sacred energy lines called 'leys' throughout Great Britain and Western Europe. The most notable of these are the Michael and Mary lines. Even before being given Christian names and associated with Archangel Michael, the Druids and Celts discerned the male and female identities of the ley energies. They assigned Celtic names of deities of light and protection to the lines.

Ley lines are, by definition, amassed flowing

telluric energy. Electrical in nature, they are the nervous system of the planet. The Michael line is the instrument of Archangel Michael, manifestations of whom have appeared along the Michael line for centuries.

The lines can be detected by dowsing and, in fact, have been mapped for millennia. They are discernable and carry a vibrant electrical pulse. I find ley energy identifiable by a projected tangible sense of 'well being' all around the areas of their path. Plant life thrives, animals seem happier, and the air seems to 'sparkle' in the proximity of ley energy.

In England, the Druids recognized the unique swirling vortex formed when two ley lines intersected. At these sites, they established sacred ritual points, initiation centers or healing refuges to utilize this amplified energy. Worship and spirituality were particularly enhanced at the powerful intersections of the Mary and Michael ley lines.

## Sacred Geometry and Freemason Architecture

Christian Freemasons came along centuries later and built churches (using sacred geometry) on top of the ancient Pagan sites situated along the ley lines, vortexes chosen by the earthwise Druid Shamans eons before. Historians speculate this was done to assist in converting the Pagan masses to Christianity. However, the illuminati amongst the Freemasons had a more divine method than simple political sway. They were aware of the amplified spiritual energy of these vortex sites and chose them with intuitive intent for construction of the great cathedrals. The amplified ley line energy flowing in these British cathedrals built along the Michael ley line is simply magnificent and must be experienced! Several cathedrals actually have the ley line channeled symmetrically down the exact center aisle of the structure. The energy is curved into circular patterns inside the brilliantly designed cathedral domes and circulates inside throughout the vaulted ceilings.

Saint Paul's in London is one such example. The powerful, reverent emotions of the thousands upon thousands of worshipers is imprinted upon, and further amplifies, the sacred energy pulsing inside many of these Freemason-designed cathedrals. The sacred geometry used in the architecture enhances these energies, somewhat in the fashion of the stone circles.

Among the beautiful cathedrals in Britain ingeniously positioned over ley line vortex crossings and nodes are Saint Paul's Cathedral, Westminster Abbey, Salisbury Cathedral, Wells Cathedral and Canterbury Cathedral.

## Earthen Zodiac Carvings

An additional Glastonbury mystery was revealed in 1927 when Katherine Maltwood, a local sculptor and illustrator, (re)discovered the 'Glastonbury Zodiac' while surveying fields surrounding Glastonbury. Also referred to as the 'Glastonbury Giants,' the zodiac had actually been referenced in various writings since medieval times but was thought to be merely part of the Glastonbury lore. Maltwood painstakingly retraced the impressive and undeniable landscape carving. These zodiac tables, etched into the actual landscape in a circular pattern about ten miles in diameter, correctly and chronologically template the twelve zodiac signs using existing landmarks, hills, rivers and land-etched boundaries.

## The Chalice Well

My favorite site in Glastonbury is the Chalice Well. The grounds are simply beautiful, a lush living spray of flowers and fountains with soft, healing energy. The famous well is located at the back of the ample garden. There are benches located throughout for relaxing and taking in the beauty. The gardens have a comforting feel and a vibrational purity. There are three distinct yet harmonic energy sources within the gardens:

- Ley line energies forming the vortex in the King's Court.
- Anionic energy formed by the Chalice well-spring and flowing waters.
- Soft energy field of the vibrant trees and plants.

All of these have tangibly different effects that vary from meditative and gently relaxing to vibrant electric intensity.

Once inside the enclosure of the Chalice Well Gardens, one feels serene and secure. The grounds are a beautifully manicured English garden, adorned with vibrant flowers, both colorful and fragrant. Two enormous Yew trees form a strong field amidst the blended energies and stand like Guardians to the King's Courtyard, where the Michael and Mary ley lines intersect and form an intense vortex. Yew and Oak trees were sacred to Druids, who sought them out for their strong protective energy. These sacred trees were considered as dignitaries, housing the living devic spirit of 'Green Man.' Their presence is soft and protective within the enclosed gardens of the Chalice Well. One is drawn to touch them and offer thanks and love, which is immediately returned in a soft loving energy-wave response from the very aware guardian Yews.

King's Court is certainly the strongest 'electric' point in the Garden. The energy near the vortex in the King's Courtyard is further embellished by ionic charges released from a seven-foot cascade of iron rich water, flowing downhill from the well. This water line energy adds both an ionic and electromagnetic charge to the vortex created by the intersecting ley lines. This vortex is rather compact, and is contained within an oscillating diameter of three to four meters. The King's Court is a potent third eye center.

The Chalice Well holds another dense energy around the wellhead area. The compact energy field is at the upthrust node of the spring, where the water movement forms a discernable anionic lattice. The Goddess speaks from within that field and is most tangible there. The wellhead is at the rear of the gardens with a perfect view of the Michael Tower atop the Tor, just a few hundred meters away. The wellhead is adorned with the sacred geometry symbol of the Vesica Pisces and is secluded by trees and shrubbery to allow for quiet meditation. There is a clear, definite presence of the feminine Guardian spirit. One feels enveloped in a protective womb of cool, moist air within this area. It is a place of creativity, rejuvenation and vitality.

The sloping western side of the Chalice Hill Dome is within the fenced garden perimeter. There are numerous areas for sitting on a bench or lying on the grass amidst pastel perfumed flowers. The devic kingdom is very present here, and one can sense faeries and happy little elves everywhere in the garden, flying around the spring, cascades and blooms, chiming an almost audible elfin laughter in the sculpted rock cascades of both the King's Court and Chalice Hill. Here, on the sloping sides of Chalice Hill, the 'veil' is very thin, easily penetrated by focused intent.

Chalice Hill is a place for visions and manifestation. One can recline comfortably on the soft, thick grass along the Chalice Hill and drift comfortably, watching the sway of branches and floating clouds. Prayers are quickened, and meditative states occur effortlessly.

The Chalice Well itself is very therapeutic. The waters have been thoroughly tested and analyzed. The spring water is slightly radioactive, rich in iron and carries a detectable magnetic charge.

There are countless documented accounts of healings taking place. For example, in the mid-1700s, an English aristocrat was healed of a long-term infirmity after he was 'instructed' by an angelic apparition to drink from the well for five consecutive weeks. The highly publicized cure created a renewed notoriety for the Chalice Well. Visitors streamed in from all areas of Europe to drink the miraculous waters.

The Druids considered the 'Red Spring' as holy water centuries before the Romans were recorded as building wellhead facilities around the sacred red spring. A stone pathway connected the red spring and the white spring to the stone circle atop the Tor. The Druids considered the red and white springs innately connected. The Michael line passes through both of them, while the feminine Mary line passes only through the red spring.

The male and female ley lines intertwine from the Chalice Well garden up the Tor in a symbolically fertile embrace of masculine and feminine energy in this sacred space.

It is noteworthy to mention that less than 100 meters from the Chalice Well flows a second and uniquely related well, the 'White Spring.' The white spring is a calcium- and energy-rich well that flows at the foot of the Tor. Rich in minerals, it is interestingly devoid of iron and has a sparkling clear, white hue. Sadly it is not part of the protected Chalice Well complex, or within the confines of the National Trust property of the Tor. The white spring is privately owned, and its water has been sold and bottled at various times as a mineral water. Its wellhead is near a stone building that has recently been both a pub and restaurant. The white spring waters flow through a cemented trough along the floor of the stone dwelling before emptying into the city water drainage.

The white spring waters bubble up from underneath the sacred chalk earth of the Tor and carry sacred water of a masculine vibration. The relationship to the Chalice Well is undeniable, yet few sacred site listings mention the white spring. There is now a grass roots movement to close off

Chilkwell Street and create a massive Glastonbury Park, connecting the Tor, Chalice Well and Whitesprings. An even more ambitious thought is to connect them all to the Glastonbury Abbey ruins, less than three quarters of a mile away. While the latter remains logistically unlikely, the concept of connecting the white and red springs at the foot of the Tor is conceivable.

The misappropriation and desecration of sacred sites saddens and frustrates me. The placement of a pub and road right through the middle of the sacred Avebury Stone Circle, the disregard of Glastonbury Whitesprings and the commercialization of the vortex sites in Sedona are all issues that, perhaps in the ascension to come, will be corrected. Our thoughts and actions can make it so, as we come to recognize these living energies.

It is possible to stay within the grounds of the Chalice Well by becoming a 'Companion' of the Chalice Well Trust. The annual cost for membership is approximately $30. Once enrolled, one can stay on the grounds of the Chalice Well in the little St Michael Retreat house, a wonderful 17th century dwelling with conference room additions and a newly renovated dining area. It can hold up to eleven guests and operates as a self-catering vegetarian B & B, with rooms as low as £17 per night. It gives one access to gardens and well after the gates close to the public at 5 p.m. I highly recommend it. The gardens at night are magnificent … and very active!

The gracious resident 'guardians' of the Well manage the operations and various functions of the Chalice Well Gardens, bookstore and St Michael Retreat. The courteous and responsible staff teamed with the site's programs contributes to the ambience and sense of well being reflected at the Chalice Gardens and Well. Each staff member exudes a spirituality and love of place that adds to the visit.

**The Tor**

Just across Well Lane Street from the Chalice Well lies the magnificent and fabled Tor. The Tor has long been recognized for its sacred power and is perhaps the most powerful site in the UK. That is quite a statement in a land teeming with ley lines and sacred energies of every genre.

The 800-foot Tor stands like a crown, towering over Glastonbury. As the highest point in the area, it is a stunning view when clearly silhouetted against the sky, with its pinnacled top sporting the sturdy, somewhat phallic, tower of the St. Michael Church at its crest.

Much has been written about the Tor. Appropriately so, as legend has long claimed the Tor to be the magical entrance to the celebrated Celtic underworld of 'Annwn,' crowned with an elaborate stone circle at its apex. The latter claim has been supported by recent archeological digs that suggest a stone circle was in place around 2000 BC, before being toppled by an earthquake.

There is strong evidence of the Tor being a religious site as early as 5000 BC. Some present day Druids claim that the Atlanteans built a holy temple atop the Tor, in a circular pattern supported by twelve columns and a dome, similar in design to the Greek Temple of Apollo. They claim it still exists there in a dimensional fold that is hidden within the misty veils of the portal atop the Tor.

The Druids and ancient Celts used the Tor as a place of sacred initiation for their priests and holy Archdruids. These ancient mystics were keenly in tune with Earth energies and were aware of how such areas could be utilized for healing and inner discovery. Celtic legends claimed the Tor to be hollow and inhabited by spirits and undergods of the Celtic spirit world, Annwn. The western slope of the Tor is said to contain a tunnel that led to the entrance to Annwn, the 'parallel world.' A huge boulder called the 'Egg Stone' marks the entrance to Annwn. It is located on the northwest side of the Tor, about 100 meters from the ground level. The Egg Stone does possess a unique electrical vibration and seems to radiate warmth, even in the cold, wet winter season. A Holy Thorn tree grows near it, brightly adorned with the prayer ties of New Age pilgrims.

The Tor labyrinth rite involves a symbolic seven-tiered walk on a sometimes discernable, steep and often slippery path that winds unconventionally around the Tor. Each completed lap represents a movement in consciousness, both correlating to the chakras and symbolizing man's backward and forward progressions in the struggle for enlightenment. There are several versions of how the labyrinth maze should be walked. The most popular route begins near the bottom of the Tor just above the entrance at Wellhouse Lane, at a large fallen standing stone just past the first bench. A clear path leads to the third level, where one takes the first turn at a stone mark on the steep vertical path. Here, one turns clockwise to begin the first lap. The encircling paths take a pattern of 3,2,1,4,7,6,5 ending at the fifth level. Prayer and permission is sought to proceed to each new level, where a new guardian guides the initiate. As the path winds upward, it becomes more difficult to follow in the thick grass and steep inclines. I found the spiraled labyrinth walk mind-altering, almost psychotropic. The Tor emits a similar charm to the ley energies that embrace its girth.

The generally straight-flowing Michael and Mary ley lines run in a most interesting pattern on the Tor. Cornish dowser and author Hamish Miller intricately mapped the Michael and Mary ley lines in 1997. He recorded that the lines traced an elaborate 'in and out' pattern between the Tor and Chalice Well. The lines seem to form a 'mating' of the energies. The Mary line forms the shape of an open cup. The Michael line forms a phallic shape entering the cup pattern.

The implications are quite astonishing. The Tor was, in fact, a center of the Pagan Beltane fertility celebrations, and the male and female ley lines seem to be following suit. The energetic synergy of the ley line bonding creates a virtual fountain, a very formidable orgasmic fountain of fertile energy that is both strengthening and expanding in its effect on the human body and mind. It is easily felt; the energy is potent and vital in its effect on the aura, body physical and spirit, blending the trinity of body, mind and spirit. The sensation is a total spiritual uplifting through the crown.

Although unusually shaped, the Tor is a natural geological formation. The top is a hard quartz capstone atop a softer chalkstone. The unusual structure was likely formed by the flow of the red and white springs. The whale-shaped Tor is adorned energetically with a powerful blend of several Earth energies – ley lines, ionic fields from the spring flows, quartz amplification from the capstone and the soothing ionic field of the calcite. The coiled nature of the ley line pattern on the sloping Tor also tend to amplify spiral energy culminating in an increased energy outlet along the top.

The presence of Archangel Michael exists and can manifest within that intense field near the Tower dedicated to his namesake. The portal holds a host of entities waiting to work with the sincere seeker. I have been to many locations of sacred energies in the world, and I can say that my first and most powerful vision (and only time I truly saw the face of my spirit guide Lam) was atop the Tor. The sense of magic, of Christ, of Joseph of Arimathea and of Camelot are here, and words cannot describe such a sacredly harmonious mélange of beautiful feelings. Go there, visit. Make the pilgrimage to Glastonbury. The site of the Tor rises above the landscape 20 minutes before one arrives by car. It is the beacon of Michael.

You may wish to take a waterproof jacket, a small blanket or tarp and foam earplugs. Often the Tor is crowded around the Michael Tower, and solitude for prayer quests and meditation is more easily found by moving a few meters down the ample slopes. The earplugs will create the uninterrupted silence, and the blanket offers a dry seat on the often rain-soaked grass. Rain can come up quickly and pass just as rapidly. This part of England generally gets the sunniest weather in the UK, but don't be dismayed if it does rain. The people of Somerset have a saying: "If you don't like the weather, just wait five minutes and it'll change."

There is no finer expression of natural beauty than a sunny day in Somerset. Likewise, there is no softer rain than the rains that green the Tor. The Tor shines. Brilliantly. For eternity.

**Abbey Ruins**

The Glastonbury Abbey was once the Crown Jewel of English cathedrals. Magnificent in architecture and the center of Christian pilgrimages, Glastonbury Abbey held a prominent and sacred position in the Christian world. Still today revered as holy grounds, the Abbey ruins are the site of the first Christian Church in Europe and are reputed to be the burial site of Joseph of Arimathea, The Virgin Mary, St. Patrick and King Arthur. And legend claims both the Holy Grail and the Ark of the Covenant were kept in the Abbey grounds.

The most powerful location on the Abbey grounds is the hallowed Lady Chapel, found just outside the museum exit, in the main body of ruins in the subterranean section of the cathedral assemblage. It is intact on three sides and topped by a low stone ceiling. A symmetrical stone altar occupies the center of the small chapel.

The Lady Chapel is located at a precise crossing of the Michael and Mary ley lines, in what was clearly the most 'Christian' employment of telluric energy in the religious mecca of Glastonbury. The heavy stone altar in the Lady Chapel was placed in the exact center of the Michael and Mary vortex. As such, it radiates a very bright, telluric energy.

## Heart Center

The seeking pilgrim should ask permission to enter and acknowledge the living energy through a prayer, offering or blessings. Despite the location now having a rather historical, museum ambience, a surprising number of visitors do recognize the sacredness of this small room and enter with respect. Many kneel at the altar in meditative prayer. In this setting, it seems most appropriate. If you place your hands on the altar, you will feel the pulsing energy emanations. Metal jewelry, rings, talismans, even water, will receive and store the energy emanations when placed on the stone altar.

The chapel and altar are still fully intact and are one of the few enclosed vortex sites I have visited. The subtle energy character of this site is different from the other open-air vortexes in Glastonbury. It is softer, a more gentle opening, influenced by the Christian chapel built around it and the saints who lived and died within its timeless telluric fountain. There is an angelic presence in the chapel, and this enclosed area and its vortex exude a deep serenity, both joy and sadness, like Holy Mary's heart. It is her presence I felt.

The Abbey ruins are on a sizeable tract of land, some 36 acres in the center of Glastonbury and owned by the Church of England. After buying a ticket at the walled entrance, you can visit a modern, well-appointed museum, charting the history of the Abbey. Complete with artifacts and large photographs, the chronological text describes each phase of the Abbey's history, and an impressive model of how the Abbey appeared before its 16th century destruction is on display.

The museum exits into the lush green grounds surrounding the great Abbey. The experience is surprisingly powerful. Despite the museum entrance and initial touristy impression, the aura of serenity and divine spirit is immediate and profound. The high walls surrounding the grounds seem to have kept out time itself, giving the enclosed area a feel of an era long past. The ambience is tranquil and holy, and a strange 'white' silence seems to blanket the grounds in a gossamer veil. Street noise is muffled or not heard against the backdrop of birds faintly chirping in the ruins. Flowers are in bloom year-round, and over 250 massive and beautifully expressed trees are scattered throughout the grounds. There are Yews, Oaks, Holly, Fir and Maple, all with a tangible presence. These centuries-old guardians are equally impressive with or without their seasonal leaves. Their reaching sprays of bare limbs make symmetrical silhouettes against the gray winter skies. I am always compelled to acknowledge and sit by them, enjoying their stunning colors in spring, summer and particularly autumn.

The ruins of the great Abbey are imprinted with emanations of sacred energy and imbued with dramatic Christian and English history. The prayers of monks and the lives of thousands are woven into the tapestry of time all through the Abbey grounds. One can easily visualize chubby monks draped in woolen robes scurrying outside the kitchen, and the senior abbots in prayer inside the cathedral walls.

There is a spring on the grounds of the Abbey, recognizable by a stone basin past the main body of buildings. It produces a soft, surrounding cloud of ionic plasma typical of aquifer fed springs. Its energy fountain is cool and relaxing, and there is usually a heavy wooden bench close by – a lovely place to sit and drift into soft tranquility.

The arteries of both ley lines pulse from northeast to southwest through the grounds.

After the Lady Chapel, they stream the breadth of the grounds to the southwest corners, up toward Wearyall Hill and the Chalice Well.

I cannot sufficiently describe the serenity available on the Abbey grounds. It is more than serenity; it is an inter-dimensional portal of peace that opens the heart. It is irradiated by an influx of cosmic heart energy, beaming through the portal above.

Mother Mary, Joseph of Arimathea and St. Patrick are said to have been buried near the site of the Lady Chapel. A prominent stone, bearing both the names of Mary and Joseph, is still visible within the walls of the Chapel.

## Abbey Construction

The great Abbey was built according to a prehistoric, Atlantean tradition of sacred geometry known to the Freemasons of the Middle Ages. According to Henrietta Bernstein in her superb book *Ark of the Covenant – Holy Grail,* the proportions of the Abbey relate to the principal numbers of the Masonic sun square. These numbers symbolize various aspects of spiritual energy and were also used in the Atlantean construction of Stonehenge, of which the Abbey was spiritual successor in its early realm. Both the stone circles and the Freemason-built cathedrals channel, amplify and isolate pure telluric energy into clear resonating notes for spiritual use. The cathedrals are far more sophisticated in this science, and several of the great cathedrals along the Michael ley line resonate to single upper-chakra musical keys!

## The Original Church Founder: Joseph of Arimathea

Joseph of Arimathea was no stranger to Glastonbury. His arrival was received with great welcome. Respected by Druids, he was given a large tract of land called the 12 Hinds. Here, he and his exiled Christians built what became the first Christian Church in Europe. It thrived for centuries and was visited by monarchs, popes and eventually Saint Patrick in 450 AD, who hailed Glastonbury as: *"the holiest earth in England."* He is said to have been buried alongside Joseph and Holy Mary's gravesites on the grounds.

## Noblis Decurio of Rome

Joseph of Arimathea was a man of great wealth and influence during the time of Jesus. According to noted author Glenn Kimball in Hidden Politics of the Crucifixion, he was one of the wealthiest men on earth at the time of Christ: *"Among his distinctions, Joseph of Arimathea was given the title of 'Noblis Decurio' by the Roman Empire, signifying his commercial role as the chief provider of tin and lead to the vast armies of Rome."* He owned massive tracts of land and mines in Gaul, and he had homes and holdings in several lands, including Egypt and inner Persia.

After the death of Jesus' father Joseph, the latter's brother assumed responsibility for the young Jesus' education, as was the custom. Arimathea was indeed an enlightened soul and recognized the light in his nephew. He understood his role as the young Jesus' mentor and benefactor, a role he would repeat as Merlin to Arthur. Through his uncle's ships and travels, Jesus received teachings in India, Iraq, Egypt and from the Druid priests in Cornwall. Between the ages of 13 and 28, Jesus had the opportunity to learn much from his travels and to minister both his learnings and his teachings from the boats of Arimathea. *"But,"* adds Kimball, *"this part of Jesus' life was all lost to historians, after the First Council of Nicea."* Only the Essene texts and foreign legends provide the missing pieces. The misdirection of the church conspiracy to gain control over the masses skewed the true message and the real life story of the man Jesus.

Kimball continues, "For centuries, Christian historians have ignored information that is common knowledge among Hindu adepts, that Jesus visited and was taught by masters in India. Jesus personally appears in legacies in India, Egypt and England. The Church of England fancies itself as the original Christian church for good reason. They were practicing Christianity in Glastonbury for 200 years before the Romans."

### Exiled From Judea: The Virgin Mary at the Abbey

According to historian Victor Dunstan's 1985 article, "Did the Virgin Mary Live and Die in England," Anna, the mother of the Virgin Mary, was born and raised in Gaul. Travel between the Middle East and Gaul was quite common during the 100 years before and after the birth of Christ. English legend claims that Jesus made at least two extended trips to England with Joseph of Arimathea and his mother. Thus when exiled from Judea, Gaul (England) would have offered the safest refuge to Arimathea and Jesus' mother, Mary. They arrived at Glastonbury in 37 AD, after being imprisoned for almost a year and allowed to flee after making arrangements with authorities for their release.

Glastonbury had long been a center for Druid priests, and Arimathea was an adept master, recognized and respected among peers. It is said that he possessed the ability to manifest, and he later reincarnated as the savant Merlin.

After an initial altar near the sacred Thorn on Wearyall Hill, the first Wattle church was built on the hallowed ground near the present Lady Chapel on the Abbey grounds. Joseph of Arimathea is credited with having brought two significant relics with him in his exodus: the Chalice, or Holy Grail, used in the Last Supper, and one of the seven replicas of the Ark of the Covenant, sacred texts stored in a copper vessel fashioned according to sacred geometry for preservation.

The church thrived and became a Christian pilgrimage site. Mother Mary is said to have died in approximately 48 AD, and Joseph 12 years later. Both are said to have been buried on the grounds of the Abbey.

### King Arthur at the Abbey

While a church was always present, the elegant structure of the Abbey was not begun until the 5th or 6th century, presumably just before the reign of the historic King Arthur. The church reached its golden age between the 8th and 14th centuries, by which time it was greatly associated with the chivalry and glory of King Arthur, his 12 knights of the Round Table and the lore of the Holy Grail.

A plaque about 50 feet from the south door of the Lady Chapel marks the gravesite of King Arthur. It was re-discovered in 1191 during the reign of Henry ll. The King was advised of the location while in a monastery in Wales. The Abbey was under renovation after a fire in 1184, and the King ordered the monks to search for the grave as depicted by ancient scrolls. Seven feet below ground at the indicated spot, they unearthed a stone slab and a leaden cross with the Latin inscription: *"HIC IACET SEPULTUS INCLITUS REX ARTURIUS IN INSULA AVALONIA,"* or *"Here lies buried the renowned King Arthur in the Isle of Avalon."*

Considerably deeper was a coffin, containing the bones of a tall man with an injury to the skull. Some smaller bones and a scrap of yellow hair, which crumbled when touched, were reputedly Guinevere's. The news spread quickly, and the bones of both Arthur and Guinevere were placed in a black stone altar in the main cathedral, where they remained until the Dissolution in 1539.

An agent of the monarchy, one Giraldus Cambrensis, made historical accounts of this exhumation. His account was tedious and included interviews with witnesses of the excavation. In 1962, Dr Raleigh Radford of the British Museum excavated the area and determined that the site did indeed serve as a grave for a member of the monarchy, based on the elaborate remains of stone linings for the crypt base. His detailed report gave credence to its being Arthur's gravesite.

My point is not to prove that Arthur lived. It is commonly agreed that there was a historic King Arthur. I aver that he was indeed a Christ Consciousness, his story being part of the repeating Christos Hologram: a symbolic truth that parallels that of Jesus Christ of Judea.

**Arthurian Metaphors**

The seeker can find many symbolic parallels to the Christ story and biblical parables within the subtle 'channeled' Arthurian verses. The twelve Knights of the Round Table mirror the twelve Disciples of Christ, the twelve tribes of Israel and the twelve zodiac signs. The seeking of the Holy Grail represents man's relentless quest for the 'unattainable' perfection.

You may recall that, in the Arthurian tales, when King Arthur and Guinevere were in harmony, England and Camelot thrived. When they grew out of harmony, the country fell into disarray. In this metaphoric parallel, Arthur, Guinevere and Camelot represent the 'trinity' components of earthbound 'man.' Their story represents the harmony / balancing aspect of body, mind and spirit. King Arthur represents the mind; Guinevere the body and 'Camelot' the spirit. When body and mind are in tune, spirit follows in kind. When separation occurs, the spirit of the union is imbalanced.

The aspect of Lancelot's love with Guinevere is a symbolic parallel to the Garden of Eden. When Eve tasted the *'forbidden'* fruit of knowledge, the idyllic world was destroyed. When Guinevere tasted the forbidden love, Camelot was

destroyed. All metaphoric truths of the plight of man through free will. The crumbling of the idyllic world leads to growth through lesson and an eventual rebirth. On the highest level, these are not judgmental but symbolic of growth and the pain associated with moving forward, outgrowing one's 'skin.' Change is the nature of the universe, of growth, and often the 'Edens' and 'Camelots' are idyllic worlds, resting places, in which growth is not stimulated and duality does not exist.

When closely studied, the interesting and somewhat bizarre parable of King Arthur and his sister Morgana La Fay represents the male and female sides of the human spirit on earth, while their 'son' Mordred, represents the ego, the lower aspect of man required for his survival in three-dimensional earth. While the ego is necessary to sustain the physical body's survival on the earth plane, it is in unavoidable conflict with the higher self. Arthur's victory over his 'son' Mordred represents man's spiritual battle to overcome the ego through truth, represented by Excalibur. In their final struggle, Arthur asks Mordred, "Why did it have to be this way? Why did destiny deem that you would destroy me?" Mordred replies, "Did you really think it could be any other way, Father? You chose to be above me."

**Destruction of the Abbey and Michael Cathedrals**

In 1536, during the 27th year of the reign of Henry VIII, there were over 800 monasteries, nunneries and friaries in Britain. By 1541, there were none. More than 10,000 monks and nuns had been dispersed, and hundreds of buildings had been seized by the Crown to be sold. Clearly, the great Glastonbury Abbey was one of the principal targets of this orgy of destruction by the divorce-seeking monarch during the era of upheaval known as the Dissolution of the Monasteries, when Henry broke from the Roman Catholic Church and formed the Church of England.

The Abbott of Glastonbury, Richard Whiting, refusing to bend to the Dissolution, was hanged and quartered by Henry VIII. He was martyred at the Michael Tower on the Tor. The Great Abbey was destroyed, including the assemblage of Archangel Michael's Cathedral on the Tor. The monastery was dissolved and placed in the hands of the 'Anglican' Church. A few years later, it fell into private hands, and its successive owners tore most of it down as building materials for walls and roads.

In 1908, the Church of England acquired the site and took wonderful, inspired actions to preserve what little was left. The ruins standing today, while sufficient to hold the imagery of the past grandeur, are but fragments of the grand structure that stood from the late 12th century onward, replacing the much older one destroyed by a fire in 1184. That said, the energy remains resplendent, and the portal is securely re-anchored. Many great and enlightened souls including, among others, the seers Wesley Tudor Pole and Dion Fortune, led the movement to reaffirm the energy of Glastonbury, beginning some 90 years ago and continuing to the present.

There is a firmly established movement in Glastonbury to build a magnificent, spiral, domed healing temple, with buttressed geometrical designs. Another petition seeks to join the 36-acre Abbey Ruins in a 500-acre Sacred Heritage Park connecting the Chalice Well, Wearyall Hill, Whitesprings and the Tor.

If you do visit, please remember to enter the Abbey site with reverence, despite its touristy museum façade. To view the site primarily from an academic perspective lessens the great potential for a profound spiritual experience, facilitated by the sacred energy available inside.

Likewise, do not let the ever-present swarm of visitors deter you from meditation and spiritual quest in this hallowed ground. The Abbey grounds are one of the most sacred places on Earth. Find a quiet spot, and meditate, contemplate and locate your center. Bring a book, umbrella and soft foam earplugs to further enhance the quiet, and plan to spend three to four hours on the grounds. Absorb what is there. You are in the true Cradle of Spirit. It shines, it sings, it balances. It is the heart of our Earth …

**Closing**

Glastonbury is an epicenter of the 'New Age,' and its energy attracts all types. The village streets are lined with historical churches, buildings and museums situated side by side with mystical shops. The High street promenade offers the full gamut of wares and services to both tourist and pilgrim. From local art galleries, vegetarian restaurants, English high tea rooms, Arthurian swords, souvenir chalices, healing arts, tarot readings, incense, crystals, wands, capes, herbs and astrological readings, it's all there. Buddhists, traditional Church of England Protestants, Druids, Wiccans, and New Age pilgrims recognize and share the potent traditions and energy of Glastonbury, each claiming it as their own. The spiritual duality is present. Like many mega-power centers, Glastonbury has an electromagnetic field that is held in balance by the integral presence of both electrical polarities, positive and negative. So when making your pilgrimage, enter the potent energy of the duality fully aware, and establish astral protection upon visiting the wondrous Avalon, for the veil is indeed thin, and both energies are present.

The powerful energy amplifies the human aura, and visitors not accustomed to this level of energy can experience an auric depletion after a few days. This is the signal to move into a lower amperage. That signal should be respected, because to overstay can result in a feeling of tiredness and erratic mood swings. Time is usually required for the human aura to adjust to the highly concentrated electromagnetic fields in power centers such as Glastonbury. Residents of such mega-energy centers develop an auric sheath that allows them to retain balance within the concentrated energy fields.

Accommodations in Glastonbury are plentiful. I highly recommend staying at the Chalice Well's 'Little St Michael's Retreat,' actually on the grounds of the Chalice Well gardens. This does require becoming a member of the Chalice Well Trust, a very worthwhile non-profit organization. Information can be obtained at: http://www.chalicewell.org.uk.

Glastonbury is easily reached in a three-hour drive from London via the M-4 to Bristol, then heading south for 25 miles on the M-5. Watch for the exit, and prepare to be enchanted when the Tor appears on the horizon.

## Tyberonn Channel

*"Now, the channel has asked about the energy of Glastonbury. We will say that it is a system of energy, the many that compose the one, you see. Much in the way that Mount Shasta is a complex of many energies that surround it, so then is Glastonbury a composite of many very ancient and very special energies.*

*This area of southern England became one of the evacuation points that the survivors of Aryan, one of the remaining three islands of Atlantis, came to just before the deluge to create new lives. Now, in the final days of Atalntis, after the second break up, Atlantis became three large islands. Poseidia, Aryan and Og, you see. Those of Poseidia evacuated primarily into North and Central America, Og into South America and Egypt, and Aryan into Portugal, the Basque region of Spain, and into England and Ireland. There were already antediluvian colonies here, you see, and there were many, such as the channel, who understood that the deluge was only a matter of time. And so*

*hordes of people left during the months before the final deluge, when the ground began to tremble and quiver more and more, you see.*

*The area of southwest England, Ireland and of the Isle of Orkney contained enclaves of mystics, those of the priesthood, one would say, that evolved into the Druids over time. The channel experienced several lives as such in this area.*

*The evidence is still there, is it not? Stonehenge was certainly built by the post Atlanteans, much earlier than you now suppose. You see, the leyline that is now called Michael once traversed Atlantis, thus its flow path and its equivalents were recognized and inhabited by the Druids across Ireland, England and western Europe. The largest of the stone circles were built through sonic frequency, although in later years the smaller ones were not. Yet all were placed upon the currents of the Earth and used to amplify them.*

*The area of Glastonbury, the Tor primarily, was a Druid enclave, as well as the grand circles of Wiltshire, Avebury and Stonehenge. These were recognized for their unique fertility and regenerative aspects.*

*This is an area in which the Earth is in parallel. By this we mean that the future and past can coexist tangibly in 3-D at times. So do many exclaim the veil is thin here, yes? Indeed. It is not the only such place on the planet but one of the most vibrant. Unique forms of the devic kingdom abide here and, again, quite tangibly visible in three dimension, although their frequency exists in the fourth. The magnetics of this area allow for the overlay.*

*Now, we spoke of the fertility of this place. You term it energy of the heart, we tell you currently it is an energy of the $2^{nd}$ chakra, in your terms, but of the $2^{nd}$ flowing with the energy of the heart. You see it is an area of harmonic sen-*

*suality, of the natural entwining of masculine to the feminine. Of telluric merging into the divine, fertilizing and combining the very polarity of the electromagnetic. We will say that atop the Tor is the feminine, and at its base the masculine. And the inverse is true at the Chalice Well, at its base the feminine, at its top the masculine, and these intertwine in helix, you see. The same occurs in Avebury Circle, though not at Stonehenge. It is a place of frequencial honeymooning, you see, of natural coupling. The energy of the Earth is very fertile here. Did not the channel speak of fence posts sprouting leaves in this region. Did not the allegorical staff at Wearyall hill grow into a Thorn tree.*

*The channel asks if the boy Jesus and his renowned uncle came to this area in the times of the Christ. We will say he did, and he didn't. The channel asks, did King Arthur and Camelot exist here. We will say again, they did, and they didn't. Both existed on a very real plane that we will refer to as a living hologramic insert. Both were dramas of higher lesson that many, many of you have expereinced as a living play, we will say, but living is the key word. How else do so many feel they were part of this experience, how else do so many feel they were knights of the table round, or disciples of the Christ, when there were but twelve?*

*The insertion of both dramas touches within the energy of this place. Both exist here on that parallel, and both can be touched within these energies. Do you understand?*

*There is a historic King Arthur and a historic Jesus, yes, in one level of understanding, in one experiential dimension, and you see, a great many beings participated in that level of understanding. Imagine this, Dear, so that you will put it in the right context. Many years from now, the same question that you asked will be asked but in a different context. They will say, was there*

*really ascension? Was there really this moment, did it happen historically, can you find it in time, or was it a symbolic event. In that same way, in the Arthurian time it is real for some, it is imagined fables for others. If you participated in it, it was very real. If you did not, it was simply a symbolic act. And so it is with those who describe the same reference, a biblical flood or many other historic events. If you participated energetically, consciously, physically, if there was an intent or desire to know, to participate or to grow via that event, it was real, and to others it is an illusion.*

*We will say that there is an energy portal for you to step into. There is an energetic grid line that transfers three forms of energies into one, a trinity into one. One that is a bridge between holographic dimensions and so a portal of thought as well, a portal of the heart. In order for you to find it, all aspects of you must be open to it, and then you will discover it, and then you will feel its magic. If all aspects of you are not open to it, you will find energy, but you will not find the portal of which we now speak.*

*How do you step into this? By removing any form of belief system. In other words, release all conceptional images. Your preconceived notions, no matter how wise or how well supported, are put forth into the third dimension based upon a third dimensional desire. To bridge the gap to higher dimension, simply clear the mind, and allow yourself the awareness of the parallel and celestial dimensional.*

*So we tell you, on an escalated level, that which you now live and breathe is but a dream, being dreamed by your higher self. So, is it real? Indeed, Dear Ones, it is real. So it is with all experience, all thought. Thoughts have their own validity, as real as your sojourn on the plane of duality. You are beloved."*

… and so it is.

# From Russia with Love ~ The Vortex of Hope for the Future

In 1944 acclaimed psychic Edgar Cayce said, *"Through Russia comes the hope of the world. Not in respect to what is sometimes termed Communism or Bolshevism – no! But of freedom – true freedom, that each man will live for his fellow man. The principle has been born there. It will take years for it to be crystallized; yet out of Russia comes again the hope of the world."*

Over six decades have passed since this remarkable channeled prophesy. Russia has transformed from a communist state to one of an evolving democracy and free trade economy. In the 90 years since the Marxist revolution, organized religion and its inherent dogma were largely absent from the Russian culture. But what was intended there was the socialist ideal of man caring for fellow man, without the mental control aspects of dogmatic religion. Russia is indeed becoming a 'cradle of hope' for the future of humanity. A bright energy pulses there.

I first traveled to Russia in 2004. My second trip was in May of 2006. Both trips included Moscow; the second took me to eastern Siberia, to wondrous Lake Baikal. My experience was profound.

## Moscow

St. Petersburg may have homed Russia's royal crown, but Moscow is its pulsing heart. Moscow is a city in which one comes face to face with all that is finest and all that is most frustrating in Russia. The gregarious geniality of its people is as evident as the extreme tensions of a city coming to terms with the confusions of rapid social change. More than anywhere else in the country, it is in Moscow where the Soviet past collides with the capitalist future. Perhaps collides is too strong a term, for truly it is a blend and becoming more harmonious. I had a very real 'déjà vu' experience within this marvelous, beautiful city. I sensed its dignity, and I loved it immediately.

As the new Moscow emerges, it is quite evident that progression into the future is shaped by the integral dignity of the city's rich and varied heritage, a timeless heritage that emphatically predates the embrace of Soviet rule. Indeed, the most striking aspect of the city today is not Moscow's much-heralded merging with Western culture but its robust revival of its own tradition and integrity. Amazing ancient cathedrals are being restored and opened, innovative theaters are reclaiming leadership in the arts, and traditional markets are coming back to life. It is a city of art, music and creativity. Moscow is once more assuming its position of world preeminence. Yet, it is ironically the 90 years of Soviet socialist influence that has had a key role in shaping the new era of the Golden Bear. The spirituality and clarity that is emerging is free from the confines of orthodox dogma. It is pure spirituality based on love of fellow man, unobstructed by canon doctrine. The potential is joyous, the city teems with creativity. The Arbat, a cobbled street mall of shops, crafts, street entertainers and artisans abounds with life in Moscow's center.

The people are surprisingly engaging and warm. But the most prominent impression was that of their piercing intelligence and zest. Having been raised in a virtual television-free environment, most Russians focused on education and arts. Many play at least one musical instrument and speak at least two languages fluently.

There is crispness, an energetic clarity through out the area. I felt a familiarity with Russia and discerned a great sense of brightness, a potent emergence of hope. The people are remarkably robust and beautiful. More than 10 million people are living in Moscow. Among them there are representatives of about one hundred nations and ethnic groups. Russians are the largest ethnic group in Moscow. There are also Jews, Ukrainians, Belorussians and Tatars, as well as increasing numbers of refugees and immigrants from Afghanistan, the Caucasus, the Baltic States and Central Asia. Orthodox Christianity is a predominant religion in Moscow. The city is embellished with onion domed, gilded cathedrals, that shine brightly like jewels over the landscape. Moscow has communities of Protestants, Roman Catholics, Judaists, Muslims and a growing circle of 'New Age' spirituality. In fact the existing religions are yet devoid of the zealot faction and seem far more open minded and accepting of differing views.

Moscow occupies more than 1,000 square kilometers. The boundary of the city corresponds to the Moscow Ring Road, which is situated at 15-17 kilometers from the city center. The city extends for 42 kilometers from the north to the south and for 35 kilometers from the east to the west. The city is clustered around the Volkhov River, and many beautiful onion domed cathedrals are situated along its path. The site of Red Square and the Kremlin is an amazing power vortex that encompasses the Cathedral of Christ the Redeemer and St Basil's Cathedral along the river front. The sacred geometry of these splendid cathedrals is extremely potent.

There are more than 20 such cathedrals in the Moscow ring. Several were built over Pagan power sites hundreds of years ago. The sacred geometry of these cathedrals is quite unique. The exquisite onion domes are often gilded in gold filigree and luminous metallic based paints of green, red and blue. This fascinating use of color is quite spectacular and adds to the potent frequency of these domed beauties. Many of these are indeed portals: magnets and holders of high-energy resonance.

## The Golden Ring

The Golden Ring of Moscow is an ovaline circle of power sites and cathedrals that circle an area of roughly 120 miles from the city center. This ring encompasses the golden vortex of the new energy of Moscow. 'The Golden Ring' is one of the oldest Russian pilgrimage routes. It goes to the northeast of Moscow and forms an ovalesque route that includes several powerpoints and sacred cathedrals. There are many interesting ancient Russian cities and sacred cathedrals along this path. The 'classical' route (counter clockwise) starts from Moscow, goes through Vladimir, Suzdal, Ivanov, Ples, Kostroma, Yaroslavl, Rostov Velikiy, Pereslavl Zalesskiy and Sergiev Posad.

Sergiev Posad is one of most sacred Cathedrals of the ring. The Sergiev Posad monastery was founded in 1340 by Sergius of Radonezh, whose name was given to the town. The massive complex is along the river, amid lush rolling hills. A holy spring is said to have risen centuries ago by divine credence and is a pilgrimage site for thousands who come to drink its curative waters.

The energy of the vortex portal of the Golden Ring centered in Moscow is simply one of the brightest energies I have ever experienced. It is powerfully anchored by Saint Germain. It is the template for the new Russia. It became anchored in 1986 and is crystalline in frequency. It is centered at the Cathedral of Christ the Redeemer and St Basil's in Red Square. It is the vortex and portal of Moscow, of the heart of Russia. It is uniquely fed and aligned to an even more powerful energy … Lake Baikal.

## Lake Baikal

Perhaps the most amazing natural site in Russia is Lake Baikal. I had the good fortune to visit Lake Baikal in May of 2006 and found it simply stunning. North America can lay claim to some pretty impressive lakes. Lake O'Hara and Lake Louise in Canada are stunning. Pyramid Lake in Nevada and the Great Salt Lake in Utah are portals. Lake Superior has the greatest surface area of any fresh water lake in the world. The mystical Crater Lake in Oregon is one of the deepest and most mystical lakes in the world. Lake Ouachita in Arkansas holds the crystalline portal. The powerful chakric portal of Lake Titicaca in Bolivia and Peru is the world's highest navigable lake, lying 12,500 feet above sea level. Italy's Lake Cuomo and Scotland's Loch Katrine are areas of tranquil beauty. Africa's largest lake is Lake Victoria, the world's second largest fresh water body; it is among the most scenic lakes in the world, straddling the equator and forming part of the borders of Uganda, Kenya and Tanzania. In the Antarctic lies the world's coldest and most southernly lake, Lake Vostok. The distinction of the world's lowest and saltiest lake goes to the Dead Sea; bordering Israel and Jordan, it lies 1,340 feet below sea level! Asia can claim the largest inland water body in the world, the Caspian Sea.

Even though these lakes and seas are all special and indeed potent, and all have roles in the planetary Ascension, Lake Baikal in eastern Siberia shines in brilliance among them. This crescent-shaped lake is more than 900 miles from the nearest ocean (the Pacific) and is about 444 miles long and 50 miles wide. Rimmed by mountains and surrounded by pristine forests, it is one of the most beautiful lake settings in the world. While it is the 7th largest lake on the globe in regards to surface area, in terms of volume of water Lake Baikal has no peers. Lake Baikal holds 20% of the world's fresh water, the largest volume of fresh water on the planet. Its greatest depth is 5,022 feet, making it by far the world's deepest lake.

Magical Lake Baikal is contained in a natural tectonic basin in an uplift highland called the Stanovoy Range. This crevice holds the waters of Lake Baikal. The immense surface of the lake is 477 meters above sea level, while its bottom plunges to 1,200 meters below. The lake is encircled by antediluvian mountain ranges rising to heights of 2,750 meters. These mountains slope steeply to the surface of the lake, embellishing a spectacular panorama of overwhelming rugged beauty.

The mountains around Baikal are rich in mica, graphite, marble, gold and other minerals, and are carpeted in rich Pine and Cedar forests. The natural resources are immense. Lake Baikal is a virtual cornucopia of precious and semi precious gemstones. Many of these are found along the massive shoreline in the crystal clear waters. These include lazurite, charoite, lapis lazuli, jade, spinel, apatite, flogopite, diopsite, pargasite, scapolite, pyrite, quartz, dolomite, calcite, malachite, giafoline, tourmaline, ortite, biotite, limonite, amazonite and aragonite.

More than 330 rivers and streams feed Lake Baikal, but the powerful Angara River is the lake's only outlet. The Angara empties into the Arctic Ocean more than 1,500 miles away. Its path is dotted with power nodes. Geologists determine Lake Baikal to be approximately 25 million years old, as such making it the world's oldest lake. Lake Baikal has tremendous clarity, the transparency of the crystalline waters is up to 40 meters. Its waters support life at incredible depths. The bottom is dotted with volcanic vents that energize and oxygenize the waters, allowing for prolific eco and bio systems of life, totally unique to the lake.

Declared a UNESCO World Heritage Site, Lake Baikal's extreme pristine beauty has long been recognized as a powerful sacred portal.

The Buryats, an indigenous people of the Lake Baikal area, have held the lake as holy for thousands of years. Their religion is shamanism, similar to that of the Native Americans. They honor the lake as a living deity. The Island of Olkhon and Shaman Rock are sacred centers of Siberian shamanism, remnants of sacred LeMuria. Buddhist monasteries and communities also have been situated along Lake Baikal's perimeter for millennia. The Buddhists consider the pristine holy lake to hold the energy of Lord Buddha.

During my visit to the lake in May of 2006, most of the holy lake was still frozen. I was delighted to find the ice had in certain parts formed geometric ice crystals that expressed themselves in amazing geometric forms. Some appeared almost in snowflake geometries, others as pinnacles. I visited a Buryat Shaman during my time in Baikal and was delighted and honored to take part in drumming ceremonies in accolade to the lake. The drums and songs, used in ceremony with a sacred fire, were strikingly similar to those of the Native American. The directions were acknowledged, and prayer songs were dedicated to the spirit of the lake.

The end of my last day at the lake was dedicated to meditation in one of the holy areas along the lake. I found a spot sheathed in granitic out-croppings, overlooking the frozen beauty of the lake. Dressed in appropriately warm clothing, I found I was able to reach a deep state very quickly. I connected to the spirit of the lake and in timeless repose had a vision of a beautiful and enormous blue eagle emerging from its depths. The eagle transformed from blue to white as it hovered high above the lake. Its body radiated the colors of the rainbow. One of these enveloped me, and I felt tremendous energy, a frequency of great peace and well-being. After a few hours, I knew my time was coming to a close. The winds whipped up and had an icy edge. I buried three crystals I had brought within the grounds, and I placed four more in the thawed waters along the shoreline. As I walked back to my waiting car and tour guide, I paused

once more to view the splendid scene. An energy pervaded me, and the Lake once again filled my heart, truly an energy of Russia, with Love.

## Tyberonn Channel

*"Greetings, Beloved! And so we speak in this hour of Russia, and indeed it is a vast land of a deep history within your past centuries. That energy that we find around what the channel terms as the Golden Ring of Moscow is an exceptionally clear energy, one that heightens what you term the intellect. The great channel you referred to, Edgar Cayce, foresaw the emergence of a new application of this ancient portal. Dear Ones, we tell you that Moscow, and indeed Russia, will be the cradle of the renewed application of spiritual principle as applied in the lives of humanity. That which you term socialism, in its true application, we tell you, is in fact the appropriate ideal for humanity in your plane. Is it not the nature of your core family to share in love and unity. We tell you it is the way of your higher selves, of higher realm. Now, how it unfolds, how it evolves in this land is yet to be seen, for there are opposing forces, you see. Now, we are not speaking of the fallen Soviet Socialist state. It was not, indeed, the true exercising of the socialist principle; it became corrupted, you see. During the advent of your second world war, the planetary leadership, as we interpret it, was largely dominated by those reincarnated from the warring faction that destroyed Atlantis, and indeed in later years the Romans. Reincarnation cycles, you see, are bound in group consciousness to a very large degree. Entire continents, countries, entire dramas in time, as you term them, often reincarnate together. They are as such somewhat tied together by past experience, like thinking, like frequency and progress of development as it were. Do you see? So, it was this group that created the war, your second world war, and such men dominated and corrupted the intent of the socialist experiment in Russia. There, an elitist faction sought power and lived in a man-*

ner of lifestyle far superior to the masses. Their primary focus was that of power, of expanding power, not truly distribution of resources for the overall well being. And as such the collapse was inevitable, you see. The initial principle was lost within those in control. Just as capitalism has, to a great degree in many areas such as the United States, lost sight of those both within and without its borders who are lacking, and thus the corruption of greed and seeking of power. It is the balance that is required, of true sharing.

Now, what we see occurring in Russia is a new influx of evolved souls in mass carrying the crystalline frequency, with a culture whose common man has for two generations lived in more unity, in greater equality, we would say. And, as the channel has mentioned, are not largely divided or controlled by organized religious creed. That is the energy of the Golden Ring. It is an insert, a hologramic frequency that can offer the potential for the rebirth of true application of human experience. Those called the Meruvians, the 6th race, are in fact the crystalline vibration. The Meruvian is not truly a racial façade or guise, rather it is the 12 stand DNA that can and is occurring in all physical biology forms. As such there is an influx of the Meruvian crystalline frequency within this area. As we have said, the Meruvian frequency influx is also occurring in South America, Scandinavia, Canada, Japan and parts of the United States. The major influx is in Russia and South America at this time, of souls in mass from the family of evolved souls, those of the 'Law of One,' those of Mu, those of Tibet, those of the golden era of Greece. These souls have accepted a specific mission and will potentially become majority forces of like ideology within these frequencial inserts.

Now, the channel asks about the energy termed Lake Baikal. We tell you it is a massive vortex and chakric center for humankind as well as for the body of the planet. Its ovaline circumference extends for over one thousand miles, and its energetic influence is global. Lake Baikal has been recognized for millennia and has always had etheric as well as human guardians along its shores. You see, Baikal carries the energy of Mu and of Lord Buddha. It was recognized in the time of LeMuria and holds that peaceful energy as a placeholder for the planet, we will say. It has long been protected by its very remoteness. The gems from this area are extremely potent, they are imbued with its tranquil energy, its balance. The gemstones of the Ural Mountains are also of key importance at this time. That of the blue lapis lazuli and the lavender charoite of Baikal, and that of the amethyst, aquamarine, topaz and demantoid garnet of the Ural Mountains are most beneficial to those that wear them. The vibration of these unique areas within Russia is of the higher activation and harmonious frequency at this time, you see.

Three potent energy vortex-portal complexes exist and triangulate in Russia's geometric template: the Golden Ring, The Ural Mountains and Lake Baikal. The most powerful of these, and understand, Dear Ones, that all three are omnificently potent, is Lake Baikal. Lake Baikal is indeed global in proportion and vibrates in harmonic oscillation with many other parts of the world, including Lake Titicaca, both LeMurian you see.

The influx of higher realm geometries and higher dimensional light is quickened above and within this lake. Above it is a precious diamond dome. This concentrated geometric sphere contains the dodecahedron and octahedron. It is irradiated with those energies of the Pleiades and Sirius B, and uniquely aligned to same. We say to the channel, you were fortunate indeed to visit this place; its energies are now within you. And so it is for all who visit there, either in body or spirit, yet both are indeed blessed. You are beloved."

… and so it is.

# Mount Shasta ~ Multidimensional Portal

Northern California is the perfect road trip, and this one began for me on a bright sunny day. I love to drive. Always have. I can really relax behind the wheel, enjoying scenery, far away from the office grind. Time to think, and that's why I came.

The road from Sacramento to Mount Shasta passes miles and miles of fertile farm fields and fruit groves. I had rented the kind of car that was perfect for rolling past flat stretches of highway and convoys of groaning harvest trucks. I eased the windows down and breathed the fresh cool air. A light rain had fallen earlier and made the air pungent with the distinctive musty aroma of wet soil.

Time flowed by seamlessly as I tuned the radio to classic rock … the Almond Brothers, "Eat A Peach." Good idea. I pulled over to a roadside fruit stand and bought fruit so juicy you needed to eat them outdoors. I didn't. Soon my pants and car were stained with fragrant juice. The sweet bouquet of peaches and plums filled the car as I continued north across the winding blue Sacramento River, a crossing I would make five times before finally leaving the river behind at the foothills of the Cascade Mountains. Life was good.

Past the river the terrain rolled into succinct golden domes of yellow-grassed hills, back-dropped by a jagged spine of steel gray mountains.

Finally the first indication I was getting near my destination. I felt the energy shift as I drove over Lake Shasta's long arched bridge. Then the amazing Castle Crags … and suddenly, voilà … Mount Shasta! Amazing Mount Shasta.

**Energy**

Mount Shasta exudes an energy quite unlike any other 'sacred site' I have visited, and I didn't expect that, not really, not at first. I have come to describe the sense of it as 'zipped space,' a sort of dimensional shrinking of space into condensed pockets of concentric overlay. That would explain the higher dimensional ET occurrences there, as well as the etheric cities neatly pocketed within the zip.

I drove onward through Shasta City on Interstate 5 to Weed and exited for Stewart Mineral Springs. Stewart Mineral Springs is the perfect place to stay when in the energy of Shasta. A sacred site in its own rite, I had stayed there on three previous trips, while attending the Lightworker Espavo Conferences from 2001 through 2003. What is both unique and glorious about the place is, of course, the natural mineral spring baths and spa. Not just the white silica springs used for the thermal baths, but also the red, iron rich spring that bubbles up alongside the white one. To my knowledge, Glastonbury, England is the only other area in the world to have both a white (male) and red (female) spring, side by side. It is an amazing place of rejuvenation, complete with a huge wood burning sauna and a crystalline creek to jump into afterward. Amazing, and so healthy and invigorating.

In fact, the entire Shasta area is embellished with 'mini' sacred sites that seem to circulate around the massif crown of the volcano. Castle Crags, Glass (obsidian) Mountain, Medicine Lake, Klamath Falls, Dunsmuir's Hedge Falls, Shasta Springs, Crystal Cave, Black Butte, Mossbrae Falls, McCloud Falls and, of course, Stewart Mineral Springs are just some of them. Each has a unique energy that contributes to and balances

Shasta. No wonder people are drawn to this land of myth and legend. The myths and legends are fascinating.

And perhaps, where there's smoke, there's fire … or at least magma!

Certainly volcanoes have been revered as places of spirit for millennia. Beyond the indigenous peoples, certain sects of Buddhism and Hinduism also consider volcanoes as living deities.

The Medoc and Shasta Indians consider Shasta to be the home of Creator-God. Over one hundred spiritual sects and groups have been attracted to the Shasta area in the past two centuries. The legends of deities and presence on and within Mount Shasta include the Ascended Masters, the Lemurian Telos City, the Hopi Lizard People, an extraterrestrial base from Sirius B, Saint Germain and White Eagle. Groups based in, and people drawn to, the area include the Radiant School of Light, Astara, Elizabeth Clare Prophet, Pepper Lewis, the California Zen Buddhist Abbey, Sri Sri Parvoo, A.S.S.K., the Essenes, Edgar Lucian Larkin, the Saint Germain Foundation ("I AM"), the Azariah group and the White Eagle Lodge. Many well-known authors, artists, channels and metaphysicians are drawn to Shasta.

**Mount Shasta**

Mount Shasta is a dormant volcano in the southern extremity of the northwestern Cascade Mountain range, or the northern reaches of the Sierra Nevada Mountains (depending on geological sources), in northern California. It rises majestically to over 14,400 feet, and as such is the largest volcanic peak in the lower 48 states. Mount Shasta is a stratovolcano and has the largest base (over 500 cubic kilometers) of any volcano in the continental USA. It last erupted 200 years ago and still produces, on average, five small earthquakes per year over the past 25 years.

Revered by Native Americans as a deity, Shasta is unquestionably a very mystical and powerful place of spirit. According to Kryon, Shasta, not Sedona, is the most potent vortex in the United States. I have spent considerable time in the energy of both, and while I am deeply drawn to the magnificent ancient energy of Sedona, Shasta is a more powerfully centered energy and exudes an extremely robust, sovereign magnetic field.

**September 2001: Up to Panther Meadows**

The first time I drove up the winding road to the holy mountain's Panther Meadows was five years earlier (with a dear sister, Lesa Michel) in route to an Espavo conference channel with Steve Rother. It was September of 2001, four days after the infamous 9-11.

Shasta's magnificent energy increased tangibly as we drove higher. The energy felt like home and was expressed in the resplendent countenance of nature. The towering Spruce and Pine that lined the serpentine road were exquisite projections of everything a tree can be, fully pulsating in symmetrical allure, embellished with iridescent lime green moss on the trunks. As I drank in the energy, I was moved to tears. To say the experience of being with 70+ Lightworkers on the mountain was magical is an understatement.

The area of Panther Meadows is a concentric overlay of all twelve dimensions, a subjacent earth-drawn stasis of the Crystalline grid into a perfect inward portal. It is exquisitely and uniquely balanced, utterly and wholly woven into an eclectic tapestry of time-space sequence, a pristine dimensional plicature.

Its complexion evolves into a majestic rock garden as the tree line is ascended. Magnificent monolithic boulders of granite and quartz are strewn about in igneous forests of towering vibrant stone of every shape. The living stones sing in the voice of the mountain, emitting a symphonic chorus of metamorphic rapture.

Is it any wonder to the adept seeker that author Guy W. Ballard entered a dimensional fold along these very slopes and encountered the "Ascended Master" Saint Germain. Ballard paused one day at a mountain spring in 1930 along Shasta's slopes, and felt a mesmerizing 'electrical' current pass through his body … and was suddenly in the presence of Saint Germain. This experience, of course led to his founding of the I AM movement and the Saint Germain Foundation, still headquartered in Shasta City. Saint Germain, as I was to discover, is among the guardian energies of Shasta.

## Transition

The year 2005 was a major transitional journey for me. My 26-year marriage had ended, and because of it I had dedicated months to deep soul searching and life review. I lost weight and felt great despair, and I searched vigorously, purposefully. I had released a lot of pain and regret, as I sought to redefine my life and my direction. Having been in metaphysics for almost 30 years I understood the change in my life had not been ambiguous, but despite being a great catalyst it hurt. I had been blessed with many soul-friends and helpers throughout the shift, but ultimately, the path of understanding is solitary. That was a big part of why I was here in Shasta.

## Lucid Dreaming

It has taken me almost a year to write of this experience, and as I do so now, I feel both the relevance and highly personal nature of it. It is an example of the dichotomy of spiritual revelation that perhaps other seekers experience, while living in two worlds and trying to balance them. I remain somewhat reluctant to share the entirety of this experience, and I do so with the caveat that this vision was, on one level, a dream horizon played out in a very real setting. It was a waking, symbolic dream. But I can no longer acquiesce to the pragmatic side of my nature that dismissed the fantastic experience as only a dream, because I was able to consciously navigate within it and learn from it, and on that level it is personally valid. These dimensions exist, but they cannot be fully realized without experiencing them oneself. It was the disciplines of the Native American traditions, practiced for seven consecutive years in vision quests, prayer, fasting and earthdance that had formed a prerequisite springboard enabling this experience.

## Tyb's Journal: July 2005

It is almost sunset, and although it is early July, the air is cold. Beds of alabaster snow still block the road to upper Panther Meadows. I am with Israel, master soul and my spiritual mother of many lives. We park the car at Bunny Flats and fumble through the backpacks in the trunk to find parkas and ponchos.

We pause to feel the energy and watch the crimson magenta of the sunset morph into burning orange and peach. It's too beautiful to watch on foot. We find a smooth boulder and sit in silent reverence as the sun dips below the western horizon.

Once white clouds are now sky borne silhouettes, deep blue, etched in silver. Venus, the evening star, emerges brightly above the fading montage of the spectacular sunset. Other stars are beginning to wake, slightly pulsing, sprinkled across the dark velvet canopy above.

We stir simultaneously from the hypnotic spell of the twilight. It is now dark, and the energy has shifted. Crickets and tree frogs twir and croak in modulated percussion, starlings sing from a distance, a snow owl coos from the trees. In the music of night, we silently rise and walk by starlight up the rocky path into the meadow above.

Shasta at night is teeming with devics. I saw flashing peripheral movements from the corner of my vision, as I focused on walking the rising footpath. It was really dark now, moonlessly dark! The wind shifted to the east and had an icy edge, as it flowed down in waves from Shasta's snow covered peak.

We carefully chose our footing as laterite pebbles crunched beneath our hiking shoes. After a brisk 30-minute walk, we parted from the trail and walked into an opening in the meadows of Bunny Flats. The stars above were now fully exposed and afforded a subtle silver light on the valley floor as we treaded over rises and falls. We found a dry crevice and walked through it until we came to a long felled tree trunk. We laid our backpacks down and sat a few feet apart in silence to begin our merkaba mediations and shamanic journey. We offered prayer songs and offerings in the Native American modality, honoring the directions, the earth, sky and creator. We honored the energy of Shasta, of all beings, and asked permissions to be here in grace and humility. Israel and I spoke for a few moments then silently, began our journey.

I lay flat on the still warm earth, and stared in amazement at the incredible starry universe above for what seemed a timeless eternity. Meteorites occasionally streaked across the sky.

## My Vision on Shasta

The night was getting colder, as I lay on the ground and stared upward at the amazing starscape. After a time, I closed my eyes, and to my delight, I could still see the stars. I felt like I was flying among them, my telltale signal of being in lucid state. Timelessness pervaded, and minutes seemed like hours within that sensation. Suddenly I sensed a powerful presence. I was overwhelmed with emotion as a cloud of beautiful energy, purple and gold, enveloped me. It was beautiful beyond words, and I felt I was in the presence of an Angelic being.

I wept in deep yearning, as the energy embraced me. The tears were cleansing, and trapped emotions leapt for expression and release. I felt so at home, so at one with the energy. This loving presence and embrace, and its resulting emotional purge, lasted about 45 minutes (as close as I could interpret time from that state). As it ebbed, I slowly sat up and came back into my body, in revelry and amazement, still emotional. I glanced about in the darkness in silence. I soon heard a distinct voice instructing me to visualize my merkaba, and to see it spin, and to tell Israel to do the same. I did, and we began the visualization.

Almost immediately, the purple energy reformed and then materialized as Saint Germain. He smiled, and instantly both Israel and I were transported inside a massive Hall inside the mountain. We were surrounded by the Ascended Masters. Some were like giants, some were reptilian in appearance, some were Indigenous shaman, all exuded an incredible love. Tyberonn was one of them. I was told to step onto a small platform, and when I did, a sphere of spinning light was placed onto my head. When this was done, I was given an immediate understanding of the changes in my life, and I knew their purpose. This portion of the higher dimensional journey was experienced conjointly by Israel and I. Israel was helping me to interpret what we were shown. Her ability to navigate and communicate in that realm were simply amazing and far greater than my own. For the next few minutes we sat in our 3-D bodies side by side and with eyes closed, and we verbally communicated what we saw in the dream state, in the Hall of Ascended Masters, inside the dimensional folds of the holy mountain.

The remainder of the night was very long and very personal. The visions were varied and complex, and dealt primarily with me being taken into pieces of my life for review, understanding, confronting and releasing energetic blocks. Much of this was to enable and learn the intricate aspects of self-love. Love of self, I was told, is essential in order to become 'crystalline.' It is more than just a feeling; it is also a frequency, a key code vibration necessary to achieve the higher levels of mastery. Love of self enables passion, to love others. I was shown that it has always been easier for me to give love than to receive it. That point stayed with me and seeded much deeper contemplation.

On the second night in the high meadows, my journeys were into a realm of geometric grids. Saint Germain was my guide, and we entered into a realm that was like a mosaic of pentagonal tiles, superimposed over everything. This was a living field, and occasionally the tiles would seem to open, and we passed though the aperture into another realm of octagonal geometry, and then a third of 12-sided tiles. Each progression had a higher frequency. I was told that sacred geometry is the language of the higher dimensions, and that each dimension, each grid, had a unique expression based on a geometric matrix. I asked about my theories of grids around the Earth with 12 dimensions, and this was confirmed. Saint Germain laughed and said that this was only the tip of the iceberg. The grids do not spin, but they

do breathe. They are aware, but not conscious, as entities. Their geometry is generally as described, dodecahedron, icosahedron and double penta dodecahedron, but it is not fixed; the geometry can alter, depending on the dimension from which it is viewed. The grids do shift within their dimensional access. I was shown parallel realities where different aspects of my oversoul worked with these energy systems. I interfaced with three of these aspects.

I was given another sphere of spinning light to absorb, and told that there were greater grids that encompassed our Universe, and that our universe had 356 dimensions. That the geometry of the Universal grid was the geometry of light, a formless geometry, not understood by humanity at this point in evolution. I was told that many of the power points and grids on our planet were activated in a variety of complex manners. That the geometry of high dimensional portals like Mount Shasta and Hawaii are faceted, in dodecahedral and icosahedral geometries, and perform a multitude of functions depending upon the faceted activation, according to solar, lunar, stellar and planetary angles in synergy with the unique mineralogy (electromagnetic field) and terraqueous nature of each. The angle in which light is received influences the effect and genre of energy function at grid points, power points and portals. Geometric shapes have consciousness and are capable of holding and organizing thought in a similar manner as crystals. Incredible synergy occurs when crystal fields and specific angles intersect.

I was shown that Shasta is about alignment of life, while Hawaii, for example, is about rebirth, creation. The Living Earth does have 12 chakras, but these shift and do not correspond on a one to one basis with the 12 major facets of the geodesic grids. Each of the planetary grids open and effect all of the human chakras, and while we often assign a planetary sacred site as a heart or root chakra, in truth, this is not really the case. They each effect all human chakras but may, in specific timings or angles of activation, have a greater effect on one human chakra than another.

The third and last night in the high meadows of Shasta was equally amazing. The lucid dreaming came faster and more fluent. Two past life personalities of mine presented themselves, one a Native American Shaman, and another my Atlantean self as Tyberonn.

Tyberonn, I was told, is my root oversoul, and he appeared massive, 60 feet or so in height. He was/is an Ascended Master. The Shaman seemed a bridge aspect between my current self and Tyberonn. I melded more easily within the Native American Shaman and felt I was inside, sharing his body, as I walked through the meadows in the darkness. I felt unworthy and was told to release that emotion. The Shaman spoke of the importance of impeccability and of applying knowledge to one's life. Walking the talk, alignment of the higher mind to the daily aspects of personality, as a frequency aspect of the crystalline vibration that facilitates integrity of self, and thus higher reality understanding.

At about 3 a.m., the visions were complete, and we knew it was time to leave. Leaving the meadows at night was an interesting journey in itself. Tired and spent, it was difficult at first to become fully in control of our bodies. It was now cloudy and very dark, and quite cold. We felt stiff and numb. We could not see clearly to walk. Winding our way through the shrubbery, rocks and trees was cumbersome, and the direction out was eluding us. It was so dark that I could not see my hand in front of my face. After stumbling and nearly falling, I stopped. And then, to my delight, I suddenly became the Native American Shaman, Medicine Bear. The change was immediate. I became energized. He exuded a vibration of serene will and safeness,

of well being. My vision transformed, and the dark moonless valley was illuminated in a strange violet light. The violet light enabled me to walk fluidly, confidently, with Israel in tow, through the dark rocky valley and onto the marked entry trail. In short time, we were on the trailhead. I felt happy and grateful as I transformed back into my own body, and the violet glow dissipated. We paused at the entrance trailhead of Bunny Flats, and gazed over the valley, somehow reluctant to leave. We were deeply grateful for the magic of this experience and for the gifts Shasta had facilitated over the past three nights. Much had been shown, and I had much to consider. We gave thanks, walked to the car and drove slowly down the mountain.

## The Shasta Template

Mount Shasta lingers in defiance of society's carefully nurtured notions of what constitutes 'reality' and what is 'fantasy.' My experience mirrors both. Having worked as a field geologist for most of my career, I am naturally attracted to Gaia's elements and mountainous expressions, especially volcanoes. And while my 'day job' keeps me quite grounded (and pressured), in many ways, it has expedited my expansion through metaphysical journeys and allowed me to circum-navigate the globe and visit many, many sacred sites.

One pragmatic researcher writes:
"Proponents of alternative realities are not scientists and shouldn't try to be – they are artists and mythmakers for a constantly changing culture, and should be respected for their abilities as poets, shamans, and mythmakers. Scientists tell us what the universe is like, and teach us about nature. Mythmakers tell us how we react to the world, and thus teach us about ourselves. For example, a discovery that the brains biochemistry might cause a certain mental state satisfies no basic emotional need in the average person.

But proposing that humans can psychically 'see' people and places across long distances inspires many of us on the deepest level. Practically all alternative reality theories and beliefs – psychic powers, reincarnation, visitors from other worlds or dimensions, Masters who monitor historical event – appeal to basic urges most of us have, frighten us deliciously, or inspire us deeply. Most have precedents in archaic myth and folk belief. But most times, a cup of coffee is just a cup of coffee."

Maybe, as the Buddhists teach, the middle road is best. Allow for all realities, but live in balance. Grounding is essential in metaphysics. Keeping one's feet on solid ground while reaching for the sky seems to fit the bill.

Perhaps Shasta is a portal to higher dimensions. Perhaps it is defined by the spiritual sense of a presence when nothing in 3-D is seen, a gust of wind ruffling one's hair when there is no wind.

What I've concluded is that Shasta (like many sacred sites and power points) provided the template for a valid experience of multi dimensionality, held juxtaposed in spatial timelessness. An undeniable sense of well being and enhanced imagination were more easily accessed within its field.

Spirituality requires understanding and developing, not simply acquiring the academic knowledge of metaphysical theories of spirituality, but also the experiential process.

My key has been enacting the discipline and ceremonial rituals of the indigenous traditions, including fasting, vision quests, shamanic journey and earthdance ceremonial rituals. These filled my understanding with experiential content ... living it. And allowed me to truly know that such experience is real and is valid.

In theory, there should be no difference between meditating in your living room or on a mountaintop ... yet for this writer, on Shasta there was a catalystic movement, an undeniable facility, which made it a whole lot easier to expand consciousness.

Is it the altitude, the minerals, the granite, the basalt (which is 50% silica), the rarified air, the tectonic stresses, the expectation or the magnetics? Or is it all and none of the above?

It would be dismissive to say that what happens at Shasta is the result of industrial slabs of anticipation served on the experiential plates of all too eager mystics. But whatever the message, for this writer the engaging paradox didn't run out of allegory, just logic and time.

One philosopher writes:
"Shoot for the moon with the effectual arrows of desire, for a mans reach must exceed his grasp, or whats a heaven for?"

Perhaps we are as small as the cages we construct for ourselves or as infinite as the cosmos, depending on the parameter of our belief. But for those seekers that have opened and been to Shasta and other like sites, I am preaching to the choir. It is real, but then again, it's only a dream ... a navigable dream.

**Tyberonn Channel**

*"Now, Mt Shasta anchors a very complex multi dimensional fold, and does so through its special geometry, complex frequencies and unique electromagnetic field. These allow light portals from many higher dimensions to coexist within the Earth dimensions precisely in the massif of Mount Shasta. Among those are the ones from Sirius B, the Pleiades and Arcturus, as well as many others, and we repeat, many others. That is correct. We ask the channel, "Do you doubt your*

*experience with them?" It was quite real. We tell you, dreams and visions are indeed actual, they are real and often the catalystic means for dimensional travel. Do not doubt them, rather learn to navigate within them.*

*Your interpretation of Shasta as condensed, zipped space is quite accurate. You see, a cubic measure of space in the upper meadows of Mount Shasta holds upward of 36 dimensional frequencies, at certain times as many as 44. It is the blend of energies, varied by celestial alignments and terrestrial magnetics that trigger the variation. Shasta is far more active in some periods than others for this reason. Dimensional gates open and narrow accordingly.*

*Now, the channel asks of the origin and significance of the energy body of Mount Shasta. We confirm that he is LeMurian, but also Atlantean. And although the volcano itself is somewhat dormant at this time, in terms of what you consider volcanic activity, in dimensional terms it is very expansive, very active. Currently, Shasta is in commissioned transition, in the task of balancing energy harmonics that exist between Atlantis and LeMuria. And for that reason it is a LeMurian area, and yet an Atlantean, masculine volcano, twinned with parity to the femine.*

*Do you understand? It is significant for both Atlantis and LeMuria. You see, Mount Shasta transfers energetic excesses from one to the other, seeking equilibrium within integral dimension. That is what creates such dynamic charge in this area. It is why one becomes dimensionally enabled and energized upon that mountain, you see?*

*Now, while the lands of LeMuria and Atlantis coexisted for over 800,000 years, their civilizations coexisted only some 50,000 years. One projected heart, the other mind. One was excessively male, one excessively female, in a*

*manner of speaking. Can you see why these must be brought into BALANCED alignment for the Ascension? Do you understand that, in a very valid sense, all time on your planet coexists in multi dimension? So we tell you that Mount Shasta is in a special role to blend these, to attune these in multi dimensionality, and accordingly Shasta is very specifically in harmonic oscillation with your islands of Hawaii and Mount Fuji in the Pacific areas and with the Canary Islands in the Atlantic; all holding aspects of LeMuria and Atlantis. Do you understand why it is volcanoes, specific ones, that are capable of such commissioned undertaking on your planet? We tell you it is because of the dimensional expansion capabilities of their electromagnetic fields.*

*Now, it is not every volcano that is so endowed, we will say that this varies according to their placement, geo magnetics and embellishment. There must, of course, first be the correct frequencial potential of sufficient raw energy there, and it must be of a specific blend. Now, as the channel has an affinity for gems, we use this analogy: one can find a rough diamond that appears to be a mere carbon deposit, but if it is burnished and proves to contain clarity and symmetry, it can be polished and faceted into a gem of luminous beauty that refracts light and energy in wondrous ways. As such do volcanoes and other sourced power points evolve into the awareness of dimensionally expanded sacred sites? But the energy potential was there first. Now indeed, when what you might refer to as a great historic event occurs in a field or valley or mountain, and multitudes of people are thereafter drawn there to visit the location of the great event, the energy they amass can also polish the location to a higher frequency, and a sacred site of sorts will evolve by amplification.*

*But it is not just the raw telluric energy, not just the geometry, it must also be embellished with the sacred. And that is so misunderstood.*

*Your mainstream physists, mathematicians and scientists currently have many concepts, many systems of thought, of belief, of paradigm that are being applied to physics as simply a complex mathematical challenge, and they omit the sacred. The two must be coupled for humankind to truly understand the nature of the Living Earth and consciousness of the Cosmos.*

*We tell you that Mount Shasta is by far the most powerful sacred site, the most omnipotent vortex-portal complex in North America. Few locations on your planet have equal capacity of multi dimensional expansion alloyed in divine synergy. You are beloved."*

……….. and so it is.

# Sacred Sites and Power Points of Gaia

## AFRICA

### Algeria
* Djemila
* Sidi Abed: Tlemcen
* Sahara Desert
* Tasilla N'Ajjir

### Chad
* Kahuzi Biega National Park

### Egypt
* Aswan
* Giza Pyramids
* Abu Simbel
* Almuharraq Coptic Monastery
* Gebel Katarina
* Mount Sinai
* Luxor: Temple of Karnac
* Dendera: Temple of Hathor
* Heliopolis: Spring of the Holy Family
* Mosque of Ibn Tulan, Fustat
* Philae: Temple of Isis
* Tell el Amarna
* Temple of Hathor
* Temple of Ra
* Nile River
* Siwa Oasis: Temple of Amun

### Ethiopia
* Axum: St Mary of Zion, Arc of the Covenant
* Bale Mountains National Park
* Dendi Volcano
* Rock-Hewn Churches of Lalibela
* Rift Valley
* Semien Mountains
* Source of the Blue Nile
* Wonchi Volcano

### Gambia
* Wassu Stone Circle

### Ghana
* Lake Bosumtwi
* Kenya

* Mount Kenya
* Mount Elgon
* Mount Longonot Volcano
* Masai Mara Reserve
* Tsavo National Park

### Libya
* Cyrene
* Leptis Magna
* Sabratha

### Mali
* Bandiagara
* Dogon Shrines
* Timbuktu

### Madagascar
* Canyon des Singes
* Lac Anivorano-Sacred Lake
* Mont Passot
* Iravoandriana Stone Megalithes

### Morocco
* Atlas Mountains
* Kutibayah Mosque
* Lixis
* Tizi'n'Toubkal
* Volubilis

### Mozambique
* Gorongosa National Park

### Niger
* The Great Mosque,Agadez

### Nigeria
* Ife
* Oshogbo

### Namimbia
* Fish River Canyon
* Etosha National Park
* Mururob: God's Finger
* Kalahari Desert

## Rwanda
- Volcanoes National Park
- Mgahinga National Park

## Somalia
- Fakhr Al-Din

## South Africa
- Table Rock, Capetown
- Ghost Mountain
- Lake Fundudzi
- Kimberely
- Pilanesburg National Park
- Kruger National Park
- Matopos National Park: Matobo Mound
- Oyoun Mossa Moses Springs
- Hammam Pharaon Thermals Waters: Pharoah Bath

## Sudan
- Faras
- Nuri: Pyramid of King Taharqa
- Pyramids of Meroe
- Temple of Jebel Barkal

## Tanzania
- Mount Kilamanjaro
- Arusha National Park: Meru Crater
- Serengeti
- Lake Victoria
- Ngorongoro Crater
- Longido

## Tunisia
- Builla Regia: Temple of Apollo
- Djemila
- Dougga: Temple of Saturn
- Nefta Mosque
- Kairouan Mosques
- Chambi Mountain
- Atlas Mtns
- Tébessa Mountains

## Uganda
- Mount Stanley
- Rwenzori Mountains
- Mount Muhavura
- Ihimba Hot Springs
- Kitagata Hot Springs
- Mount Mikeno
- Nyamasizi Hot Springs
- Semuliki Hot Springs
- Buranga Hot Springs

## Zaire
- Sanga, Lake Kisale

## Zambia and Zimbabwe
- Gulubabwe Cave
- Victoria Falls

# THE AMERICAS

## Argentina
- Cueva de los Manos, Perito Moreno
- Difunta Correa Shrine
- Patagonia
- Nahuel Huapi National Park
- Mount Uritorco
- Perito Moreno National Park
- Tierra del Fuego
- Aconcagua Provincial Park, Los Herras
- Sierra de las Quijadas National Park: San Luis
- Lanín National Park: Neuquén
- Ojos del Salado, Nevados

## Belize
- Altun Ha Pyramids
- Caracol Mayan Pyrmaid
- Cerros
- Lamanai Pyramids
- San Ignacio
- Xunantunich El Castillo

## Bolivia
- Lake Titicaca: Island of the Sun, Island of the Moon
- Copacabana Cathedral
- Nevado Sajama
- Samaipata
- Salar de Uyuni
- Tiajuanaco
- Mount Illampu

## Brazil
- Diamantina

- Igreja de Bonfim, Bahia
- Manaus, Amazonas
- Marajo Island, Amazonas
- Sao Tome de Lietras
- Sete Cidades
- Corcovado Mountain Rio de Janeiro
- Iguasu Falls
- Caparaó National Park, Mineas Gerais
- Aparados da Serra National Park, Ro Grande de Sur
- Monte Pascoal
- Monte Roraima

## Canada
- Banff Springs, Sulpher Mountain
- Banff Falls
- Bannock Point, Ontario
- Dreamers Rock, Ontario
- Lake Louise, Alberta
- Lake O Hara, British Colombia
- Emerald Lake, British Colombia
- Lake Moraine, Alberta
- Kananaskis Provincial Park
- Majorville Medicine Wheel, Alberta
- Minton Turtle: Native American Medicine Wheel, Saskatchewan
- Mount Edith Cavell
- Peyto Lake
- Pyramid Mountain, Alberta
- Spirit Lake, Jasper National Park
- Lake Superior
- Niagara Falls, Ontario
- Bon Echo Provencal Park
- Vancouver Island, British Colombia
- Waterton National Park, Alberta
- Moose Mountain Medicine Wheel, Saskatchewan
- Sproat Lake, Vancouver
- Sundial Butte Medicine Wheel, Alberta
- Gros Morne, Newfoundland
- Tuktut Nogait, Northwest Territory
- Mingan Archipelago National Park, Quebec
- Forillon National Park, Quebec
- Mount Logan, Kluane National Park, Yukon
- Cape Breton Highlands, Nova Scotia
- Ungara, Quebec

## Caribbean
- Bimini Island

- Jamaica: Blue Mountains, Dunn Falls
- Bermuda
- St Lucia
- Aruba: Gold Fields

## Chile
- La Serena, Elqui Valley
- La Valle Encanto, Ovalle
- Minas de Lapis Lazuli, Coquimbo
- Pintados
- The Giant of Atacama
- Torres del Paine
- Ojos del Salado
- Osorno
- Petrohue Falls
- Atacama Desert
- Easter Island
- Santiago, Cerro El Plomo
- Volcan Parinacota

## Colombia
- Cerro Huaika
- La Ciudade Perdida
- Lago Guatavita
- Sierra Nevada de Santa Marta
- Nevada de Huila
- Lago Iguaque
- Parque Nacional Los Nevados
- San Augustine

## Costa Rica
- La Basilica de Nuestra Senora de Los Angeles
- Vocan Irazu
- Arenal Volcano and Hot Springs
- Poas Volcano
- Parque Nacional Volcán Arenal

## Ecuador
- Cerro El Corazón, Quito
- Cochasqui
- Ingapirca
- Pululahua Natural Monument
- Galapagos Island
- La Cordillera de los Llanganates
- Mount Chimborazo
- Mount Cotapaxi
- Mount Tungurhua

- Ruins of Ingapirca
- Ruins and pyramids of Cochasqui
- Banos; Church of the Holy Water

**El Salvador**
- Tazumal
- San Andres

**Guatemala**
- Cahyup
- Piedras Negras
- Tikal Pyramids
- Uaxactun Pyramids
- Ruins of El Mirador
- Lago Atitlan
- Vulcan Acatenango
- Vulcan de Fuego
- Vulcan Tacana

**Honduras**
- Copan
- Volcan & Lago Yojoa

**Mexico**
- Baja California
- Chitzen Itza
- Chiapas-Mayan Pyramids
- Cholula
- Coba
- Cozumel
- Edzna
- Palenque
- **Great Pyramid of Cholula**
- Teotihuacan
- Izamal
- La Venta
- Las Limas
- Mitla
- Mount Iztacchihuatl
- Monterrey
- Oxtotitlan
- Citlaltepetl  Pico de Orizaba
- Mount Popocatepetl
- Nevada de Colima
- Sierra Negra / Tliltepetl
- Tula
- Tulum

- Volcan Popocatepetl
- Uxmal
- Yucatan: Cenotes and Springs
- Zayil

**Nicaragua**
- San Cristobal Volcano
- Momotombo Volcano
- Mombacho Volcano Reserve
- Volcan Masaya

**Peru**
- Ancon
- Aramu Muru
- Cerro Santa Apolonia
- Chavin de Huantar
- Cusco
- Pisac
- Sacred Valley
- Machu Picchu
- Nazca
- Temple de Pachacamac
- Temples of Sunand& Moon, Trujillo
- Tres Cruces
- Volcan Pichu Pichu
- Volcan Sabancaya
- Volcan Tutupaca
- Ollantaytambo
- Lake Titicaca

**Venezuela**
- Angel Falls, **Canaima National Parque**
- Parque National Sierra Nevada-Los Frailles
- Mount Sorte, Chivacoa
- Orinoco National Reserve
- El Limon, Maracay
- Autana Mountain: Wahari-Kawai
- Colonia Tovar Mountains

**United States (USA), Southwest**
- Grand Canyon, Arizona
- Havasu Falls, Arizona
- Lake Powell, Arizona
- Sedona, Arizona
- Montezuma's Well, Arizona
- San Francisco Peaks Volcano, Arizona
- Canyon de Chelly, Arizona

- Moab, Utah
- Chaco Canyon, New Mexico
- Bandelier, New Mexico
- Sangre de Cristo Mountains, New Mexico
- Pyramid Lake, Nevada
- Enchanted Rock, Texas
- Moody Pyramids, Galveston Island, Texas
- Big Bend National Park, Texas
- Zion National Park, Utah
- Monument Valley, Utah
- Canyon Lands, Utah
- Arches National Park, Utah
- Bryce Canyon, Utah

**USA, Northwest**
- Craters of the Moon National Monument, Idaho
- City of Rocks National Monument, Idaho
- Nez Perce National Reserve Mountains, Idaho
- Wizard Island, Crater Lake, Oregon
- Mount Hood, Oregon
- Mount St Helens, Oregon
- Multinomah Falls, Oregon
- Mount Baker, Washington
- Mount Ranier, Washington
- Beacon Rock, Washington
- Mount Adams, Washington
- Colombia Gorge Stonehenge, Washington

**USA, Western**
- Mount Shasta, California
- Mount Lassen, California
- Joshua Tree, California
- Death Valley, California
- Channel Islands, California
- Tlamco, (LeMurian Site) San Francisco, California
- Napa Valley, California
- Esselen Creek: Big Sur, California
- Yosemite National Park, California
- Mount Cuchamama- Tecate, California
- Sequoia National Park, California
- Chief Mountain, Montana
- Glacier National Park, Montana
- Black Canyon of the Gunnison, Colorado
- Mesa Verde, Colorado
- Crestone Needle, Colorado
- Needles Rock, Colorado

- Canyon of the Ancients National Monument, Colorado
- Garden of the Gods, Colorado
- Manitou Springs, Colorado
- Colorado National Monument
- Black Hills, South Dakota
- Bad Lands, South Dakota
- Harney Peak, South Dakota
- Bear Butte: Black Hills South Dakota
- Turtle Mountain, North Dakota
- Devils Tower, Wyoming
- Bighorn Medicine Wheel, Wyoming
- Medicine Wheel, Medicine Mountain, Wyoming
- Grand Tetons National Park, Wyoming
- Beartooth Mountains, Wyoming
- Yellowstone National Park, Wyoming

**USA, Midwest**
- Hot Springs National Park, Arkansas
- Eureka Springs, Arkansas
- Toltec Mounds, Arkansas
- Queen Wilamena State Park, Arkansas
- Crater of Diamonds State Park, Arkansas
- Buffalo National River, Arkansas
- Emerald Mounds , Mississippi
- Angel Mounds, Indiana
- Mounds State Park, Indiana
- Great Circle Mounds, Indiana
- Gold Pyramid House, Illinois
- Cahokia Mound, Illonois
- Effigy Mounds National Monument, Iowa
- Pipestone National Monument, Minnesota
- Norton Mounds, Michigan
- Maremac Springs, Missouri
- Fantastic Caverns, Missouri
- Towosaghy, Missouri
- Serpent Mounds, Ohio
- Octagon Earthworks, Ohio
- Spiro Mounds, Oklahoma
- Quartz Mountain State Park, Oklahoma
- Red Rock Canyon State Park, Oklahoma
- Talimena State Park, Oklahoma
- Temple Mounds, Wisconsin
- Aztalan Mounds, Wisconsin
- Devils Lake State Park, Wisconsin
- Lizards Mound, Wisconsin

## USA, Southeast

- Mound State Monument, Alabama
- Russell Cave, Alabama
- Crystal River Mounds, Florida
- Great Temple Mound, Florida
- Everglades Mounds, Florida
- Stone Mountain, Georgia
- Ocmulgee National Park, Georgia
- The Georgia Guidestones, Elbert County Georgia
- Rock Eagle Mound, Georgia
- Wickliffe Mounds, Kentucky
- Poverty Point Mounds, Louisiana
- Natchez Mounds, Louisiana
- Tchefuncte Mounds, Louisiana
- Emerald Mound, Mississippi
- Asheville, North Carolina
- Pilot Mountain, North Carolina
- Judaculla Rock, North Carolina
- Sauls Mound, Pinson Mounds, Tennessee
- Gatlinburg, Tennessee-Great Smokey Mountains
- Parthenon, Nashville, Tennessee
- Ruby Falls, Lookout Mountain, Tennessee
- Cades Cove, Tennessee
- Virginia Beach, Virginia
- Fairy Stone State Park, Stonecross, Virginia
- Shenandoah National Park, Virginia

## USA, Northeast

- Catoctin Mountain Park, Maryland
- Washington D.C.
- Gettysberg, Pennsilvania
- Appalachian Mountains, Pennsylvania
- Pocono Moutinas, Pennsylvania
- Mount Katahdin, Maine
- Acadia National Park, Maine
- Mount Washington, New Hampshire
- Mystery Hill, New Hampshire
- Mammoth Cave, Kentucky
- America's Stonehenge, New Hampshire
- Tripod Rock, New Jersey
- Niagra Falls, New York
- Herkimer, New York
- Liberty Island, New York
- Green Mountains, Vermont
- Moundsville, West Virginia
- Blue Stone State Park, West Virginia

## USA, Hawaii

- Haleakala Volcanoe, Maui
- Moku'ula, Maui
- Mauna Kea, Hawaii
- Mount Kilauea, Hawaii

## USA, Alaska

- Mount Denali
- Kenai Penninsula
- Mount Sanford
- Mount Blackburn
- Mount Churchill

## Mid Atlantic

- Azores Islands

# ASIA

## Afghanistan

- Blue Mosque
- Bamiyan Buddhist Shrines
- Dacht-i-Navar Volcanoes
- Badakshan Lapis Lazuli Deposits
- Mount Nowshak

## Australia

- Argyle Diamond Pipe
- Anthwerrke
- Ball's Pyramid, Lord Howe Island
- Nyungar
- Bennets Brook
- Kunkuwarra
- Warmalana Island
- Noonkanbah
- Umpampurru: Goddess Site of Fertility
- Wullunggnari
- Melville Island: Dreamtime Site
- Kulaluk
- Laura, Queensland: Home of Spirti Gods
- Uluru
- Kata Tjuta National Park
- Big Ben Volcano: Heard Island
- Blue Mountains: Sacred Caves
- Boonuloolu
- Bungle Bungle
- Devil's Marble
- Hanging Rock, near Woodend, Victoria

- Glasshouse Mountains, Queensland
- The Pinnacles
- Budawang National Park
- Lake Narran
- Kata Tjuta
- Great Barrier Reef
- Murramarang National Park
- Morton National Park
- Mount Fox, Queensland
- Mount Kooroocheang
- Mount Noorat Crater
- Mount Bingingerra
- The Escarpment in Kakadu
- The 12 Apostles
- The Olgas: Kata Tjuta
- Cathedral Gorge
- N'Dhala Gorge
- Undara, Queensland
- Warrumbungle National Park
- Cradle Mountain: Lake St Clair National Park, Tasmania
- Mount Field National Park-Tasmania

**Bangladesh**
- Bagerhat
- Mainimati Ruins

**Burma (Myenmar)**
- Lake Inle
- Mount Popa
- Pagan
- Shwemawdaw Pagoda
- Shwedagon
- Sri Ksetra

**Cambodia**
- Angkor
- Phnom Chisor
- Wat Phnom
- Ta Prom Temple
- Wat Preah Keo

**China: Major Sacred Mountains**
The Buddhist *Four Sacred Mountains* are:
- Wǔtái Shân: Five Dimension Mountain, Shânxî
- Éméi Shân: Gentle Brow Mountain, Sìchuân
- Jiǔhuá Shân: NineGlories Mountain, Ânhuî
- Pǔtuó Shân: Potalaka Mountain, Zhèjiâng

The Taoist *Five Great Mountains* are arranged according to the five cardinal directionsof Chinese geomancy which includes the center as a direction:
- Tài Shân: East – Leading Peaceful Mountain, Shândông
- Huà Shân: West – Splendid Mountain, Shǎnxî
- (Nán) Héng Shân: South – Balancing Mountain, Húnán
- (Běi) Héng Shân: North – Eternal Mountain, Shânxî
- Sông Shân: Center – Heavenly Spiral Mountain, Hénán

**China**
- Confucius Temple, Tianjin
- Dragons in the Cloud Hill, Jiangsu
- Gao Temple, Ningxia
- Emeishan, Sichuan
- Huánglóng
- Hengshan, Hunan
- Higher Daxiong Baodian Temple, Jiuhua Shan
- Huang Shan Mtns and Thermal Springs
- Jade Dragon Snow Mountain
- Jinggang Sacred Mountains
- Jiuzhaigou Valley and Falls
- Jinci Temple, Shanxi
- Monastery of Divine Light, Sichuan
- Mount Cangyan
- Mount Jiuhua: Nine Sacred Peaks
- Mount Gasherbrum (26,400 feet): Border China - Pakistan
- Mount Gongga/Minya Konka, Sichuan
- Mount Hua
- Mount Emei
- Mount Heng Shan
- Mount Kailas (Kahlesh on Tibet side): Crown Chakra of the planet
- K2 Mount Godwin Austen: Border of China - Pakistan (28,200 feet)
- Konqi Stone Circle, Sinkiang
- Longmen Grottos and Sacred Buddhist Carvings
- Luomen, Gansu
- Luohen Temple, Sichuan
- Lushan Quaternary Glaciation National Geopark
- Mount Jizu Sacred Mountain, Yunnan
- Mount Lao, Shandong
- Mount Lu
- Mount Luofu

- Mount Putuo, Shanghai
- Mount Qiyun
- Mount Qingcheng
- Mount Song: Shaolin Temple
- Mount Tai
- Mystery Valley: Tianzhu Mountain
- Putoshan temple, Zhejiang
- Qinghai Lake
- Qian Shan
- Qinghengschan, Sichuan
- San Qing Mountain, Taoist Holy Mountain
- Shaolin Monastery, Henan
- Taishan
- The Grand Buddha, Sichuan
- Temple of Heaven, Beijing
- Temple of Six Banyon, Guangzhou
- Yuantong Temple, Kunming
- White Horse Temple, henan
- Wudang Mountains

## Fiji Islands
- Labasa
- Navatu Rocks
- Korolamalama

## Indonesia
- Dieng Plateau
- Double Temples: Lombok
- Java: Bourobudar
- Java: Gedung Songo Hindu Temples
- Karang Tretes Cave
- Lemo
- Mendut Buddhist Temple
- Mount Bromo Volcano
- Mount Merapi
- Mt Rinjani
- Krakatoa Volcano, Rakata Island
- Semeru Volcano
- Surunadi

## Indonesia: Bali
- Besakah Hindu Temple
- Lake Bratan
- Mount Agung Volcano
- Mount Batur Volcano
- Puru Luhur Ulu Watu
- Puru Sada

- Puru Taman Ayun
- Tanahlot Sea Temple

## India
- Allahabad
- Alampur
- Ayodhya
- Barren Island Volcano, Andaman Islands
- Bhubansewar
- Haridwar-Ganges River
- Elephanta Island: Shiva Shrines
- Golden Temple, Punjab
- Mount Abu
- Mount Kanchenjunga (28,000 feet)
- Ratnagiri
- Sun Temple ,Orissa
- Taj Mahal
- Tirumala

## India: Sacred Chakric Cities
There are seven sacred cities in Hindu India, which are the principal pilgrimage centers:
- **Varanasi** on the River Ganges
- **Hardwar** on the River Ganges
- **Ayodhya**, the birthplace of Lord Rama
- **Mathura**, Lord Krishna's Birthplace
- **Dwarka**, where Krishna ruled and where the Krishna Vasudeva was born
- **Kanchipuram**, the great Shaivite temple city of Tamil Nadu
- **Ujjan**, site every twelve years of Kumbha Mela

The most holy pilgrimage for a Hindu to make is around the four divine direction "*abodes*" that stand at the cardinal compass points of the mythological map of India:
- **Badrinath:** North – High in the Himalayas Lord Shiva
- **Puri**: *East* – Lord Krishna
- **Rameshwaram Island**: South – Lord Rama
- **Dwarka**: West – Lord Krishna

## India: Sri Lanka
- Anuradhapura: Temple and 2000 Year Old Tree
- Aluvihara
- Golden Temple of Dambulla
- Mihintale Mountain

- Temple of Buddha Tooth

## Japan
- Beppu Thermal Springs
- Dewa Sanzan Temples
- Eihei Ji, Fukui
- Ise
- Izumo Taisha
- Mount Fuji
- Mount Asama San
- Mount Haku
- Mount Kirishima
- Mount Koyo
- Mount Ontake Volcano
- Mount Osore: Sacred Volcano
- Mount Tateyama
- Nachi No Taki Waterfall
- Nara
- Nikko
- Nonakado Stone Circle
- Oshoro Stone Circle
- Dewa Sanzan: 3 Sacred Mountains
- Mount Aso San
- Shiroku Island
- Tamagawa Hot Springs
- Zenko-Ji Temple, Nagano

## Korea North
- Kumgangsan
- Mount Paektu

## Korea South
- T'Aebaeksan
- Hallasan
- Sokkuram Grotto

## Laos
- Pha That Luang
- Pak Ou Caves
- Wat Phu
- Wat Si Munag

## Malaysia
- Cheng Hoon Teng
- Gunung Jerai
- Ipoh Cave Temples
- Niah Caves

## Mongolia
- Amarbayasgalant Monastery
- Erdenezeu Hiid Buddhist Temple: Hatroin
- Gandantegchinlen Hiid Temple Complex: Ulan Bator
- Gobi Desert
- Gobi Altai Mountains
- Gundgavirlan Hiid Temple and Monastery
- Mount Khuiten
- Tavan Bogd Mountains, Bayan Ulgii Aimag
- Khorgo-Terkhiin Tsagaan Lake National Park
- The Four Holy Mountains: Ulan Bator
- Dariganga Volcano Ulaanbaatar
- Middle Gobi Volcano
- Taryatu-Chulutu Volcano

## Nepal
- Janakpur
- Kathmandu Valley
- Kanchanjanga Mountain (3rd highest in the world)
- Krystal Mountain: Mustang
- Pashupatinath
- Lumbini Temple
- Swayambhu Stupa

## New Zealand
- Arahura
- Cape Reinga
- Taranaki (Egmont)
- Lake Taupo
- Egmont National Park
- Fiordland
- Hokitika Josef Glacier and Gold Field
- Mokoia Island
- One Tree Hill
- Ngauruhoe
- Mount Cook National Park
- Pukekaikoir: Tongariro National Park
- Mount Raoul Kermadec Islands
- Paparoa National Park
- Ruapehu Tongariro
- Mount Tongariro
- Tarawera: Okataina
- Waiheke Island
- White Island
- Westland National Park

## Pakistan
- Badshahi Mosque
- Court of Many Stupas: Buddhist Holy Site
- Ilam Mountain
- K2 – Mount Chogori (world's 2nd highest mtn)
- Mehrgahr
- Neza e Sultan Volcano
- Panja Sahib
- Satpara and Gilgit Buddhas

## Polynesia
- Tonga: Ha Amonga – A Maui Sun Gate
- Tonga: Paepae'O Tela Pyramid
- Kosrae- Micronesia – Ancient Mu City
- Pohnpei: Nandauwas Temple
- Society Islands: Raiatea Island
- Tahiti: Moorea Island
- Western Samoa: Pulemelei Pyramid Mound
- Western Samoa: Mount Lata

## Sakhalin Island: Russia
- Volcanoes

## Taiwan
- Pei-Kang

## Thailand
- Ayuthaya
- Doi Suthep
- Lak Muang Shrine
- Stone Mountain: Prasat Hin Knao Phanom
- Wat Pho
- Wat Tham Seua

## Tibet
- Mount Kailash
- Lhasa Temples
- Tashilhunpo
- Toling

## Vietnam
- Emperor of Jade Pagoda
- My Son
- Nga Hanh Son
- Sam Mountain
- Tam Son Hoi Quan Pagoda

## EUROPE

## Albania
- Butrint Ancient Sacred Site
- Kruje-Dollma Treke: Pagan and Sufi Shrine

## Armenia
- St Gregory the Illumionator: Site of Pagan and Christian Shrines
- Yerevan
- Garni: Greek Style Temple to Pagan God Mithras

## Austria
- Spirit Rock: Teufelsteine – Kapfenberg
- Magdelenesburg Peak: Klagenfurt
- Melk Abbey
- Saint Stephan Cathedral: Vienna
- Salzburg
- Georgenberg: St George Cathedral

## Belgium
- Weris, Erezee, Oppagne: Standing Stones and Megalithic Complex

## Bosnia Herzegovina
- Mithraic Temple
- Medjugorie: Hill of Apparitions
- Nin Sacred Springs
- Stecci Stones
- Zborna Gomilla

## Bulgaria
- Pchelina Hill
- Bulgarian Mountains
- Kazanluk: Thracian Goddess Site
- Kozhuh: Thermal Springs
- Madara: Pagan Sacred Carving
- Baba Vanga Church
- Pirin National Park
- Rila National Park and Monastery
- Rotunda of St. George: Sofia
- Rupite
- Stone Forest: Varna
- Musala
- Strandja

## Croatia
- Basilica of Euphrasius

- Split Cathedral

**Cypress**
- Rock of Aphrodite

**Czech Republic**
- Libenice Sacred Celtic Pagan Site
- Odry Stone Circle
- Prague Monasteries and Cathedral of Infant Jesus
- Mount Hostyn
- Bystrice Cathedral and Sacred Spring
- Zavist Celtic Fortress

**Denmark**
- Bavnehøj
- Bildso Megalithic Site
- Budolfi Cathedral
- Dolmen near Stenvad
- Frejlev Skov Dolmens and Stone Circle
- Bornholm Isle-Templars
- Jelling- Viking Burial Mounds and Runestones
- Lindholm Hoje
- Mols Stone Mound: Knebal
- Trundholm: Ritual Sun Disc Mound
- Tustrup Dolmen and Megalithic Chamber

**Finland**
- Halti Mountain
- Pihtsusköngäs
- Enontekio
- Kallioparta: Lake Inari
- Saana
- Surtsey Vocanic Isle
- Ukkosaari Island
- Vasarainen

**France**
- Mont Saint Michel
- Alet les Bains
- Ariège Pyreenes Grottos and Underground River
- Bagneux –Megalithic Stones and Cave
- Carcassonne: La Cite
- Collioure: Chateau Royal Templar
- Notre Dame
- Noves Fertility Stones
- Cojoux Standing Stones
- Chateau Peyreperteuse

- Chateau des Comtes de Foix
- Chateau de Queribus
- Gorge Galamus
- Mount Blanc
- Lascaux
- Lourdes
- Pic de Vignemale
- Chartres
- Rennes de la Chateau
- Carnac Stones
- Carn Island: Finistere
- Brittany Monolithes
- Fairy Stone: Le Grand Menhir Base
- Montsegur Cathor
- Puilaurens
- Reims
- Roche Tuilière and Roche Sanadoire, Mont Dore, Auvergne
- Eveonne
- Douvries la Delivrande
- Isle de Sein
- Sources de la Seine
- Mont Lozère
- Romamadour
- Paray le Monial
- Montagne Noire
- Vezeley
- Chaine des Puys
- Volcan de Ardeche
- Puy de Lemptegy
- Saint Sernin Church: Toulouse

**France: Corsica**
- Stantari
- Filitosa
- Fontanaccia
- Rhinaghiu
- Calanche

**Germany**
- Aachen: Charlemagne's Imperial City
- Externesteine: Sacred Rocks and Teutoburg Forest
- Brutkamp
- Cologne Cathedral
- Goloring Henge Monument
- Kurburg Stone Circle
- Kirnach Mounds

- Cairn of Barnenez
- Heuneberg
- Oesterholz
- Zwölf Apostel, Bavaria
- Berchtesgaden
- Manching Celtic Site
- Mt Brocken, Harz Mtns
- Mount Zugspitze
- Mumling Grumbach: Holy Well and Fertility Site – Pagan Celtic
- Degernau Monolith Stone
- Speyer Cathedral
- Steinkreis Werpeloh
- Trier

## Gibralter
- Rock of Gibralter

## Greece
- Delphi: Temple and Uracle Site
- Mycenae
- Olympia
- Methana Volcano
- Santorini Volcano
- Metoera Monaliths and Monasteries
- Parthenon
- Temple of Apollo
- Pathos: Cave of John
- Ikaria Hot Springs
- Santorini Island

## Greece: Crete
- Caves of Zeus
- Mount Ida
- Knossos
- Palace of Minos

## Holland
- Havelterberg Dolman near Havelte
- Megalithic Stones Kniphorstbos between Anloo and Schipborg
- Anloo Stones in Forest
- Basilica of St. Servatius: Maastricht, Holland
- Neolithic Stone Mound and Medieval Church in Rolde
- Domkerk Cathedral
- Cathedral of Saint Martin, Utrecht
- Castle of Muiden: Muiderslot (Powernode)

- Utrecht Cathedral
- Papeloze Kirke
- Schimmeres Neolithic Chamber
- Toterfout-Hlave Mijl Barrows Bronze Age Sacred Pagan Site

## Hungary
- Baradla Cave
- Bodrokeresztur: Neolithic Mound
- Aggtelek National Park
- Thermal Springs on Margitsziget
- St Stephen's Basilica: Budapest
- Benedictine Pannonhalma Archabbey
- Matthias Church
- Hevis Thermal Springs
- Buddapest Thermal Springs

## Iceland
- Thingvellir

## Ireland
- Drumbeg Stone Circle
- Kiladare: St Brigids Cathedral – previously Pagan Holy Site
- Lough Gur: Stone Circle
- Skellig Michael
- Ring of Kerry
- Mayo: Knock – Hill of Apparitions
- New Grange
- Poulnabroune Dolman
- Labby Dolman
- Rock of Cashel
- The Burrens
- Cliffs of Mohr
- Glen Garry National Park
- Tara Hill

## Italy
- St Peter's Basilica and Vatican, Forum: Rome
- Florence Cathedral
- Assisi
- Sardinia: Barumini, Cagliara, Anghelu Ruju, Li Lolghi
- Castelluccio: Sicily
- Cerveteri
- Mount Vesuvius: Naples
- Mount Etna: Sicily

- St. Marks Cathedral: Venice
- Syracuse Cathedral
- Lake Cuomo
- The Dolomites
- Mount Blanco
- Subiaco Sacred Grotto of St. Benedict
- Cervo Cathedral
- Tarquinia
- Veii: Temple of Apollo

## Lithuania
- House of Perkunas: Pagan Site to Thunder God
- Vilnius Cathedral

## Luxembourg
- Rindschleiden: Holy Well of St Willibord and Church

## Malta
- Hagar Qim
- Ggantija Temple
- Church and Grotto of St. Paul

## Norway
- Alta
- Borgund Stave
- Gamle Aker Kirke
- Gorkstad
- Jan Mayan Volcano
- Finnafjord
- Lysefjorden
- Geirangerfjord
- Jostedalsbreen National Park
- Oseberg
- Thermal Springs at Bockfjorden, Svalbard
- Nærøyfjord Landscape Preservation Area
- Northwest Spitsbergen National Park
- Steinsetninger: Stone Circles

## Poland
- Church of the Virgen Mary: Krakow
- Mount Grabarka
- Lichen Cathedral
- Carpathian Mountains
- Gaj: Megalithic Mound
- Wieliczka Salt Mine Near Krakow
- Salt Chapel of Saint Kinga

- Sarnovo Mounds: Wloclawek
- St Annes Churchl: Warsaw
- Grodcyzn Volcano

## Portugal
- Antelas- Megalithic Site
- Ante Grande e Zambujeiro
- Almedras Stone Circle
- Zambujal Megalithic Site

## Romania
- Retezat-Godeanu Mountains
- Sambata Monastery
- Piatra Craiului Mountain
- Fagaras Mountains
- Mangalia: Ancient Basilica
- Sarmizeget: Carpathian Mtnsusa
- Sucevita Monastery: Putna
- **Volcanoes of** Paclele
- Bucegi Mountains

## Russia
- Abhkasia-Georgia
- Alaverdei Cathedral: Georgia
- Cathedral of the Assumption: Vladmir
- Elbrus Volcano
- Ivolginsk Buddhist Monastery: Siberia
- Ipateyev Monastery
- Lake Baikal
- Moscow Golden Ring
- Kazan Cathedral: St. Petersburg
- Kizhi Island: KareliyaPagan Sacred Mounds
- Khamar Dban Buddhist Monastery: Siberia
- Kremlin
- Maikop: Pagan Megalithic Site – Caucasus Mtns
- Mtatsminda Holy Mountain and Anchiskhatai Basilica: Georgia
- Church of Christ the Redeemer: Moscow
- Azas Plateau Volcano
- Ural Mountains
- Sergai Posad Springs and Cathedral
- Solovyetsky Monastery
- Sakhalin Island Volcano
- St Basil's: Moscow
- Trinity Cathedral: Pskov

## Serbia

- Lependski Vir: Pagan Sacred Site

**Spain**
- Antequera: Milagra
- Burgos Cathedral
- Christo de la Luz, Toledo
- Great Mosque at Cordoba: Sacred to Pagans, Christians and Muslims
- Montserrat
- Mulhacen: Sierra Nevada
- Olot Volcanic Field northeast Spain
- Granada: Abbey de St Secillio-Sacre Monte
- Santiago de Compostella
- Pyrenees: Pico de Aneto
- Sierra de Pena de Francia
- Trepuco-Minorca

**Spain: Canary Islands**
- Pico de Teide: Tenerife
- El Hierro
- Vulcan La Palma

**Switzerland**
- Convent of St. John
- Matterhorn
- La Tene Celtic: Pagan Site
- La Petit Chasseur: Standing Stones – Megalithic **Site**
- Lake Lucerne
- Alps
- Einsiedein Cathedral
- Lake Bieler: Druid Island

**Sweden**
- Ale's Stone Circle
- Anundshogen
- Gamla
- Hagestad
- Gratrask
- Lund Cathedral
- Lugnaro Mound
- Gotland Island

**United Kingdom (UK): England**
- Arbor Low
- Castlerigg Stone Circle: Ley Site
- Michaels Mount: Cornwall

- Tintagel: Cornwall
- Landsend: Cornwall
- Boscawen Un Stone Circle: Cornwall
- Merry maidens Circle: Cornwall
- Trethhevy Quoit-Stone Circle Porthole: Entrance to Other World
- Ilkley Moor
- Glastonbury: Tor, Chalice Well, Abbey
- St Paul's Cathedral
- Rollright Stones
- Canterbury Cathedral
- Avebury Circle: Wiltshire
- Stonehenge: Wiltshire
- Westminster Abbey
- Salisbury Cathedral and Old Sarum
- Keswick; Castle Rigg Stone Ring
- Knaresborough: Mother Shipton's Oracular Cave
- Rudston:Great Megaliths
- Lake Windamere: Lake District
- Lincoln Cathedral
- Walsingham Cathedral and Holy Well
- Wells Cathedral and Springs
- Bath Roman Springs
- Canterbury Cathedral
- Winchester Cathedral
- Cerne Abas Giant
- Chiswick House
- Ben Nevis

**UK: Scotland**
- Ballachroy Astronomical Stone Circle
- Callanish
- Iona: Abbey and Cobhan Cuilteach Circle
- Staffa Island
- Hebrides
- Cullerlie Stone Circle: Aberdeenshire
- Machrie Moor Arran
- Isle of Lewis: Callanish Circle
- Kingside Hill: Stone Ring – Edinburgh
- Findhorn
- Loch Ness: near Urquart Castle
- Loch Katrine
- Trossachs: Waterfall Area
- Glenn Coe
- Temple Wood Stone Circle, Argyll
- River Dee near Braemar
- Rosslyn Chapel

- Rosslyn Glen
- Tomnaverie Circle: Aberdeenshire
- Arthur's Seat: Edinburgh
- Loch Lomond
- Orkney: Skara Brae – Ring of Brodgar
- Edburgh Castle
- Ben Lomond
- Isle of Skye
- Dunotter Castle
- Dunfillan Hill, Megaliths
- Holy Well and Rock of St. Fillan
- New Scone Shien Fairy Hill
- Sterling Castle
- Glen Eagles near Perth
- River Dee near Abbeymore

**UK: Wales**
- Bryn Celli Ddu
- Carn Ingli Sacred Mountain
- Cader Idris Holy Mountain
- Clynnog Fawr; Gegaliths, Holy Well, Shrine of St. Beuno
- Dinas Emrhys: Merlin Magical Fortress
- Holy Island
- Gors Fawr
- Snowdonen Mountains
- Trelleck: Megaliths and Well of St. Anne
- Llangolen: Castel Dinas Bran
- Holywell: Church of St. Winifred
- St. David Cathedral
- St. Govans Chapel and Holy Well

**Ukraine**
- Caves Monastery: Kiev
- Santa Sofia Church
- Neaplois

# MIDDLE EAST

**Armenia**
- Agartsin Monastery
- Cathedral: St Gregory the Illunianor – Former Pagan Site
- Garni

**Azerbaijan**
- Babek Mineral Springs

- Boyuk Khanizadagh and Turaghai Mud Volcanoes
- Kobustan Caves
- Lake Chaechasta
- My Gapydijek
- Mount Ushenal
- Praying Hands of Allah: Mtn Peak near Baku
- Surakhany Temple
- Maiden Tower and Ferhad Cave, Sharur
- Nakhchivan Mineral Springs

**Bahrain**
- Barabar Temples
- Tree of Life: Eden

**Georgia**
- Mount Mtatsminda
- Vardzia
- Anchiskhati Basilica
- Tsminda Samebo

**Iran**
- Kelisa-Ye Hazrat-E Sarkis
- Qum
- La Susa
- Fire Temple: Takht-I Sulaiman – Birthplace of Zoraster
- Masjid-Iman
- Kelisa-Ye Hazrite-E Lugha: Birthplace of St. Luke
- Kuh-E Kahje
- St. Bartholomew Church: St Stephan – Kelisa Darre Sham
- Ateshkade
- Mahan Sufi Site

**Iraq**
- Babylon
- Ur
- Ninevah
- Samarrah
- Kazimayn Mosque
- Kerbela
- Najaf
- Mosque of Nabi Yunus: Tomb of Jonah
- Hatra
- Uruk
- Nippur- Sumerian Creation Site

- Ashur

**Israel**
- Beatitudes Mount
- Bethlehem
- Dead Sea
- Haifa: Elijah's Cave
- Jerusalem
- Mount of Olives
- Mount Zion
- Nazareth
- Sea of Galilee
- Solomon's Mound
- Temple Mount Dome of the Rock

**Jordan**
- Citadel El Qala Amman
- Petra
- Kerak Castle
- Mount Nebo Church
- Shobak Castle

**Kazakhstan**
- Bezeklik
- Mausoleum of Hodja Akhmed Yasavi: Sufi Dome

**Lebanon**
- Barouk Cedar Forest
- Mount Lebanon
- Mount Hermon

**Saudi Arabia**
- Madain Salah
- Mecca
- Medina

**Syria**
- Apamea
- Jabal ad Druze Volcano
- **Basilica of St. Sergius**
- Bosra
- Church of St. Simeon, Qal'a Sim'an
- Convent of Our Lady, Seidnaya
- Great Mosque (Umayyad Mosque), Aleppo
- Harrat Ash Shamah Volcanic Field
- Damascus-Chapel of St. Paul and Shrine of Sayidda Zeinab

- Krak des Chevaliers
- Monastery of Mar Mousa al-Habashi
- Mosque of Umar
- Palmyra

**Turkey**
- Antioch
- Aphrodisias: Temple of Aphrodite
- Blue Mosque- Istanbul
- Bolu Thermals
- Cappadocia Uchisar
- Cesme Thermals
- Didyma: Apollo Oracle Site
- Dolmens of Kirklareli
- Goreme
- Labranda: Zeus Temple
- Mount Ararat
- Mount Ida
- Mount Nemrut
- Mount Nimrod
- Mount Duzgunbaba
- Mount Suphan
- Olba: Zeus Site
- Olympos: Chimaera
- Pinara: Lycia
- Santa Sophia
- Suleymaniye Camii Ottoman Mosque
- Tendurek Volcano
- Troy
- Konya
- Yazilikaya: Hittites Temple

**Uzbekistan**
- Samarkand
- Kalyan Mosque
- Khiva

**Yemen**
- Friday Mosque
- Great Mosque of San'a
- Temples of Sun and Moon: Ma'rib

# Earth Energy Glossary

The following glossary of terms are my take on the 'Living Earth's' nervous system, chakras and aura … I will note that portions of the below glossary are based on my own interpretation of Gaia and her energy fields, with assistance from channeled intuitive sources.

**Apex Grid Point**: Corner points that occur on facets of the polyhedral grids.

**Conductive Energy Fields**: Area of high quartz contents (granite, sandstone, and quartzite) or metallic mineralogy (iron, copper, silver, gold) that attract, conduct and amplify telluric energies.

**Dragon Lines**: Another term for leylines, normally used in the Orient, specifically Japan, China, India and Tibet. The Dragon symbolizes the kundalini force. Dragon lines are referred to in the Orient as the kundalini energy of the Living Earth, or Gaia.

**Gaia**: The living, self aware, spirit of Earth.

**Grid**: The templates surrounding the Earth. Geometric domes with specific functions relating to the gravitation field, electromagnetic and light ascension.
- **Crystal 144 Grid**: The Earth's ascended merkaba. Anchored after the Harmonic Convergence. The geometry is the double penta dodecahedron. Extends to the 9th dimension. It is the matrix for the ascension.
- **Electromagnetic Grid**: The grid is an icosahedron. The Earth's vital energy is tuned with this grid. Leylines and telluric energies are a function of this grid. In a wide analogy, the Earth's nervous system.
- **Gravitational Grid**: This grid is a dodecahedron. The simplest spherical platonic solid. It is the tool used for tuning the planet's duality.
- **Polyhedron 120 Grid**: Extends from dimensions 9-12. This polyhedron has 120 triangular faces, 180 edges, and 62 vertices. The 120 Polyhedron provides a way to include the regular Dodecahedron and the Icosahedron into a single polyhedral system. All the Platonic "solids" share their vertices with the 120 Polyhedron. It has a higher frequency than the 144 grid, resonating to 182. It encompasses the 144 double penta dodecahedron.

**Grid Lines**: The facet edges of the icosahedron geodesic sphere. Energy lines connecting corner points of the triangles and pentagons composing the grids. These differ from leylines, although the energy is electrical in nature. These lines connect apex points and do have a linear movement along surface edges of the facets of the polyhedron.

**Hydro Lines**: The energetic field created when water is moving in a uniform direction, such as rivers, tide inlets and underground aquifers. The energy line is anionic in nature and quite pleasant to experience, creating plasmic fields of charged ions. Very calming, creating a sense of well being.

**Ions / Ionic Fields**: An ion is an atom that has either a positive or negative charge due to having either an excess of deficiency of electrons.
- **Anionic**: An atom with an excess of electrons, resulting in a negative charge. Negative ionic fields are actually benevolent. Waterfalls, moving water (hydro-lines) and ocean surfs create anionic fields.
- **Cationic**: An atom with a deficiency of (negatively charged) electrons, creating a positively charged particle field. An excess of cationic charges in the atmosphere can be detrimental and create feelings of imbalance.

**Ionic Plasma Field**: Fields of charged particles. These exist in almost all telluric power points and can create physiological effects.

**Lateral Flow**: Energy streams with a horizontal energetic flow. Often occurring in cave openings or anticlines.

**Ley Lines**: Flow lines of the Earth's electromagnetic current. Telluric energy normally flows along natural paths of conductive mineralogy, such as quartz, metals or water and can in some cases be manipulated and directed. The Michael Line in the UK and Europe has been directed into stone circles and great cathedrals.

**Major Leylines and Routes**
- **AA Michael Heart Line**: From Banff Canada triangulating Lake Louise, Lake O'Hara and Emerald Lake, extending north to Spirit Lake in Jasper and west to Vancouver Island.
- **Apollo and Athena Leylines**: Begin at Delphi in Greece and extend to Africa and into Northern Germany.
- **Atlantean Line**: Originates in the Sargasso Sea, thru Bimini, into Florida, through Stone Mountain near

Atlanta, Georgia, forking northeast to Asheville, North Carolina along the BlueRidge Mountains to upstate New York. From Stone Mountain it forks west to Hot Springs, Arkansas on to the Talimena Ridge bordering Arkansas and Oklahoma.

- **Condor Line**: The Condor Leylines extend from Cusco, Peru with myriad lines to Machu Picchu, Diamantina Brazil, Tierra del Fuego, Lake Titicaca, Easter Island and north to the Yucatan.
- **Dragon Leyline**: Connecting Mount Fuji to Mount Kahlish in Tibet, and Fuji to Lake Baikal in Siberia.
- **Eagle Line**: The Eagle Lines extend from Sedona Arizona to Lake Tahoe, Yosemite Park, to Mount Shasta to the Cascades of Oregon and Washington, to British Colombia and to Denali Alaska.
- **Hawk Line**: From Sedona to San Francisco Peaks, north and eastward thru Zion National Park to Monument Valley. From San Francisco Peaks westward to Grand Canyon.
- **Giza Line**: From Giza southward to Mt. Kilamanjaro, to Victoria Falls and to Capetown.
- **Mayan Leylines**: Begin in the Yucatan area of Mexico at Chitzen Itza and extend to Monterey, to Sedona in the northwest and Austin, Texas in the northeast. They extend southward from the Yucatan to Cusco, Peru.
- **LeMurian Leyline**: Connects Mount Shasta to Hawaii, Tahiti and Easter Island.
- **Michael and Mary Lines**: Extend from Skellig Michael Island in southwest Ireland through England, France, Italy to Mount Carmel In Israel.
- **Mecca Line**: From Mecca in Saudi Arabia through Iraq to Kashmir, to eastern Pakistan-K2 and to Mt. Kahlish.
- **Roseline**: From Orkney Scotland through UK and France to Santiago de Compostella, to Montserrat and to Rome.
- **Serpent Line**: From Poverty Point Louisiana thru Toltec Mounds in Arkansas, to Spiro Mounds, Great Serpent Mounds, Cahokia and to Lizard and Aztalan Mounds in Wisconsin.

**Platonic Solids**: A Platonic solid is a polyhedron whose faces are identical regular polygons. The ancient Greeks were able to show that there are exactly five such Platonic solids: the tetrahedron, hexahedron, octahedron, dodecahedron and icosahedron.
- Tetrahedron: Geometric polyhedron solid contained by four identical triangular surfaces.
- **Hexahedron**: Geometric solid, contained by six identical square surfaces, a cube.
- **Octahedron**: Geometric solid contained by eight identical triangles, double pyramid.
- **Dodecahedron**: A geometric solid having twelve faces. The regular dodecahedron is bounded by twelve equal and regular pentagons; the pyritohedron is related to it. The rhombic dodecahedron is bounded by twelve equal rhombic faces. Represents the gravity grid.
- **Icosahedron**: A platonic solid having 12 vertices, 30 polyhedron edges and 20 identical equilateral triangular faces. The geodesic sphere represents the electromagnetic 'human grid' aspect of the 3 in 1 Crystal Grid.

**Portal**: A 'white hole' interdimensional conduit that allows for higher dimensional energies to flow within a focal planetary window. A function of correlating the crystal 144 grid in alignment with the electromagnetic and gravitational grids.

**Quartz Fields**: Electromagnetic energy fields that are produced by and exist around quartz in nature. Amplifying in effect.

**Rhomb** (Rhombic / Rhomboid):An equilateral parallelogram rhombohedron or quadrilateral figure whose sides are equal and the opposite sides parallel. The angles may be unequal, two being obtuse and two acute, as in the cut, or the angles may be equal, in which case it is usually called a square.

**Telluric**: Relating to the Earth. Telluric energies are Earth energies, Earth electricity. A naturally occurring phenomenon. Telluric energy has a 'male' and female aspect. This can be thought of as yin and yang.

**Vortex**: A circular swirling motion of energy. A vortex will in general be characterized by the direction of motion as clockwise or counterclockwise; and the direction relating to the Earth surface, either an outward flow (electrical) or inward pull (magnetic).
- **Electrical Vortex**: A classification of vortex that spirals energy from inside the Earth. Electrical vortexes can vary in diameter from a few feet wide to mega vortexes, such as Sedona and Lake Titicaca. The latter is up to 75 miles in diameter.
- **Magnetic Vortex**: A classification of vortex that pulls energy inward from above into the Earth. Magnetic vortexes are less frequent that electrical vortexes and are generally larger in diameter.
- **Electromagnetic Vortex**: A vortex exhibiting both inward and outward energy sources. These are generally a vortex inside a vortex.

# About the Author

Tyberonn has worked as an engineer and geologist for the past 30 years in the energy sector. He is a native of Arkansas but has lived abroad for 20 years and has traveled to over 50 countries in his geology work. He has lived as an expatriate in Brazil, India, Venezuela, Gabon, Congo, United Arab Emirates and Scotland. He studied gemology while in Brazil. He has had a great interest in metaphysics, sacred sites, spirituality and music. He has visited over 200 sacred sites across the globe over the past three decades. He has been a guest speaker at the Elders Speak Conference in Sedona, Arizona, Lightworker Conferences with Ronna Herman and Steve Rother and a guest on metaphysical radio programs. He has mixed Native American heritage and has completed six 5-day vision quests and numerous shamanic journeys in Mexico and in South America. He is a staunch environmentalist and member of the Sierra Club. He believes in renewable energy sources and has worked from the 'inside' to help effect environmental change. He currently resides in Texas, where he continues work as a geologist, writer, musician and speaker. He is writing his second book on the metaphysical healing properties of gemstones. He can be contacted for speaking engagements via his website: www.Earth-Keeper.com